Facilitating Communication in Young Children with Handicapping Conditions:

A Guide for Special Educators

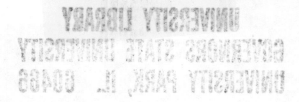
Advisory Editor

Michael Bender, Ed.D.
Vice President of Educational Programs
The Kennedy Institute
Professor of Education
Johns Hopkins University
Joint Appointment, Department of Pediatrics
Johns Hopkins School of Medicine
Baltimore, Maryland

Facilitating Communication in Young Children with Handicapping Conditions:
A Guide for Special Educators

Peter J. Valletutti, Ed.D.
Dean of Graduate Studies and
Professor of Special Education,
Coppin State College,
Baltimore, Maryland

Mary McKnight–Taylor, Ed.D.
Associate Professor,
Department of Special Education and
Rehabilitation Counseling,
Hofstra University,
Hempstead, New York

Audrey Smith Hoffnung, Ph.D.
Associate Professor,
Department of Speech-Language Pathology,
St. John's University,
Jamaica, New York

With a contribution by
Michael Bender, Ed.D.

A College-Hill Publication
Little, Brown and Company
Boston/Toronto/London

College-Hill Press
A Division of
Little, Brown and Company (Inc.)
34 Beacon Street
Boston, Massachusetts 02108

© 1989 by Peter J. Valletutti, Mary McKnight–Taylor, and Audrey Smith
Hoffnung
First Edition

Library of Congress Cataloging in Publication Data

Main entry under title:

Valletutti, Peter, J.
    Facilitating communication in young children with handicapping
    conditions : a guide for special educators / Peter J. Valletutti,
    Mary McKnight–Taylor, Audrey Smith Hoffnung.
          p.   cm.
    "A College-Hill publication."
    Bibliography: p.
    Includes index.
    ISBN 0-316-89542-3
    1. Handicapped children — Language.   2. Handicapped children —
    Education — Language arts.   3. Oral communication — Study and
    teaching.   I. McKnight–Taylor, Mary, 1930–   .   II. Hoffnung, Audrey
    Smith, 1928–   .   III. Title.
    LC4028.V35   1989
    371.9'044 — dc 19   89-2831
                                                                     CIP

ISBN 0-316-89542-3

Printed in the United States of America
EB

To Helen, Donald, and Clare Adanuncio; Eleanor and Doug Banks; Dolores and Frank Parra; Mildred and Dave Verticchio; and to the memory of my beloved uncle, Jimmy

P. J. V.

To my mentors at the University of Virginia, my colleagues at Hofstra University, and my family — especially Tamar and Courtney

M. M.–T.

To my supportive, understanding, and loving husband, Joe

A. S. H.

Contents

Preface

Early intervention in the lives of children with handicaps has long been professionally championed because it may prevent secondary disabilities and because it allows professionals to take full advantage of the still developing and more "plastic" brain and nervous system. However, never before in the field of education have nationwide attempts been made to provide special educational and related habilitative experiences from the very beginning of a child's life. Because educational goals and emphases change as the child matures, most special education teachers may not necessarily be knowledgeable or skilled in providing early education, especially during infancy and the toddler years.

Facilitating Communication in Young Children with Handicapping Conditions is designed to provide a guide for special education teachers so that they might develop and implement educationally relevant experiences for young children with handicaps in the essential area of communication skills. The basic premise of this text is that special educators have a professional responsibility to provide instruction that will facilitate communication skills, especially in the areas of nonverbal and oral language.

Teachers who are concerned about teaching communication skills to young children with handicaps need to concentrate their studies on the nature and the needs of children from birth to 8 years of age. They should be able to discuss the nature of nonverbal and oral language and its development so that they, the educators, may more productively interact with parents, communicate with other professionals, and facilitate the nonverbal and oral language of the young children they teach. They must become familiar with the assessment procedures of other professions, be able to interpret their findings, translate data from these other human service professions into educational prescriptions and programs, and integrate relevant methods and approaches into a unified treatment program. A case in point is the use of augmentative communication. Whenever a speech-language pathologist uses computer technology to augment the communication of severely neurologically damaged children, the classroom teacher must be cognizant of and able to use adaptive devices, hardware, and interactive software. Teachers should be able to carry out both informal and formal assessment techniques available to them so that they may directly translate educational evaluations into programming decisions. Most of all, teachers need the skill and the knowledge essential for stimulating language in a variety of settings and to diverse groups with wide-ranging heterogeneity in terms of type and degree of handicap.

Further, teachers must understand the singular and specialized role that speech-language pathologists play in the speech and language functioning of children who deviate sufficiently from normal developmental patterns. It is necessary for special education teachers to identify and use those methods and approaches appropriate to educational practice while relinquishing to speech-language pathologists those problems that require the attention of these specialists.

Teachers must direct their attention to the ways in which language skills can assist in the development of cognition, which is especially relevant to the educational task when a variety of therapeutic interventions address motoric, affective, and functional activities of daily living. The role of special educators is constantly changing and expanding, and if mainstreaming is to be successful, special education teachers must serve as consultants to regular classroom teachers.

The authors' mission is to blend the knowledge of two professions — speech-language pathology and special education — so that teachers of young children who are handicapped may interact more productively with speech-language pathologists and, in this manner, provide the children they teach with a school experience that facilitates effective communication. Teachers should benefit greatly as they learn special methods, as they explore needed competencies and strategies for stimulating language, and as they become more familiar with the nature of language and how problems in this area may be remediated and minimized.

Although the principal audience for this text is the special educator, regular classroom teachers and speech-language pathologists should also benefit. It is hoped that, as a result, educators working in the mainstream and speech-language pathologists may more effectively cooperate with special educators in achieving a more fully realized school-based experience that is truly interdisciplinary in nature and that uses the clinical setting, the home, and the community as learning centers.

P. J. V.
M. M.-T.
A. S. H.

CHAPTER 1

Introduction and Overview

PETER J. VALLETUTTI

The Education for All Handicapped Children Act (EAHCA), PL 94-142, and companion state statutes have had a tremendous impact on the total educational system: local education agencies, state education agencies, and institutions of higher education. For example, the concept of the least restrictive environment, a cornerstone of both federal and state legislation, has required that regular classroom teachers acquire the necessary attitude, the classroom management approaches, the behavioral modification techniques, and the instructional strategies that will help ensure the benefits believed to accrue both to children without handicaps and to children with handicaps who have been mainstreamed. The integration of those students with handicaps who are capable of being introduced into the educational mainstream provides the most normalized of the least restrictive environments.

THE IMPACT OF ZERO REJECTION

Perhaps the greatest impact of federal and state legislation, however, arises from the requirement to educate *all* children regardless of type or degree of handicap. As a result of PL 99-457, education is now mandated at age 3 rather than age 5, as previously specified in PL 94-142. Public Law 99-457, passed in 1986, also provides incentives for states to create programs for the newborn to 3-years-old age group, and many forward-looking states have already mandated service from birth through 21 years of age. This zero-rejection aspect of the law will continue to affect both teachers and teacher educators.

At the same time, it is clear that despite current state-level and probable future federal-level mandates, education from birth is an unlikely enterprise; the several processes of identification (Child Find), screening, assessment, official labeling, and program planning are time-consuming procedures. These processes guarantee not only that education will be delayed until late infancy at the earliest but also that critical time will be wasted — time that might have been more beneficially spent on direct service both to the children and to their parents or principal caregivers.

Nevertheless, despite such procedural delays making education from birth an unlikely possibility, many school systems throughout the country are now attempting to provide educational programs for students with handicaps at an earlier age than was contemplated a mere generation ago.

Furthermore, it is apparent that the rapidity with which children with handicaps are brought into the educational system depends not only on the sophistication of parents and other advocates but also on their assertiveness. Moreover, the promptness of bringing such children into the educational system is largely a function of the presence of a handicapping condition whose symptoms are severe enough to alert physicians or parents to the probable existence of a disabling condition that requires early and continuing special education and related habilitative and other services. Thus, special education for very young children is, in reality, the education of those children whose behavioral and learning problems are so patently severe that they cannot be easily ignored, rationalized away ("He'll outgrow it!"), or otherwise denied. Teachers of children with handicaps must therefore be prepared to work with a unique population, not only because of the age of the students and the curricular implications but also because of the likely nature and severity of the handicapping condition.

It is necessary, then, to examine those elements that are certain to stimulate early identification of a disabling condition so that the nature of very young children with handicaps can be better appreciated. Structural anomalies in which the physical characteristics of the child glaringly deviate from the normal (e.g., the stereotypical stigmata of the child with Down syndrome, the cranial abnormality of the child with microcephaly, and the structural defect of the child with cleft palate) are readily recognized by even the most unsophisticated observer and will lead to some type of intervention. Motor performance deficiencies such as those found in severely neuromuscularly involved children with marked cerebral palsy are not likely to go undetected (if not immediately, then in the first years of life) because the very young child is primarily a sensorimotor being whose motor behavior is carefully monitored and scrutinized by doting and even minimally involved caregivers. Sensory impairments of a severe and profound nature, with the accompanying absence of the child's response to substantial auditory or visual stimuli, are apt to disturb even the most naive parents, who will become concerned when they are not reinforced by their child's response to parent-tendered auditory or visual stimuli. Unfortunately, the child disabled by a mild to moderate sensory loss will often go unnoticed, even by sophisticated observers, because the relative mildness of the handicapping condition does not preclude responsiveness to gross sensory stimuli. It is only later, when the school-age child fails to adapt to the diverse demands of school life, that teachers and parents are more likely to note the confusion and errors resulting from the less severe sensory handicap. Severe behavioral deviations are also likely to create parental anxiety (e.g., when a child is unresponsive to and shrinks from human contact — so typical of autistic children who withdraw from touch, fail to communicate with smiles or through eye contact, and demonstrate marked language delay). Finally, as in the case of children who suffer from a progressive degenerative disorder that, at first, may not be manifested, the untoward condition in the early years becomes cruelly and gradually obvious to the caregiver (e.g., the child with Tay–Sachs disease whose apparently normal development begins to deteriorate progressively, leading typically and ineluctably to a vegetative state and to death). Indeed, whatever, the underlying pathology, it is the seriousness of the delay or deviation that invariably leads to the early identification of those young children as handicapped.

THE NEED FOR SPECIALIZED KNOWLEDGE

Because teachers of very young children with handicaps are typically providing individualized programs to students who are severely handicapped, they must have an unusual breadth and depth of knowledge about the nature of diverse handicapping conditions and about the nature of the multidisciplinary services these children invariably require. In addition, teachers must be skilled educational diagnosticians, skillful programmers, and highly competent communicators who must interact with an array of professionals, parents, and concerned members of the community. Obviously, an educational progam for very young children involves continuous and effective interaction with parents or other caregivers because they are crucial to the educational process:

- They are an invaluable source of information about the child's abilities as demonstrated both in the home and in the community.

- They are able to provide insight into the child's interests and thus about potential reinforcers.

- They are an essential source of information needed to prioritize educational goals and instructional objectives in terms of their potential effect on the daily functioning of the child.

- They play a critical role in helping to ensure program consistency, especially in programs designed to modify behavior.

- They must play a major role in the carry-over process, helping make certain that skills either partially or completely mastered in the educational setting are practiced and demonstrated in the home setting as the child functions in the activities of his or her daily life.

Thus it may be seen that teachers of these children require specialized knowledge (e.g., of medical problems and interventions) and skills (e.g., communicating with parents and with other professionals) that are not needed to the same degree by teachers who serve older children with handicaps.

Teachers of young children with handicaps must concentrate on curricular areas different from those areas whose importance increases as the student passes through the elementary, middle, and later years of school life. In the middle years of education, social, academic, and prevocational skills are emphasized, whereas the later school years concentrate on social, vocational, and other adult functional skills. However, the preschool and early school years must be concerned with the key maturational areas of motor development, self-care, preacademic learning, cognitive development, and the development of nonverbal and verbal aspects of language. Although most teachers are prepared to teach preacademic and cognitive skills to young children who are handicapped, they are not as prepared or as conditioned to program for motor, self-care, and both nonverbal and verbal language skills. In fact, early in the rehabilitation movement, several other professional groups emerged to deal with these important areas of human development in individuals with disabling conditions.

Physical and occupational therapists have assumed major responsibility for the motor development of people with handicaps in hospital and clinical settings, and more recently, in schools. As special education has achieved greater prominence, there has been greater emphasis on the role of educators, resulting in the addition of teacher specialists such as adaptive physical educators who are primarily concerned with the motor facilitation of students with handicaps. Occupational therapists have long dealt with the so-called activities of daily living (ADL), which to a great degree mirror the self-care curriculum typically provided by special educators. Although speech-language pathologists have the major responsibility for the development of oral language when there have been significant discrepancies in that domain, it is clear that teachers of very young children who are handicapped must accept some responsibility for the development of oral language, not only for its own sake but because of its singular role in the development of cognition.

THE PROBLEMS OF DEFINING DOMAIN

If the very young child, by legal mandate, is to be the primary responsibility of the public schools and their teachers, then these teachers must operate in largely unfamiliar and perhaps inadequately understood areas. They must also separate those aspects of the program that involve the direct services of related professionals from aspects that should be implemented by the teachers themselves. However, this separation is not easily done; any profession is usually unwilling to relinquish territory or power.

The first problem of increasing teacher competency in poorly delineated or unchartered areas needs to be solved by institutions of higher education, state departments of education, and local education agencies working in concert to prepare preservice teachers, beginning teachers, experienced teachers, and master or mentor teachers. The problem of special teacher preparation is particularly acute when special education teacher certification is not age specific. Teaching a 1½-year-old child who is handicapped is clearly a different task from teaching a 9-year-old child who is handicapped, not only because of the age difference but because of the likely difference in the severity of the disabling condition; that is, the 1½-year-old is more likely to be severely handicapped, whereas the 9-year-old may be found at any point along the severity continuum from mild to profound. It must also be remembered that curriculum priorities must be changed for various age groups as societal demands and expectations change and as motivational factors, interest factors, and functioning levels change within the child.

The second problem of identifying professional domains and their overlapping dimensions needs to be solved by professional organizations and recognized leaders in the respective competitive or overlapping fields; however, although this is a consummation devoutly to be wished, it is unlikely to occur without great difficulty. Clearly, the question of domain is not resolved merely by logical examination because it is closely tied to professional status, training, and economic factors. So, in the absence of professional consensus, decisions will continue to be made at local levels and in individual schools on an ad hoc basis, thus postponing decisions that may be vital to effective programming for children who require clarity in program delivery systems.

THE IMPORTANCE OF
COMMUNICATION SKILL DEVELOPMENT

Thus it is evident that teachers of infants, toddlers, and nursery- and primary-level children who are handicapped require extraordinary preparation in all key areas of maturation. This fact is particularly so in the area of communication skill development — especially when one considers that most teacher preparation programs place inordinate emphasis on written language (reading in particular) despite the primacy of oral language; despite the fact that facility in written language is less likely to be realized, given the severity of the disability in those who are identified as handicapped when they are very young; and despite the fact that effective oral communication has greater functional value than written language as the individual develops as a person, as a social being, and as a responsive and responsible member of the community.

This book is designed to assist teachers in developing the requisite knowledge and skills that will make it possible for them to competently facilitate communication in young children who are handicapped.

CHAPTER 2

Facilitating Communication: Teacher Competencies

MARY McKNIGHT–TAYLOR

Competence in any profession demands a broad range of positive personal and professional qualities, including comprehensive knowledge of the field, with particular attention to the area of personal responsibility. In addition, the competent practitioner must possess a high level of skill in interpreting and implementing sound professional practices. The National Commission on Excellence in Education (1983) makes the following recommendation:

Persons preparing to teach should be required to meet high educational standards, to demonstrate an aptitude for teaching and to demonstrate competence in an academic discipline. Colleges and universities offering teacher preparation programs should be judged by how well their graduates meet these criteria. (p. 30)

Administrators and supervisors of educational programs are also concerned about the level of skill and the strength of teacher commitment to education. Doll (1983) described the changes that are taking place in supervision and administrative procedures to ensure quality teaching practices. He suggested that the two main efforts of supervision in earlier times were directed toward helping people change their behavior on the job (in a positive, productive way) and toward helping those they supervise to perform more effectively. Doll presented a summary of the information that various studies have provided about teaching and the teacher's role. Some of the competencies discussed by Doll (1983) include the following:

1. The intervention of teachers between pupils and the subject matter they are to learn is essential.
2. What teachers should do in classrooms to aid learning can depend on the nature of the subject matter to be learned. In teaching certain subject matter, teachers need to be rigorous taskmasters. In teaching other subject matter, they need to step aside to permit their pupils to experience freely, openly, and without inhibition. (p. 13)

Some of the other points made by Doll in the same passage are specific to administration and supervision, but two are relevant to this discussion and support the need for development of teacher competence in other areas. Individualizing instruction and personalizing tasks to the learning and behavioral characteristic of the students are important skills. Doll continued with the following ideas:

- Teaching should be specific to the educational level and other characteristics of the group (not to mention the individuals) being taught.

- There are three sets of factors that produce learning by pupils: (1) the pupil's own ability and motivation, (2) the qualities of the home environments from which pupils come, and (3) the amount and nature of instruction within congenial classroom environments. (p. 14)

These factors and others have been considered in developing a list of competencies crucial to success in the area of language and communication.

Special educators must demonstrate knowledge of the course of language development as well as knowledge of the causes for delays, disorders, and disabilities that affect the teaching and learning processes. This knowledge provides a basis for long- and short-range planning, establishes realistic expectations for students, and sets the time lines and framework for the curriculum. The knowledge of normal language development provides a basis for realistically appraising the progress of a wide range of exceptional children with varying degrees of mental, physical, and emotional challenges.

The presence of a child with special needs creates a family with special needs whose dynamics are likely to be distorted. It has been suggested that the child with special needs performs a specific function in family interaction, and that the labeling of the symptoms and of the behavioral or emotional functioning of that child provides a basis for each of the other family members to interact with the child and each other (Turnbull, Summers, and Bothersome, 1984). The home and learning environment of exceptional children are likely to be substantially different from those of nonhandicapped children. Special needs youngsters often do not participate in the usual primary family unit attributed to stereotypical, middle-class cultural and familial interactions. Special education teachers who are sensitive to these factors will be alert to the compensatory experiences and adapted teaching strategies needed. The physical stamina of teachers, and their mental and emotional reserves, may be subjected to enormous drains because of the demands made by the diverse types and degrees of disability found in a self-contained classroom.

This chapter discusses the competencies seen to be vital to teacher success and pupil progress, with particular reference to the development of language and communication skills in young children with handicaps. Eight separate categories of competence are discussed. The special educator should demonstate competence in

Diagnosis and evaluation
Classroom organization
Behavioral management techniques
Curricular approaches
Instructional methods and materials
Communicating with parents, other professionals, and the community
Self-monitoring and self-development
Professional and career development

DIAGNOSIS AND EVALUATION

Diagnostic competencies include the ability to obtain instructionally relevant information, interpret it, and plan appropriate instructional and remedial activities for children. Diagnostic and assessment skills include the ability to adapt testing materials, test sessions, schedules for testing (the amount of time to be allotted, the time of day), and the testing environment to accommodate the special needs of young children with handicapping conditions. The disabling conditions may not always be directly related to language and communications, but they may be related to the physical functioning that makes test material difficult to manipulate. There may also be a need for alternative strategies designed to obtain and keep the child focused on the tasks being presented. There is often a need for extended relationship building before the assessment level of functioning may be viewed as accurate.

The special education teacher is supplied with data from many sources. The concept of a multidisciplinary team is a good one because it is designed to provide intensive multifaceted intervention for the child. However, use caution when interpreting formal data without direct communication from those evaluators who have gathered the information and made specific recommendations for instruction. And remember, although recommendations can provide valuable instructional insights, classroom teachers have the professional responsibility of designing the instructional program. Not only can interdisciplinary information be helpful in this effort, but the classroom teacher must also base instructional planning on more personalized assessment techniques such as observation of the child in activities with both receptive and expressive language demands.

Such observations may be conducted for specific periods or in specific subject areas, or they may be devoted to a specific area of communication. This permits the teacher to develop more accurately the strength-and-weakness profile upon which planning will be based. Ecological observations are observations made in various settings with attention to factors in the environment that in some way influence behavioral outcomes. Wiederholt, Hammill, and Brown (1983) described ecological observations as an important diagnostic procedure.

The developmental milestones for social and emotional development need to be considered because they affect language development in children. There are informal diagnostic measures that reveal inhibitors to ready communication or to the development of skills that help children express their emotions and understand those of peers and adults. Informal data-gathering devices include dramatic play, in which children are encouraged to play with a variety of objects and to create their own scenarios. The language and emotion content would indicate feelings and ideas, as well as the child's ability and willingness to express them openly. Puppetry, for example, provides an opportunity for children to vent hostilities verbally and physically while still being able to undo the dreadful punishments they deal out to the objects of their anger (Woltman, 1968). Interpreting the verbal and emotional content enables teachers to schedule activities, plan lessons, and select materials that develop and extend the communication capabilities of their children appropriately.

Planning and using diagnostic data enables the teacher to be objective when choosing topics, time, and materials that can be personalized for individual and group sessions. Mager (1962) stated that behavioral planning, which focuses on observable, measurable behaviors, helps the teacher and the child. This is possible because the data provide the profile of need, as well as a road map for achieving chosen goals.

The special education teacher must be sufficiently skillful to:

1. *Identify the cognitive, physical, and emotional strengths and weaknesses of each pupil.* This activity includes such determining factors as the student's energy level, medical problems, and general emotional set. Is the child able to place objects in functional categories? Is the student aggressive? Withdrawn? Responsive to other children? Does the student interact with adults in the environment? On what level of sensory and motor functioning does the student perform? What objects or activities seem to appeal to the child?

2. *Identify the optimal conditions under which learning takes place for students.* First, the teacher must draw on observational data as well as review and interpret data in the child's record to establish the best time of day for language programming. The teacher is then able to match physical functioning levels with instructional demands appropriate to the child's typical performance. Another factor in determining optimal conditions is the physical setting that a particular child requires, or in which the child functions best. This factor includes the amount of space needed and the amount of stimuli, both visual and auditory, that can be tolerated by the child. Second, the careful monitoring of social environment is also important; it includes individual sessions or sessions that pair children with similar needs. Positive planning also includes pairing children whose dissimilar needs might serve as motivation or reinforcement for the others in the group. If, for instance, one child has a physical limitation and cannot hold or manipulate curriculum materials, a child who has those skills should be considered for inclusion in the group. This pairing is likely to build constructive interpersonal relations, establishing empathy in the physically capable child while helping the child with the limitations to accept help when it is needed. Conversely, the child receiving help must have an opportunity to give help in other contexts.

3. *Identify the hierarchy of prerequisite skills and subskills that are necessary to acquire the various communication functions.* This process has been called task analysis, and it involves breaking tasks into small increments of behavior that lead to a terminal goal. The task-analysis approach tells the teacher at which point in the educational sequence instruction should begin. In addition, the degree of success can be measured more precisely because a task analysis is behaviorally articulated so that the teacher becomes alert to the student's demonstration of specific behaviors. Task analysis helps reduce frustration and boredom in children and teachers because it maximizes the power of challenge and success. This is possible because task selection, and the entry point at which the task selection is made, is matched to the child's level of skill in that particular area. For example, if a child repeats accurately (without reminders or hesitations) two things presented orally (auditory memory), the next task might be to have the child listen to and repeat three words similar to those already mastered. In this case, they would be similar in length, in phonetic structure, or in category (e.g., toothbrush, toothpaste, and mouthwash).

4. *Engage in trial teaching.* Trial teaching involves experimenting with various instructional techniques and materials to ascertain what the most successful instructional approach appears to be. It includes attention to the demands of the task, the mode of presentation, the type of materials used, and the sensory channels stimulated. Trial teaching reveals the supports required, the amount of success obtained, and the degree of mastery and retention achieved for each approach attempted. Diagnostic information thus learned provides the teacher with the basis for subsequent lessons.

5. *Identify the child's tolerance for stimulation and personal accountability.* It is important to know when to alternate individual sessions with group sessions. Teachers should not bombard students with stimuli. They should watch for sensory overload and change the pace, the approach, or the medium. For example, if a session has been largely visual and auditory (spoken language), change it to music, perhaps instrumental, classics, lullabies, or other familiar music.

6. *Review on a periodic basis the milestones and approximate ages of normal speech and communication patterns.* Teachers should review and compare diagnostic material and other indicators of cognitive and emotional functioning.

7. *Assemble information from other disciplines, parents, and various subject-area tests to create a profile of functioning in dimensions related to language and communication development.* For example, specialized vocabulary is developed, both expressive and receptive, which is associated with emotional and general development, movement, art, and music, as well as with the physical health of students, siblings, and caregivers. Individualized Educational Plans (IEPs) must be created, based not only on the input provided in terms of the goals prepared by other team members but also upon the interpretation by the classroom teacher of the ways in which those goals will be introduced, monitored, and evaluated. Teachers must also gauge the contribution of those goals to the development of basic competence in the area of communication; that is, they must judge the appropriateness of the goals according to the curricular scope, the sequence charts, and the child's level of readiness.

8. *Identify special conditions for classroom testing.* Teachers should assess procedures that may give a more accurate level of a student's cognitive, language, and communication ability by using adapted equipment, prosthetic devices, tape recorders, listening stations, language masters, computers, typewriters, and communication boards, or by using pantomime and puppetry as expressive or response modalities.

9. *Adhere to a test and evaluate criterion-based assessment models.* Broad assessment statements such as *Malika doesn't play with other children* do not give enough information for planning interventions. A better way of communicating the nature of her play or nonplay is, *Malika does not respond when other children invite her to join in an activity.* This statement is more useful because it has diagnostic value. Play involves initiating contact with others, being receptive to the contacts or ventures of others, and sharing or expressing feelings, desires, and attitudes. What Malika does or does not do in the situations noted may reflect a pattern of behavior that needs to be addressed by the teacher in making plans for group work and in choosing play activities. Describing performance behaviorally also

establishes a behavioral orientation to goal setting. Behaviorally stated goals are essential to the establishment of an educational program based on assessment data.

CLASSROOM ORGANIZATION

The organization of a classroom in which children learn and grow is a complex, time-consuming task. Once done, however, the task of teaching is made less difficult. The initial organizational structure may need to be modified as children move through the school year because children learn at various rates and respond in various ways to the same routines or environments. Special education classrooms must be places in which children are challenged mentally and physically, nurtured emotionally, and supported in social growth by consistency in the application of rules and expectations for behavior. These are necessay considerations for all classrooms, but those classrooms containing children with special needs should especially be structured so that children are provided maximum support in their efforts to learn. A self-contained classroom may have students in it who have severe disabilities in one or more areas of functioning. Some children may be physically intact but may have perceptual-motor deficits such as an inability to listen to and remember verbal information (directions, sequences of numbers, or similar learning tasks). They may have difficulty with activities that use printed material, or they may find it difficult to trace, spell, or match sample material.

Teachers can use space and seating arrangements to help children compensate for problems with mobility (those in wheelchairs, with crutches, or with walkers) and sight (visually limited students with assessments of capability ranging from legally blind [20/100] to those with other limitations such as tunnel vision or strabismus) (Rosenthal, 1975). Classroom furniture, floor covering, and materials should also be designed to minimize distracting noises resulting from movement or use of materials. Children with attention deficits (hyperactive, short attention span) and children with hearing impairments need to have extraneous noises blocked out so that the focus of their attention will be on the lessons presented (Allen, Clark, Gallagher, and Scofield, 1982).

The following suggestions may present some solutions to the problems posed by disabilities represented in the classroom. For children who are limited in mobility, teachers should arrange desks and interest areas so that there is ample space for movement and so that materials are readily accessible. Children who have low vision should be given a step-by-step tour of the classroom so that they can begin to make mental notes about the location of their seats and about the distance and location of doorways, teacher's desk, special areas, and so forth. Those students who are nearsighted should be seated as close as possible to boards or screens on which information is being shown. Children with hearing impairment should be encouraged to move close to activities such as storytelling when teachers read aloud to small groups. Children who are highly distractible, or who are confused with a great deal of visual stimuli, should be seated in a plain grey (or other muted color) study carrell (a three-sided screen that shuts out all visual information except that placed on the student's desk). Carpeting or well-insulated tile helps reduce distractions created by movement (walking, crawling, or movement aided by assistive devices such as motorized wheelchairs).

Classroom organization skills require that the teacher consider all facets of the instructional process, which include the following:

- *The scheduling of activities.* Consider not only the amount of time allotted but also the time of day when activities are planned. This consideration is made in order to determine the best times for introducing new material, reviewing or reinforcing concepts, and scheduling free or unstructured time.

- *The materials used.* Pay particular attention to the format and structure of the curriculum material (what it is made of, what kind of appeal the material has for children).

- *The personnel involved in the classroom.* Consider both the number (pupil/teacher ratio) and the level of skill (the attitude toward and understanding of the special education process).

- *The influence of the physical environment.* What kind of activities may be presented? What is the impact of decoration, equipment, and arrangement of interest and instructional centers?

Teacher competence in organizing classrooms for infants and young children requires that teachers be sufficiently skilled to:

1. *Establish an appropriate environment.* Strive for an environment that is aesthetically satisfying and that includes early childhood materials for perceptual-motor, language, dramatic play, science, art, and music activities.

2. *Provide a healthy, safe environment that is free from clutter and distracting materials.* Children with special needs require adaptive equipment, mats, and changing tables, as well as appropriate medical and antiseptic/sterile equipment or materials. Provide locked cabinets for potentially dangerous equipment or materials. Infants and toddlers with various disabilities sometimes require medicines (salve, ointments, sprays) that should not be handled, or used by others. Germicide should be available for cleaning the surface of changing tables and for washing hands. There should be a supply of tissues, swabs, cotton balls, and rubber gloves available to teachers and classroom staff. Covered pails for soiled and discarded materials should also be readily available.

3. *Provide publication possibilities for children's language and communication efforts.* To help create a sense of class membership and personal pride, bulletin boards, progress charts, display tables, big books, and textured books should be created by working with the children, and ownership should be attributed to the child and to the classroom.

4. *Plan change-of-pace activities.* These should take into account the disabilities of the children, their attention span, and their frustration and tolerance levels. They should include class activities, quiet groups, and individual work. Further considerations in changing the pace of activities include the amount of teacher-assisted versus independent work and the selection of activities that provide positive energy outlets; preschool children need an active, highly motoric curriculum. Children who have specific physical disabilities (e.g., paralysis, amputations, or cardiac or respiratory difficulties) will often need a change of position and pace to allow for systemic relief and alternating periods of stimulation and relaxation. Be sure to build in quiet time when listening and reflective behavior are required. After verbalizing, ask children to think about a song, poem, or story and then either draw, make a model figure, or in some other way share their thoughts about the experience.

5. *Schedule times, space, and equipment for follow-up and review lessons, based on the child's level of response to the tasks presented.* Teachers should be able to anticipate instructional needs — if their diagnostic notes are sufficiently detailed and explicitly stated. For example, notes on the progress of the lesson might include such comments as cooperative, stopped after first try, cried and refused to try, needed full or partial prompt (verbal or physical help), not able to do any of the required elements, or able to say or do the task on the first attempt.

6. *Establish classroom routines and responsibilities.* It is important that classroom aides, volunteers, or student teachers know what their general responsibilities are as well as special procedures to be followed in the event of fire drills, seizure activity, or any other crisis situation that may arise. For example, individual conferences might be held, or written guidelines provided, that include specific instructions ("When Maceo starts to bang his head, I will go to him; you take over my group" or "When Cynthia throws a toy, we require her to retrieve the thrown object"). Some guidelines should specifically address safety factors such as urging the removal of objects that are potentially dangerous or fragile. Established routines for emergency situations allow the teaching team to move quickly and to minimize anxiety in the children.

7. *Shift instructional gears.* Although teachers should plan activities according to diagnostically based curricular objectives, they should be flexible enough to alter planned experiences to take advantage of serendipitous occasions and unanticipated incidents. If a child has been struggling toward mastering some skill and does so, let the other children applaud that child's triumph. A child might make a discovery while painting (when accidentally overlapped, red and yellow make orange). Digression from the planned project to discuss the discovery is a wonderful language-building, ego-boosting, strategy.

8. *Schedule activities that make varied language demands on children.* Teachers should give the children labelling tasks, descriptive and elaborative tasks, and tasks that require children to make associations, comparisons, and judgments.

9 *Have back-up activities and equipment.* Be prepared in case of medical or emotional crisis, equipment failure, or the absence of persons without whom planned activities are impossible.

10. *Have a broad repertoire of songs, nursery rhymes, action poems, and finger plays.* Much of language stimulation involves singing nursery rhymes and lullabies or telling story poems to children.

11. *Agree on common prompts for teaching sessions.* The signals and directions at school and at home must match. Train parents to use the same approaches and the same criteria for success.

12. *Be skilled in pantomime.* This skill adds a fun dimension to classroom management. The teacher may sometimes motion silently for a student to approach; at another time signal with a pleasant voice, "Come here"; or mimic a voice resonating over a make-believe loud speaker, "Arthur, Come here!"

13. *Physically aid a student in producing speech.* The teacher may help the child achieve lip closure for the articulation of the /p/ sound by gently pressing the child's lips together.

14. *Fade physical prompts.* Rely solely on verbal prompts as soon as possible.

15. *Take advantage of unexpected events and seize the teachable moment.* A bird momentarily resting on a windowsill may provide the impetus for a fantasy game that involves chirping, cooing, fluttering "wings," hopping, pecking, and using "bird talk" such as the owl's "who-o-o-o."

16. *Take advantage of language related to seasonal events.* As snow is falling, children can imitate the floating snowflakes while the teacher emphasizes the silence of the snow. They may later compare it to pelting rain or thunderstorms. Teachers should also encourage parents to point out the sounds of nature, and should explain how that helps build language and communication skill.

17. *Identify the impact on speech and communication patterns that may result because of differences in child-rearing practices among various ethnic, cultural, and social classes.* For example, some cultures value compliant, docile, dependent children who quickly obey adults, whereas others prize those who question, experiment, and independently pursue thoughts and projects.

18. *Provide opportunities for group responses.* When asking the class to repeat a word, hear only the correct response and say, "You're right! It is an apple."

19. *Arrange materials both for independent access and for responsible return when activities are finished.* Establish pictorial labels that indicate where materials belong. Establish an early sense of order and responsibility for care of materials. The principles of autoeducation proposed by Maria Montessori (1964) can be used as a basis for training in critical thinking, evaluation, and comparison of the properties of materials. The materials themselves help structure the learning sessions.

20. *Schedule at regular intervals ways to monitor student progress in the areas of skill attainment, motivation, effort, and attitude.* This is best accomplished by establishing regular assessment procedures (weekly, monthly, or at times dependent on the functioning level of the student and the type of material to be mastered).

BEHAVIORAL MANAGEMENT TECHNIQUES

Managing classrooms effectively requires skill in a number of areas. Behaviors such as attentiveness, cooperation, and sharing need to be reinforced, and activities must be planned to enhance their growth. Other behaviors need to be decreased, if not extinguished, and include negative acts such as stealing, self-abusive acts, or inappropriate verbalization. Still other behaviors may need to be introduced before planning activities that sustain them once they have appeared. Behaviors in this class include such acts as establishing eye contact, volunteering to speak, joining group activities, or becoming more independent about securing materials and actually working on individual assignments.

Behavioral management techniques may be psychotherapeutically oriented; that is, they may be designed to change behavior by attempting to address the causes, and they may do so in ways that help the children understand why they behave as they do (Redl, 1980). However, behavior modification techniques are based on another theory — that behavior, unless it is metabolically or genetically based, is learned; therefore, it can be unlearned or modified. Other assumptions are that behaviors are learned separately, and though there may be a cluster of behaviors with which the teacher must struggle, behaviors that are in need of change can generally be manipulated one at a time.

A cluster of behaviors might be formed around a single behavior such as out-of-seat behavior. The resultant cluster of behaviors might range from inattentiveness to physical aggression that may be self-directed or directed toward other children, or toward the teacher. Out-of-seat and off-task behaviors generally result in a lack of achievement for the children who demonstrate them.

Brickmayer (1987) defined discipline (behavior management) in her book *Discipline Is Not A Dirty Word*. She suggested that there are three essential qualities that ought to be present in order for a person to be characterized as a good disciplinarian with children. A good disciplinarian is

a person children find interesting and full of good ideas,
a person who makes rules and expectations clear and understandable, and
a person who demonstrates appropriate behavior through speech and actions.

The teacher who is strong in the area of behavior management will have an appreciation of what Fritz Redl (1968) calls a "therapeutic milieu," and will be able to create an atmosphere in which children can explore, in which trials and failures can occur without fear or embarrassment, and in which children can feel a sense of acceptance and warmth. Teacher competencies in the area of behavioral management include the ability to:

1. *Appreciate the psychological principles known as Thorndike's Law of Effect.* These principles suggest that those behaviors that are positively reinforced tend to reoccur or to gain strength, whereas those that are not reinforced tend not to be repeated or are weakened (Madsen, 1981).

2. *Appreciate the strength of the dynamics at work when behavior is managed using the Premack Principle, or what has been dubbed "Grandma's Law."* (Madsen and Madsen, 1980). This principle refers to a process in which persons are asked to do something they do not want to do (low priority event), do not know how to do, or do not do well. For attempting these behaviors, persons are rewarded by being premitted to do something they like very much (high priority event), spend time with someone they choose, or receive edible rewards or other items that are highly desirable. "Grandma's Law" is, first the spinach, then the strawberries.

3. *Recognize that a triad of interactions occurs that must be recorded and interpreted if meaningful behavior change is to occur.* Teachers must observe antecedent events and target behavior and must manage the consequences placed on the behavior. *Antecedent events* include demands or tasks imposed on the child. *Target behaviors* are those acts, verbalizations, or lack of action that are problematic to the child, other children, and to the teacher. The behavior might be one that needs to be increased. Some examples are in-seat behavior, on-task behavior, or establishing eye contact when speaking to others. Target behaviors that might need to be decreased or extinguished would be hitting, out-of-seat behavior, spitting, biting, tantrums, and negative behavior. *Consequences* are those sanctions, rewards, or responses that occur after the behavior.

4. *Record events and activities that seem to be particularly motivating.* Teachers should note those activities or materials to which the student seems drawn during free or unstructured time.

5. *Anticipate problems for the class that typically result from the disruptive behavior of one or more students.* Plan for management of the student who is out of control as well as for the rest of the students who should be helped to remain on task. Immediate reinforcement (with verbal praise, hugs, and edibles) of those students who remain on task tends to create a climate in which being on task may be far more appealing than responding to the acting-out behavior. Praise should be specific to what the child is doing appropriately. *Good Boy!* or *Good Girl!* is not a desirable form of praise. Rather, teachers should say, "That was good looking and listening, Joan. You looked right at me while I was talking and ignored Mark's shouting."

6. *Identify what is reinforcing for a child.* Create a reinforcement menu for each child (Homme, Casnyi, Gonzales, and Rechs, 1977). Although general categories may work for most children, there will be specific types of toys, books, or materials that some children will particularly want. Be aware, too, that the same activity, materials, or person will not always appeal to the child. Satiation, maturation, and new trends require constant updating and revision of a reinforcement menu. Some reinforcers, particularly edibles, are no longer powerful if the child is full. Cookies rarely work as a reinforcer after a snack or lunch. Interests invariably change, and the sought-after toy will no longer be desired. Cabbage Patch dolls, formerly highly coveted toys, have largely been replaced by Pound Puppies, and in turn, they have been replaced in some groups by GoBots, which will be replaced by new fads. Some will become classics, whereas most will pass into toy oblivion.

7. *Recognize the positive traits that others possess and the constructive things that others do.* Sharing, good humor, patience, kindness, persistence in the face of defeat, helpfulness, and other positive personality attributes are as important to reinforce as are specific skills and knowledge. These character traits contribute to the total development of the individual and to the well-being of the class. Teachers should demonstrate the value of those social traits by acknowledging them when they occur and by praising them.

8. *Concentrate on the strengths and achievements of the students.* Use those strengths as a basis for planning instructional and remedial activities. You must begin

with strengths and proceed from the known to the unknown — from the achieved to the soon-to-be achieved.

9. *Involve the student in planning.* Involve infants and toddlers in choosing activities and toys. Share with youngsters how well they are doing in their attempts, no matter how small the achievement or how far removed the skill seems to be from identified goals or instructional objectives.

10. *Attempt to seize the moment when the child is doing well.* Quickly praise or otherwise reinforce the positive behavior demonstrated, however fleeting it may be. Ignore the child and the behavior that is unacceptable, if it is possible to do so without endangering the child, other children, or property (Long and Newman, 1980).

11. *Create an air of warmth, approval, acceptance, and positive expectations through verbal, postural, and gestural communication.* Introduce a task with "You worked for a long time this morning; this is going to be easy for you." Another way to set up positive expectations is to illustrate graphically the progress made by the student over time. Let children know they are doing well. A tape recording that shows growth in oral expression may show the child that his or her language skills have improved over a given period. Reward effort as well as achievement.

12. *Create an environment that ensures success.* Leave the child with a sense of accomplishment. It is so easy to tune out learning when failure is an omnipresent condition of the school experience. Meeting the challenge of learning is a magic stimulus for children, and teachers aware of this work hard to keep children tuned-in.

13. *Choose activities that foster the growth of a positive self-concept in each child.* Help children make favorable comparisons between themselves and other children. Teachers should help children focus on how much they are like other children and on accepting the differences that exist as proof of their uniqueness.

14. *Help children understand acceptable ways of behaving by telling them what they can do instead of what they are not to do.* Brickmayer (1987) urged that teachers, parents, and other caregivers focus on permitted (encouraged) acts rather than focusing on acts that are not permitted (discouraged). Brickmayer believes that children begin to tune out all adult verbalizations if what they hear most are negatives ("No," "Don't," "Stop that!"). This tuning out is not only annoying to the caregiver, it can lead to a dangerous situation if a young child cannot discriminate between the tone in the teacher's voice saying "No" as the child moves to touch something fragile (such as a flower) and the tone of urgency in "No" when the child reaches up toward a steaming cup of coffee. Brickmayer suggests positive ways to state behavioral expectations. Instead of saying "Don't throw the bread," say "Put the bread on the plate," or "See if you can put little pieces of bread into the cup." Another example is saying "Carry the egg in both hands," instead of saying "Don't drop the egg."

In addition to the principle already discussed, Brickmayer (1987) presents six others.

1. Protect and preserve children's feelings that they are lovable and capable.
2. Offer children choices only when you are willing to abide by their decision.

3. Change the environment instead of the child's behavior.
4. Work with children instead of against them. [Here Brickmayer uses the analogy of refinishing furniture when one is very careful to work with the grain. She reminded the reader that children too have a special way of doing things, and if we try to accommodate their style, situations may be improved if not made more pleasant altogether.]
5. Give children safe limits they can understand. Recognize their feelings without accepting their actions. Maintain your authority calmly and consistently. When children break rules, allow them to experience the consequences of their behavior.
6. Set a good example. Speak and act only in the ways you want children to speak and act. (pp. 8–19)

CURRICULAR APPROACHES

Select curricular packages and materials whose format and content are appropriate to the particular needs of the infant or preschooler with handicapping conditions. Visual, auditory, physical, mental, and emotional deficits may create problems for the child in the reception, organization, or expression of thoughts, feelings, and ideas. Attention to this area is crucial to teacher and learner success. With the passage of PL 94-142, both special and regular educators were faced with the challenge of choosing appropriate materials for children having an array of physical, mental, and emotional problems. To be effective, teachers must choose curricular materials that provide for individual differences in the ability to manipulate the material; educators must also determine the learner's receptivity to the teacher and the material being taught, as well as the learner's physical stamina, motivational level, attention span, and tolerance for frustration. Teachers should review curricular packets that contain sample plans or materials to be used in lessons designed to teach language and communication skills, and some record should be kept of the response the lessons triggered in the children being taught.

These sample plans and the record of sessions provide insight into the type of format that seems to be most helpful to the child. In curriculum selection, the visual qualities, or face value of the material, should be considered:

- The size of letters, numbers, and so forth

- The spacing of material

- The number of concepts presented at one time

- The versatility of the material.

A special consideration is the appropriateness of the material for the chronological and mental age of the children for whom the curriculum is designed. Early childhood curricula materials should be sturdy, colorful, safe (use nontoxic paints, be free of sharp edges, have no splinters, and have no harmful coverings). They should provide opportunities for structured and unstructured sessions.

Allen (1974) described the social behaviors that appear in the normally developing child's repertoire for various age ranges, beginning with newborn to twelve months, and ending with the social skills that should be present in children up to the second grade. She made several points that should be considered when teachers are selecting curricular materials that would be beneficial to children who are developing in an atypical pattern physically, mentally, or socially. "Social development, cognitive development, language development, and physical development, are inseparably interwoven . . . Furthermore, motor development contributes heavily to cognitive development, and both depend on socialization — on the development of certain refined social skills" (p. 153).

A social learning curriculum has been built around the creative arts. Activities and a rationale for their inclusion can be found in a module developed by McKnight-Taylor (1985), in which she suggested that the area of creative arts is rich with opportunities for developing in all disability groups and in all ages a sense of self-worth and competence. Carefully structured activities, and judicial selection of projects and experiences, help exceptional learners develop a sense of appreciation of their contribution to groups of which they are members, as well as an appreciation for others in their environment. McKnight–Taylor believed in the potential for free expression and in the joy of creating, and she believed that with proper guidance, experience would be successful and censure-free. She pointed to the various forms of media involved in creative arts and to the possibilities for discovering, sharing, belonging to a group, and participating in experiences that bring personal satisfaction and pride.

Three additional curriculum options offer solutions to a great number of problems related to the physical or mental limitations on the ability of young children to generate recognizable depictions of common objects. One is computer art; another is photography, particularly using a Polaroid camera that gives immediate feedback (Li, 1987). Some 110 cameras match the sharpness and detail of a skillfully used 35 mm. The third option is the use of videotapes or videorecorders.

Many instructional systems evolved through the cooperation of planning units that incorporated the need of several schools, or school districts. One such system is the PLAN (Program for Learning in Accordance with Needs). The PLAN began as a program for grades one, five, and nine (Gronlund, 1974). The language arts component is the only part that is discussed in this section.

The PLAN program is individualized so that students works at their own pace. Basically the system is made up of Teaching Learning Units (TLUs), each of which is based on a specific behavioral objective that specifies what the student should be able to do when the unit is completed. In some areas, especially the primary unit, objectives are carefully sequenced. (This brief discussion of one curricular approach should alert special education teachers to the fact that opportunities exist for developing, field testing, and providing research data on the effectiveness of curricular materials for children with special needs.)

The importance of curricular packages cannot be dismissed; they are responsible for the presentation of both concepts and information, and they offer a form of organizational structure for the classroom. Teachers need to be sufficiently skilled to:

1. *Select appropriate materials.* The format and content of curricular materials should be appropriate to the level of their students' ability and should provide ways for the students to learn that overcome disabilities or weaknesses.

2. *Select nonstereotypical material.* Racial and sex models should be presented in an unbiased, nonstereotypic light.

3. *Use a variety of commerically prepared materials along with those that are made by teachers and students.*

4. *Select from various subject areas, materials that will introduce new experiences to children as they learn concepts and facts.* Music, for example, can help teach concepts such as fast and slow, or loud and soft. The Hap Palmer music series of records and cassette tapes has a sprightly beat; some are syncopated and sound very much like today's current top songs. They teach basic information, and one, *Getting to Know Myself,* helps build a positive self-image in the children.

5. *Use material that reflects the cultural diversity of this country, being certain to include those races and cultures represented in the classroom.*

6. *Choose materials that are structured toward the learning style of students with various needs.* Use programmed materials that present small pieces of information, review it, test to see whether it has been mastered, and give immediate feedback about the correctness of the answers given by the children.

7. *Use material that has multisensory qualities.* Children with learning problems generally benefit from intensive sensory stimulation, varied material, and repetition of the material to be mastered.

8. *Identify behavior that indicates the student may not be able to learn by using the material as it is presented.* Changes of material to the concrete level might be indicated, or another form of presentation might help develop language. Common things in the environment can be used. For example, to teach *light,* or *on,* or *off,* the teacher might use a lamp with either a push button or a chain to turn the light on and off. (A chain is preferable because the action is more defined.) Teachers say, "The light is off." They pull the chain (or push the button) and say, "The light is on!" The wall light in the classroom can be used in place of, or along with, the lamp.

9. *Locate specialized materials.* For example, locate materials that help children with perceptual-motor deficits improve their skills in those areas that have been diagnosed. Physical education materials such as balls of various sizes and weights can be used. Mat activities are also good for young children; rolling and crawling and paired pushing/pulling activities develop motor systems and increase opportunities for socialization.

10. *Use computers and other assistive technology in initial teaching sessions and in drill and practice sessions.*

11. *Use readiness materials.* Such materials include sand and water tables, building blocks, and large pegs that have been adapted in size (made larger),

perhaps with a head on them so that they can be grasped by children with poor motor control.

12. *Choose a wide variety of dramatic play materials.* Be sure to include many types of dolls or puppets so that various family constellations can be created to fit the differing backgrounds from which the students may come.

13. *Provide many creative outlets for students.* A great part of their learning depends on guided discovery and experimentation.

14. *Select materials that are appropriate for students' motor ability and that provide outlets for whole-body movement, if such movement is possible.*

15. *Provide materials that can be used on the floor, on mats, on wheelchair trays, and on other surfaces where the child with special needs may need to be placed.*

INSTRUCTIONAL METHODS AND MATERIALS

An important skill in this area is the ability to choose methods of teaching that respond to student needs, that are in keeping with special education mandates, and that are within the guidelines of the administrative structure in which the teacher operates. Special education techniques sometimes seem strange to those persons trained in traditional education programs. What seems like coddling or a failure to hold students fully accountable for their behavior or for their achievement is in fact an appropriate response, given the infant or toddler's developmental level. The concept of developmental delays, disorders, and disabilities provides the basis for selection of materials and approaches that develop growth in students with a range of handicapping conditions.

Contingent on the type of disability and the kind of alternative approaches required, teachers may change one or more of the following: the task, the way the task is presented, the way the child is asked to respond, or the material used. If a child has a short attention span, the teacher might plan two or three minilessons with one set of interactions in each, rather than having the child respond to three tasks in a single session. If a student has problems focusing on individual items on a page that has several sets of pictures, letters, or words, the teacher can make the picture larger, or make the outlines of the pictures bolder or darker; increase the span between the items on the page; or present the items (pictures, letters, or words) on individual cards, one at a time. The materials can be lined up on a chalkboard ledge or attached to the board with double-faced tape so that the child can select the item the teacher has asked for.

Teachers will find excellent reference sources in some of the material generated by Dean's Grants (federally funded projects that were administered by schools of education in various universities). Another source of information is the material generated by the Division of Personnel Preparation, Special Education Programs, Office of Special Education and Rehabilitative Services, U.S. Office of Education. *Classroom Strategies for Accommodating Exceptional Learners* (Allen, Clark, Gallagher, and Scofield, 1982) is part of a series developed by the University of Minnesota under Grant No. OEG 007 902045. Allen and colleagues suggested that teachers view instructional practices for all learners (especially those with special needs) as more than assignments, and they suggested matching students with materials based on readability or other formulas. Five steps that help learners learn were listed by Herbert (1982):

1. Teach needed vocabulary, explain the way in which the lesson will proceed, and establish the structure for the lesson.
2. Give additional information that will help children understand what they are being asked to do, say, or suggest. Link the suggestions or clues to experiences that the children may have had.
3. Sometimes interact with the students on a one-to-one basis; at other times encourage them to interact with each other.
4. Let children know that they are expected to succeed. Make positive statements such as, "You can do it. I'll show you how."
5. Requirements made on students should be varied to meet their levels of strength with provisions for their weaknesses.

Teachers must be able to use a variety of approaches if they are to overcome the problems presented in developing language and communication skills in young children with developmental delays, disorders, or disabilities. They must be alert to opportunities to:

1. *Utilize resource people in various areas who may have some appeal to children.* Artists, doctors, nurses, builders, writers, lawyers, judges, actors, sports people, politicians, community helpers, pilots or astronauts, and business persons (if given assistance in preparing their presentations) may be valuable motivators for dramatic play with resultant language and communication growth. The help provided guest presenters might include some background information on particular handicapping conditions and any limitations those conditions might place on the student's performance or ability to comprehend what is said. Presenters might also need help in translating or concretizing concepts related to their fields. Builders, architects, and carpenters, for example, might add a dimension of reality to their presentation by using the visual aid of a cardboard or "box city" in which recycled cat and dog food cans serve as fish ponds, boats, tables, towers, flower pots, and other miniature parts that simulate a real environment.

2. *Master, use, and teach basic manual communication techniques.* Teachers must be able to instruct children with severe hearing impairments in a program of total communication and children with sufficient hearing but with intellectual or motor functioning deficits in an alternative communication system such as communication boards and computers. Alternative communication systems may include manual signing as well as pantomime and gestures that indicate what is expected from the child in speech or action.

3. *Be thoroughly familiar with diagnostic packages.* Assessment data from such instruments as the Brigance, The Denver Developmental Scale, The Portage Project, The DIAL, and the Gesell Developmental Scales suggest curricular approaches and materials (Freeman, 1977, pp. 60–61).

4. *Collect, maintain, and use books, pictures, and movies that depict persons with handicapping conditions in various roles.* Use literature that does not necessarily depict the child with handicapping conditions in either a super hero's or a pathetic victim's role. The idea is to use materials that highlight the similarities of children with disabilities to children who have no major challenges. It helps children and adults to see pictures and books that include children with visible handicaps going about ordinary pursuits, coping, enjoying, and working with whatever resources are available to them.

5. *Compile a list of resource persons with visible as well as invisible handicapping conditions.* These resource persons in various occupations can be invited to share their skills and their experiences in lessons, field trips, or other experiences.

6. *Mix activities, people, and materials that stimulate or reinforce speech.* Television programs geared toward young children often ask children to root for a character, to clap, or to sing-along. These are good programs for relaxed, fun-filled activity.

7. *Reward thoughtful, reflective answers as well as spontaneous responses.* After initially rewarding any and all verbalizations, children must be conditioned not to shout or blurt out answers. They should be taught to adhere to established rules for group participation. Children who think more quickly or who answer impulsively with the first thing that comes to mind will prevent children who are shy or unsure of themselves from answering. Value each response; do not permit children to ridicule responses of others. Be accepting of approximations of the desired response. Encourage children to be reflective when their responses require thought or verbal mediation. Leave children with the correct information. If a response has been incorrect, give the correct response, and encourage the child to repeat it.

8. *Use good questioning techniques.* Questions that help the child analyze a situation aid the child in developing critical thinking skills. Picture-interpretation exercises help focus questions and the ensuing discussion. *What happened? Why? How could this situation be changed?* Include questions that facilitate affective development. For example, *How do you think the children felt when their guinea pig escaped?* or *What do you think will help make them feel better?*

9. *Be acquainted with current games and songs popular with the child's social group.* Use them because they are already familiar and may encourage the child to participate in individual sessions and in group activities with peers who are also familiar with these current cultural clichés and fads. Keep informed about meaningful dates and events in the child's home and community, and use them as a focus for language activities.

10. *Develop a sense of capability in children.* By building lists with children, teachers take an important step toward building a personal profile. Such lists should include topics similar to the following:

- Things I can do

- Things I like to eat, to wear, to hear, to see

- Places I like to go

- Places I have visited

- People I have visited

- My wish list

In developing a wish list, teachers should steer children toward wishes that begin with themselves and their world. They should later move toward helping children think about and wish for positive changes for others.

11. *Develop resource files for science concepts that help the children understand and make analogies between their body systems and simple machines.* Children who have physical limitations may be helped to understand what is malfunctioning in their own system and what in nature or in technology duplicates the motion denied to them. Children in wheelchairs can address the upper torso, arms, shoulders, neck, and face (sample teeth, jaws, and chins — models from a local dentist may be used or models and charts secured from science/health catalogs). An additional source would be The Heart and Lung Association and special foundations for various disabilities. Children with visual or auditory limitations may use models of those systems, and under the teacher's guidance, instruments that duplicate the production of sounds may be used.

COMMUNICATION WITH PARENTS, OTHER PROFESSIONALS, AND THE COMMUNITY

The communication between school and community has historically been channeled through such organizations as the Parent-Teacher Association (PTA) and, with special children, the Special Education Parent-Teacher Association (SEPTA). However, formal mechanisms, do not take the place of the special interaction that the teacher of children with special needs provides. Informal contacts provide the basis for transmitting information about children's progress and needs on a much more personal level. Teachers have a great responsibility to relay accurately and promptly resources and information to parents, community leaders, and other professionals, which will enhance the quality of educational services. Contacts, both formal (report cards, test reports, and progress reports) and informal (good news notes, invitations to special events, and telephone calls) provide a basis for communication among the parents, the community, and the other professionals. Thus teachers must be competent to:

1. *Model teaching strategies for parents, aides, and volunteers.* Ask for feedback from those being trained so that questions or concerns will be aired. Provide many opportunities for practice under teacher supervision.

2. *Develop good interpersonal skills.* The success of the program depends on how well one is accepted.

3. *Make recommendations.* Teachers must provide to administrators, related personnel, and parents the rationale for current and future programming.

4. *Participate in special events in the community such as city or state fairs.* These field trips or parent-guided experiences provide motivation for experience stories and art or music activities that stimulate expressive language.

5. *Know the games, activities, commercials, and TV programs that children are likely to see,* and be alert to opportunities for steering parents and other caregivers toward stimulating TV programs and other video or audio materials.

6. *Plan cooperatively with parents, team members, and family advocates.*

7. *Listen to and guide parents toward solutions or resources that will aid them in securing services for themselves or their children.*

8. *Be acquainted with materials and research developed by organizations concerned with the development of language and communication skills.*

9. *Negotiate with local museums, botanical gardens, historical societies, libraries, and private collectors to secure entry to special sensory exhibits and other experiences tailored to the requirements of children with special needs.* Children who are visually impaired will profit from visits to gardens and exhibits that include items with varied identifiable textures and shapes. Gardens that contain aromatic herbs and flowers provide still another sensory experience. Teachers foster language and communication skills by explaining and reinforcing the experiences in lessons taught both before and after the visit.

10. *Sensitize lawmakers, school board members, and philanthropic groups to the special needs and abilities of children with handicapping conditions.* It is important that the local community, as well as politicians on the state and federal levels, develop an advocacy stance in order to provide opportunities for exceptional persons from infancy throughout their life span.

11. *Channel to parents information about impending bills that will have some impact on the quality of education for their children.* Many organizations mounted a tremendous letter-writing campaign when PL 99-457 was being considered. They informed parents and the community at large of the implications of the bill. It was projected that children between ages of 3 and 5 throughout the United States would be affected, and it was possible that parents would no longer have a choice of infant and preschool programs. Some therapeutic and social options were also threatened (Lewis, 1987).

SELF-MONITORING AND SELF-DEVELOPMENT

Skills and attitudes vital to teacher success have been examined throughout the history of teacher preparation programs. The list of competencies in this area is extensive. McKnight–Taylor (1976) developed a list of strategies and questions that teachers might use to monitor themselves as they move through their careers. Teachers were urged to pinpoint those factors in their lives they could control and those they could not change. In addition to the characteristics already listed, a successful teacher should also:

1. *Develop good interpersonal skills.* The success of the program is dependent on how teachers are perceived. Are they industrious, creative, emphatic, and

conscientious? How are they accepted by peers, administrators, parents, and the community? These are important elements in fostering positive public relations.

2. *Know how to handle stress.* Teachers must know when to renew themselves; introspection enables them to know their limits. They are then able to recognize and heed the signals indicating that personal and professional demands have depleted their reserves.

3. *Maintain an enthusiastic, playful attitude.* Teachers should enjoy playing with children and should introduce humor into the teaching sessions. They should be able to help children laugh at themselves and at truly funny situations.

4. *Be spontaneous and energetic.* Teachers should be able to plan activities that help compensate for impaired health or other energy drains presented by the handicapping conditions of their students.

5. *Be relaxed.* Be able to get down on the floor mats alongside the children.

6. *Be able to communicate enjoyment.* Let children see that they create joy by communicating with others.

7. *Keep confidences.* It is important to maintain confidentiality when possible. Physical and sexual abuse, however, or other threats to a child's emotional or physical health require that appropriate disclosure be made to safeguard the child. Some of the information or feelings shared with teachers need not, and should not, be passed along. Casual gossip is damaging and hurtful. A true professional does not gossip. Teachers often receive very sensitive information. There may be a great deal of pain, dissatisfaction, and disappointment in the lives of parents and children. This is true for those with special conditions as well as for those developing normally.

8. *Conduct yourself in a manner that demonstrates your competence in the field of special education and your respect for the importance of the interventions provided by special education programs.* Teachers who work with severely impaired children must often point out the difference between their efforts and what lay people see as mere "baby sitting." The structured and consistent approaches applied in sensorimotor learning, in self-help areas, and in beginning communication training have been carefully researched and are constantly being monitored and evaluated. When explaining the rationale for their activities to administrators and parents, teachers should be able to transmit the purpose of what seems to be merely play or basic physical care and maintenance.

9. *Keep abreast of medical and technological innovations in the field of special education and express confidence in the methodology employed in special education.*

10. *Prepare students for a child's extended absence.* A child may be absent due to operations or illness. The teacher should have the class draw pictures and send notes or taped messages to the child. They might also take class pictures and send individual messages to the child and the child's family, letting them know that the teacher and the class are preparing for the child's return. A class book might weave into it the settings and people that the child who is recuperating will recognize and be able to name. For example, if the child is in a hospital setting, doctors, nurses, hospital beds, and nurses' station can be a part of the teacher/class-made story. If there are specialized pieces of equipment used in the retraining and recuperative process (e.g., standing chairs, walkers, wheelchairs, braces, or casts), they should also be a part of the book.

11. *Prepare students for teacher absences (e.g., personal leave or needed medical procedures).* Teachers can work with the class or with individual children for whom their absence will pose a problem. Such problems include fear that the teacher will not return, feelings of abandonment, or the inability to accept changes in routine or personnel. Teachers can mark the calendar saying, "This is (these are) the day(s) that I will be gone. I will be back on this day." Plans and activities that may be going on can be discussed in the class during the teacher's absence, or the teacher may leave surprise packets and notes to be opened. These packets may be foam-rubber puzzles, inexpensive toys such as a jar of bubbles with wire or plastic rings, or books. Teachers may choose to make books of photocopied or mimeographed pictures, including scenes with pronounced themes or actions — pictures about which the child could talk or pictures that would provoke questions. Although D'Angelo (1981) suggests wordless picture books as a mechanism for motivating children with language disabilities, such books could also serve a very useful purpose in this context. The teacher might sign a single note for the children, telling them that they remain in the teacher's thoughts and saying the teacher thinks the toy (book or whatever has been left) is special.

12. *Freely express approval and affection for students.* A warm, caring, accepting attitude lets the children know that they are valued. Children are more willing to attempt assigned tasks if they are confident that failure at the task does not mean that they are personal failures. Greet the children with enthusiasm, using that time to stimulate communication. End the day's work with the same warmth, helping the children remember the day's successes and planning for the next day's efforts. By tone and language, let the children know that they should expect to be successful.

PROFESSIONAL AND CAREER DEVELOPMENT

The status of teaching as a profession has come increasingly under fire from inside and outside the ranks of the educational community. Literacy levels of teachers have been challenged, as has their ability to perform in an increasingly technological society. Revised standards for teacher preparation and certification are being implemented on a national basis. The recent report, *A Nation At Risk: The Imperative for Educational Reform* (National Commission on Excellence in Education, 1983) and the outcry for demonstrated excellence in education provide a clear mandate. Teachers must be discerning consumers of information and philosophy, and they must develop resources for humanistic and aesthetic growth. The National Committee on Excellence in Education (1983) framed its recommendation using a world view of the demands that will be placed on our citizens.

We must dedicate ourselves to the reform of our educational system for the benefit of all — old and young alike, affluent and poor, majority and minority. Learning is the indispensable investment required for success in the "information age" we are entering.

Our concern, however, goes well beyond matters such as industry and commerce. It also includes the intellectual, moral, and spiritual strengths of our people which knit together the very fabric of our society. The people of the United States need to know that individuals in our society who do not possess the levels of skill, literacy, and training essential to this new era will be effectively disenfranchised, not simply from the material rewards that accompany competent performance, but also from the chance to participate fully in our national life. (p. 7)

Teachers must also scrutinize program emphases, training possibilities, and educational opportunities that may be available. They must present a model of intellectual curiosity, professional confidence, and dedication to the field of education. To improve their skills and their professional standing teachers can:

1. *Participate in professional conferences by sharing innovative strategies for teaching language and communication skills.*
2. *Serve on community boards as a representative of special education interests.*
3. *Submit to publishing houses, advertisers, and news services information and suggestions that give a positive view of the gains being made in special education curricula.*
4. *Alert legislators to issues that would improve educational services to children with special needs.*
5. *Enroll in college courses and special seminars designed to upgrade skills and to provide new techniques for working with children with special needs.*
6. *Serve on boards of day-care centers to ensure that special education interests are served.* Early identification measures and alternative approaches to teaching can be provided if special education teachers provide guidelines and reference materials.
7. *Master the professional vocabularies associated with special areas of speech, language, and communication development, especially as it relates to exceptional conditions.*
8. *Keep abreast of current issues in world, national, local, regular, and special education.*
9. *Prepare for teaching, reporting, and other presentations with carefully researched facts and accurate summations of data.*
10. *Secure credentials that indicate an increased understanding of the objectives and theories in the field.*
11. *Sense the need for responsible participation, not only in the conduct of your own classroom but also in the program in which you teach.* This means that teachers must have an appreciation for their duties as members of an interdisciplinary team in terms of reporting, interpreting, and implementing those portions of team decisions that apply to classroom procedures. This also means that teachers should belong to and attend SEPTA meetings, and teachers should belong to professional organizations such as the Council for Exceptional Children (CEC), which is concerned with all exceptional conditions, and join special chapters of this organization whose major concern is specific age groups (e.g., the Division of Early Childhood [DEC]). Other organizations, both national and local, are concerned with particular groups included under the title *Developmental Disabilities.* The six exceptional conditions listed under this classification are mental retardation,

autism, cerebral palsy, cerebral dysfunction, sensory disorders (blindness and deafness), and epilepsy (Ehlers, Prothero, & Langone, 1982).

SUMMARY

One of the most important skills for teachers is the ability to monitor their performance in the variety of roles in which they function. Because infants and other young children with handicapping conditions present with diverse needs, teachers must continuously strive to expand their professional competencies to meet those needs. They, therefore, must develop diagnostic and evaluation skills that will enable them to plan and implement appropriate instructional procedures. In addition to developing diagnostic and programming skills, the successful teacher must communicate effectively the goals and methods of the program to other professionals and parents. Continuous renewal and the development of additional competencies must be central elements in the teacher's professional vision. This development is particularly important for the teacher who works with young children with significant speech and language handicaps.

REFERENCES

Allen, J., Clark, F., Gallagher, P., and Scofield, F. (1982). *Classroom strategies for accommodating exceptional learners* (University of Minnesota, Grant No. OEG 007-902045). Washington, DC: United States Office of Education.

Allen, K. E. (1974). The acquisition of social skills in the young child. In N. G. Haring (Ed.), *Behavior of exceptional children: An introduction to special education* (pp. 332–340). Columbus, OH: Merrill.

Brickmayer, J. (1987). *Discipline is not a dirty word.* Ithaca, NY: Cornell University.

D'Angelo, K. (1981, September). Wordless picture books and the young language-disabled child. *Teaching Exceptional Children,* pp. 34–37.

Doll, R. C. (1983). *Supervision for staff development: Ideas and application.* Boston: Allyn & Bacon.

Ehlers, W. H., Prothero, J. C., and Langone, J. (1982). *Mental retardation and other developmental disabilities: A programmed introduction.* Columbus, OH: Merrill.

Freeman, G. G. (1977). *Speech and language services and the classroom teacher.* Minneapolis, MN: University of Minnesota.

Gronlund, N. E. (1974). *Individualizing classroom instruction.* New York: Macmillan.

Herbert, H. (1982). *Developing comprehension, nature or nurture?* Emporia, KS: Kansas International Reading Association.

Homme, L., Casnyi, A. P., Gonzales, M. A., and Rechs, J. R. (1977). *How to use contingency contracting in the classroom.* Champaign, IL: Research Press.

Lewis, E. (1987, February). Spotlite on Down syndrome. *Association for Children with Down Syndrome Newsletter,* p. 1.

Li, P. (1987, September). Contests, contests, contests. *Classroom Computer Learning.* pp. 54–56.

Madsen, C. K. (1981). *Music therapy: A behavioral guide for the mentally retarded.* Lawrence, KS: National Association for Music Therapy.

Madsen, C. K, and Madsen, C. H., Jr. (1980). *Teaching discipline: A positive approach for educational development* (3rd ed.). Boston: Allyn & Bacon.

Mager, R. (1962). *Preparing instructional objectives*. Palo Alto, CA: Fearon.

McKnight–Taylor, M. (1976). Lesson 2: Teacher attitude 1. In *Teaching children with special needs: A teacher education series for K–3 teachers* (pp. 5, 6). Owing Mills, MD: Maryland State Department of Instructional Television.

McKnight–Taylor, M. (1985, Spring). Special education and the arts. *Focus 4* (p. 3). New York State Association for Childhood Education International.

Montessori, M. (1964). *The Montessori method*. New York: Schocken Books.

The National Commission on Excellence in Education (1983). *A nation at risk: The imperative for educational reform*. Washington, DC: U.S. Department of Education.

Palmer, H. (1974). *Getting to know myself*. Freeport, NY: Activity Records.

Redl, F. (1968). A therapeutic milieu: What's in it? In N. J. Long, W. C. Morse, and R. G. Newman (Eds.), *Conflict in the classroom: The education of emotionally disturbed children* (pp. 363–374). Belmont, CA: Wadsworth.

Redl, F. (1980). The concept of the life space interview. In N. J. Long, W. C. Morse, and R. G. Newman (Eds.), *Conflict in the classroom: The education of emotionally disturbed children* (4th ed.) (pp. 257–271). Belmont, CA: Wadsworth.

Rosenthal, A. B. (1975). Visual disorders. In E. E. Bleck and D. A. Nagel (Eds.), *Physically handicapped children: A medical atlas for teachers* (pp. 261–273). New York: Grune & Stratton.

Turnbull, A. F., Summers, J. A., and Bothersome, M. J. (1984). *Working with families with disabled members: A family system approach*. Lawrence, KS: The University of Kansas.

Wiederholt, J. L., Hammill, D. D., and Brown, V. L. (1983). *The resource room teacher: A guide to effective practices*. Newton, MA: Allyn & Bacon.

Woltman, A. G. (1968). The use of puppetry in therapy. In N. J. Long, W. C. Morse, and R. G. Newman (Eds.), *Conflict in the classroom: The education of emotionally disturbed children* (pp. 202–208). Belmont, CA: Wadsworth.

CHAPTER 3

The Nature of Language

AUDREY SMITH HOFFNUNG

The American Speech-Language-Hearing Association (ASHA) is devoted to the development, habilitation, and rehabilitation of children and adults, and it has recently drafted a definition of that complex system called language (ASHA, 1983). In the definition proposed, the use of language requires the interaction of many variables. Using the ASHA definition as a base, language is here examined in its many aspects (ASHA, 1983, p. 44):

Language evolves within specific historical, social, and cultural contexts; language as a rule-governed behavior is described by at least five parameters — phonologic, morphologic, syntactic, semantic, and pragmatic; language learning and use are determined by the interaction of biological, cognitive, psychosocial, and environmental factors; effective use of language or communication requires a broad understanding of human interaction including such associated factors as nonverbal cues, motivation, and sociocultural roles.

LANGUAGE EVOLVES WITHIN SPECIFIC HISTORICAL, SOCIAL, AND CULTURAL CONTEXTS

Language has developed over time in various social and cultural settings. Language is not static; it is a dynamic, constantly changing system. For instance, the language of Shakespeare, poetic and beautiful as it may be, is no longer used. "Shall I compare thee to a Summer's day? Thou art more lovely and more temperate . . ." (Sonnet XVIII, William Shakespeare) would probably be replaced today by "You are lovelier than a summer's day." And "Romeo, Romeo, wherefore art thou Romeo" (Romeo and Juliet, William Shakespeare) would today probably become, "Where are you Romeo?" New words are constantly being added as the social values and conditions change and as events occur. The abbreviation *Ms* is not to be found in a 1969 dictionary, whereas *Miss, mistress,* and *Mrs.* are. The word reflects a social change in the role of women. We *rap* when we discuss; we are *uptight* when we are nervous; and because our technology has created a new occupation, we send an *astronaut,* not a pilot, to the moon.

The geographical and cultural setting dictate the type of dialect we speak. People who use a particular dialect of a language are speaking the *same* language as are others who speak a different dialect of that language. The people who use the various dialects of a language are mutually intelligible to each other (Gleason, 1961); that is, the communicators can understand each other. Geographically, the dialectal differences may be found in the sounds, words, and structures used; for example, in the midwest, the *r* is included in the pronunciation of the word *western,* whereas in the eastern and southern areas of the United States, the final syllable of *western* would be more likely to rhyme with the final syllable in *piston.* In addition, because people in the eastern and southern parts of the United States do not pronounce the final *r* at the end of words, *sore* and *saw* are pronounced similarly. *Merry, Mary,* and *marry* are pronounced similarly west of the Alleghenies but are pronounced differently east of the Alleghenies (Gleason, 1961). Speakers of British English and American English generally understand each other though the speakers of British English use *lift* for *elevator, subway* for an *underground crossway,* and *bobby* for *policeman.*

In the south, *evening* describes any time of day after noon, and the use of *tote* in North Carolina for *carry* is based, according to linguists, on the word *tot* from the English-based Creole of Sierra Leone (Dillard, 1972). The use of the "perfect" structure varies from southern dialect to northern dialect and varies within the southern dialect itself. The southern dialect includes: (1) *I done gone,* and (2) *I done went.* In addition to (1) and (2) the southern dialect also includes *I've done gone* and *I've done went,* whereas the black dialect includes *I done go* (Dillard, 1972).

These differences are not produced randomly; they are based on a rule system of that particular dialect. The sociolinguist Labov (1970) stratified the classes of white New York City adults as lower class, working class, lower-middle class, and upper-middle class. Using this stratification system, distinct differences were recognized among the groups; for example, the –*ing,* as in *going,* was pronounced as /in/ rather than /iŋ/ with greater or lesser frequency for each group — the upper-middle class using /in/ less frequently in casual speech (20 in 100 times) than the lower class (80 in 100 times).*

Dialectical differences are based on geographical location, with further differentiation by socioeconomic status and by ethnic or racial differences. Labov's (1972) studies are a plea to those who work with children (who speak a dialect that is not considered a standard middle-class dialect) to understand the child's dialect, to recognize that each dialect is governed by specific rules, and to respect the dialect as well as the speakers of the dialect. It has been found that some dialects of a language are generally considered more acceptable than others, just as certain accents are considered to be more acceptable than others; for example, a French accent in some company is considered to be cultured or sophisticated. A teacher's preconception of people who speak a specific dialect may cause a teacher to judge children based on the dialect they speak. A teacher's expectancies of the children are an important factor in their overall accomplishments.

LANGUAGE AS A RULE-GOVERNED BEHAVIOR IS DESCRIBED BY AT LEAST FIVE PARAMETERS: PHONOLOGIC, MORPHOLOGIC, SYNTACTIC, SEMANTIC, AND PRAGMATIC

It is the capacity to use language, a system of conventional symbols, that separates the human being from the other creatures of the world. Symbols are one type of sign. There are three kinds of signs that are analyzed extensively in the literature: the icon, the index, and the symbol. The **icon** bears a visual resemblance to the item it represents; for example, a photograph or a map is an icon. The **index** is related physically to the item it represents; for example, smoke is found where there is fire. The **symbol** "is something that stands for something else" (Muma, 1978, p. 378). "It stands for other things that bear no real relationship to them." (DeVito, 1970, p. 7). It is arbitrary . In our language, *chair* has

---

* The Merriam Webster Pronunciation Symbols are used.

come to mean something you sit on. It could have conceivably been called a table or a foot or a desk. The dictionary lists the word as stemming from Middle English *chaiere*, from Latin *cathedra*, from Greek *Kathedra*, and from "*Kata– cata–+ hedra* seat — more at sit" (Webster's, 1969, p. 137), but does not explain why those particular sounds, combined in that particular manner — not /re(a)ch/ or /e(a)rch/, but /che(a)r/ indicate an item of that particular function. Of course, each symbolic "relationship is learned as part of a specific culture" (Traugott and Pratt, 1980).

This learned convention may be used for oral language or for communication that does not use oral language, such as the Red Cross symbol. Rees (1980) differentiated between oral language and communication, noting that oral language is dependent on a set of rules. It is a structured system that is used for both understanding and producing spoken language, and it serves as a means of communication. Emotions (smile or frown) are demonstrated in facial expressions and in body language. Bloom and Lahey (1978) divided language into three dimensions: content, form, and use. They stated that language users use an arbitrary code to classify the world. The content is the idea or experience users wish to communicate. Words are selected to convey the meaning. The form is a sound or a rule-governed combination of sounds that form a word; for example, *state* but not *szate* is found in English; the *sz*– is not an accepted sound combination in English. The rule-governed combination of sounds or words can be combined into a rule-governed combination of words, for example, the declarative sentence *I wash a sock,* or the question *Do I wash a sock?* Rule-governed inflectional endings can be added to the words, for example, plural [–s] and past tense [-ed] in *I washed socks.* An intonation pattern using, for example, stress and pitch change (called prosodic features) is superimposed on the words. For example, *I wash socks* has the falling pitch of a declarative at the end of the sentence, whereas *Do I wash socks?* has the rising pitch of a yes/no question at the end of the sentence. The speaker uses this novel creation of content and form for a specific purpose, that is, to inform, persuade, describe, or suggest. The following pages describe the five parameters of language.

Phonology

Rules are said to exist in all areas of language. Starting with the smaller elements of phonology, each of the elements can be examined individually, and each of them can be combined into the larger totality.

Phonology is the study of the sound system and sound patterns of language. Its smallest element is the phoneme, which is based on an abstract concept (Ladefoged, 1982). The **phoneme** is not the sound as it is produced, but it is the smallest unit that differentiates meaning. There are 46 phonemes in English (Gleason, 1961). Each language contains its own set of phonemes; for example, a nasalized vowel is listed as part of the French vowel system but does not appear on the list of American English vowels (Ladefoged, 1982). A phoneme is composed of a combination of a number of distinctive features. Jakobson, Fant, and Halle (1967) were interested in the discrimination between isolated words, that is, words presented without the use of context or syntax (_bill-pill_), and they provided an early version of the Distinctive Feature Theory. They suggested that (in example just noted) one distinctive feature, −voice, changes the perception of the listener from /b/ to /p/. The vocal folds are in vibration for the voiced /b/, so it contains the +voice feature; there is no periodic vibration of the vocal folds for the voiceless sound /p/, so it has a −voice feature. This binary opposition indicates that the feature is present (+) or absent (−). Only one feature sets the /b/ and /p/ apart; therefore, the difference between them is minimal.

Chomsky and Halle (1968) later proposed a different universal system of distinctive features, limiting the number to 13 features and stressing the articulatory features, or placement and use of the articulators. Their system is used on a clinical level for judging articulation development and articulation errors and for establishing clinical intervention programs (McReynolds and Bennett, 1972; McReynolds and Engmann, 1975; McReynolds and Huston, 1971). This method provides relative ease in analyzing the rule-governed speech problems of the child. The type of error that occurs when the distinctive feature has not developed, or when it is misused, is considered a linguistic error, in contrast to an error committed when producing a phone. A **phone** is the sound actually produced. Phonetics is the study of how a phone is produced (Muma, 1978). A phone is not based on the linguistic rules of the language. Infants babble phones. They play with sounds but do not use conventional meaning at this point; they do not use sounds to contrast meaning.

Traditionally, a speech-language pathologist (SLP) may have said that the child is substituting a /d/ for a /g/, when the child says _dough_ for _go_ or _dame_ for _game_. (Spoken words are best judged by sound and not by spelling). They might have said that, instead of bringing the back of the tongue back and up, the tip is being raised to the alveolar ridge of the palate or the roof of the mouth. But, using Chomsky and Halle's Distinctive Feature Theory, the error would be noted as not using two distinctive features +back and +high. By definition, the distinctive feature +back occurs when the body of the tongue is brought back or is retracted from the central or neutral position, and +high occurs when the body of the tongue is elevated above the central or neutral position (Chomsky and Halle, 1963). The body of the tongue lies under the hard palate (Ladefoged, 1982) in contrast to the blade of the tongue, which lies under the alveolar ridge. By using Distinctive Feature Theory, the SLP can detect the pattern of errors, which is a more effective approach than just noting whether the error has occurred in one phoneme. They look for other sounds that might be affected, reasoning that if the child does not have a distinctive feature in one phoneme, it will probably not be present in other phonemes that contain the same feature (Compton, 1970; Costello and Onstine, 1976; Pollack and Rees, 1972). This approach provides an economy of analysis. The likelihood is that if the child does not use the /g/ in _girl_, the back sound /k/ will not be used in _key_ and _cup_, and the back sound /ŋ/ will not be used in _sing_ because both of these sounds also contain the +back and +high distinctive features. This does not mean that the child cannot physically produce the sound. Imitation of the sounds _kakaka_ may be present but the /k/, /ŋ/, and /g/ may not be used when uttering words to communicate meaning.

In contrast, examples of phonetic or production errors are (1) a dentalized *t*, for which the sound is produced by hitting the back of the front top teeth (maxillary central incisors) rather than the gum ridge (alveolar ridge) of the palate; (2) an interdental *s* lisp, when the tongue is placed between the teeth (interdental position) rather than behind the teeth; (3) hypernasality, when a cleft palate or structural bone and tissue defect prevents a complete separation of the oral and nasal cavity (in this instance, the abnormally formed palate or roof of the mouth allows air to escape through the nose when speaking, causing the child to produce the sounds with too much nasal resonance, that is, with hypernasal resonance); and (4) the production of slow, uncoordinated, inaccurate movements of the articulators (lips, tongue, vocal cords, and soft palate), when a neurological problem exists as in a child with cerebral palsy. In this instance, when producing the word *pat*, for example, the lips may not close for the *p*, the vocal folds may not vibrate for the vowel *a*, and the tongue may not elevate to produce a clear, crisp, plosive *t*. The effect will be a slurred, unintelligible production. The lip closure, the vocal cord vibration, and the tongue elevation must be sequenced and timed with precision. Other neurological problems may result in a paresis, or an inability to move the muscle. A different type of limited movement occurs with damage to the nerve that innervates, or provides nerve stimulation to the muscle. Damage to the hypoglossal nerve (cranial nerve XII), which innervates the tongue, may weaken and limit the elevation of the tongue so that it does not reach the alveolar ridge to form *t, l, n,* or *d* in *dot* or *lane*. It is important to realize the difference between phonemic and phonetic errors in a child's speech. If a child's problem is with a phoneme, the error is with a rule or is a linguistic error; if the child's problem is with a phone, the error is one of production.

A more recent method of analyzing the production errors of a child (or an adult) is the Phonological Process Method. Hodson (1980) listed more than 42 processes that a child may use when speaking. Again, the investigator is expected to look at patterns. If children with language disorders produce *pi/pit, pi/pick, si/sip*, they may be using their own phonological process for production. In this example, the type of phonological process used is labeled the final consonant deletion process, or the post vocalic (after the vowel), obstruent (plosives and fricatives), singleton (only one sound), omission. (See Table 3-1.) The behavior is not a random product of the child's but is a production behavior that theoretically is based on the developing linguistic rule system of the child. Using the Phonological Process Method, the use of the *d* for the *g* is termed **velar fronting** (Hodson, 1980). The *g* is a velar sound; the velar sound should be made at the back of the mouth, but when it is made in the *d* position, it is made on the alveolar ridge or toward the front of the mouth. (See Table 3-2.) Studies have been conducted using the Phonological Process Procedure (Camarata and Gandour, 1985; Edwards and Shriberg, 1983; Hodson and Paden, 1983; Shriberg and Kwiatowski, 1985). Research, new thought, new approaches, new hypotheses, and continuing discussions are to be found in the literature.

Table 3-1. DEVELOPMENTAL HIERARCHY OF SOUNDS

Approximate Age	Nasals	Plosives		Glides	Fricatives		Affricatives		Liquids
		Voiceless	Voiced		Voiceless	Voiced	Voiceless	Voiced	
2:6	m	p	b	w					
3:0	n	t	d						
3:6	ŋ (sing)	k	g	y (yes)					
4:0					f				
4:6					s sh (shoe)	z			
5:0						v	ch (chop)	j (jaw)	
6:0					th (thin)	th (the) zh (beige)			r
7:0									l

This chart is a composite, with some modifications, of the research findings of Poole (1934), Sander (1972), and Templin (1957).
[a] Children may not use all sounds in all positions during their developmental stages. For example, the child may use a sound such as /b/in the initial position (boy) and not in the final position (tub) or may use the /s/ in the final position (house) and not in the initial position (sit).

Place of formation:

m,p,b — lip sounds
w — lip and velar sound
n, t, d, l, s, z — lingua-alveolar sound; tongue tip to the alveolar ridge
ŋ, k, g, y, r — back or velar sound
f, v — labio-dental sound; lower lip under the top teeth
th, th — lingua-dental sound; tongue tip to the back of the top teeth
sh, ch, zh, j — post alveolar; the body of the tongue is raised to a point posterior to the alveolar ridge

Table 3-2. EXAMPLES OF PHONOLOGICAL PROCESSES

Phonological processes	Strategy	Example
1. Final consonant deletion	Children omit the final sound of the word.	haɫ, beɖ, hug̸, baɫk, waɫɫ
2. Fronting	The child produces a sound in the front of the mouth when the sound should be formed further back in the mouth. Front sounds are developed before back sounds.	
	e.g., Lingua-alveolar sound for velar.	tē/key do/go
	e.g. Lingua-alveolar sound for post-alveolar sound.	tü/shoe
3. Stopping	The child produces a plosive for a fricative	por/four tüp/soup
	or for an affricative	t ip/chip
4. Prevocalic voicing	The child changes a voiceless sound to a voiced sound before a vowel.	gap/cap, gis/kis zu/Sue, dāk/take
5. Cluster reduction	The child deletes one consonant of the cluster.	
	e.g., /s/ reduction	ʃteam, ʃkip, miʃʃed, miʃt, maʃk
	e.g., /n/ reduction	had/hand wet/went
	e.g., /l/ reduction	bü/blue mik/milk

Based on Hodson, 1980.
Note: It is theorized that children develop their own strategies when producing words. This table lists strategies used by young children. Children may use a combination of strategies. For example, dē/take = prevocalic voicing + final consonant deletion, and dē/steak = cluster reduction + prevocalic voicing + final consonant deletion. Remember to think of sound, not spelling.

Shriberg and Kwiatowski (1985) used the term *phonological* to represent the entire speech production process, from the underlying representations to the production of the surface phonetic forms. The child is said to build a phonological rule after being presented with repeated stimulations of that rule being used in a sound in a word. The child may learn to differentiate a /b/ from a /p/ after hearing the /b/ and /p/ used in words in context in social interaction (Say *bye bye*, Where's the *bat*? Give me a *big* hug. Mommy has *pie*. *Pat* the doggie. Give me the *pig*.) The /b/ and /p/ are phonemes, and as phonemes they are sounds that differentiate one meaningful word from another, for example, *bye-pie*, *bat-pat*, and *big-pig*. The child builds the rule aided by the contextual setting, the meaning of the phrase, the syntactic structure, and the intonation pattern. The use of the rule may be limited at first to a particular person or to a limited number of words and, later, may generalize to a variety of people using that rule and to a variety of words that include the same phoneme and therefore are based on the same rule; that is, the child builds an internal representation of the rule and later (after hearing the sound being used in a word by people of different ages, sexes, and dialects) builds a composite image of the sound, which by then has developed into a phonemic category (Locke, 1980). This internal representation of the rule enables the child to understand the /p/ as in *pie* as it is said by a young or old speaker, by a male or female speaker, by a native speaker, or by speakers of different dialects or accents (e.g., one who speaks English as a second language). It enables him to perceive a /p/ phoneme that is formed in a stressed syllable (im-'por-tant), in an unstressed syllable (pa-'ja-mas), or before a consonant (cap-tain) as the same phoneme /p/, even though variations of that sound (allophones) are produced in words.

Because the /p/ in *important* is stressed, a great deal of air is exploded through the lips; the /p/ in an unstressed syllable produces less aspiration or air; and a /p/ that completes one syllable and occurs before the initial consonant of the second syllable does not produce released air — yet they are all heard as /p/ by the native speaker. A normal child who has the ability to differentiate the sound will eventually be able to produce it. Perhaps he can differentiate it because he can produce it (Locke, 1980). Locke (1983) cautioned that, when the child with language delay does not use particular features, the tendency by members of the profession is to label rather than to look for the reason for the use of the different rule. He suggested that published tests have been used for determining auditory perception or auditory discrimination *rather* than recognizing that production difficulties may be the basis for discrimination errors (Locke, 1980). In other words, when the child's production error of *dough* for *go*, is noted, an auditory discrimination test is administered (e.g., Wepman's 1958 test), during which the child is asked to state whether *thief-sheaf* and *wedge-wedge* are the same or different. When the child fails the test, it is concluded that the problem is in the area of auditory discrimination, without considering the alternative view (Locke, 1980) that the child's production error may be the basis for the observed discrimination error. A child with a production problem may not always be able to discriminate the sounds he is not able to produce (Locke, 1980). Thus, a child with articulation problems may have more difficulty differentiating the sounds that are in error in his production. The child's production of a sound may help in his discrimination. It is the phone that is actually produced and is considered the surface structure.

The terms *clinical phonology* (Grunwell, 1982) and *phonological disorders* (Locke, 1983) are growing in use. Locke suggested that the single term *clinical phonology* is needed to describe speech disorders rather than the separate terms *articulation* and *phonological.* As stated previously, speech problems have been separated into articulatory disorders, which involve the "peripheral speech-motor activity," or the use of the muscles relating to speech (e.g., the tongue, lips, and soft palate), and phonetic errors and phonological errors, which are the errors the speaker uses when the problem is in the "pre-articulatory" acquired rule system or the linguistic system (Locke, 1983, p. 339). It is necessary to look for the levels within the sound system, sounds being a part of phonology, to define and refine the method of classifying raw data and to retain a flexibility or opennesss so that theories may be revised as the need arises. Some suggestions for teaching some of the features will be found at the end of the Phoneme section in Chapter 4.

Morphemes

A **morpheme** may be just one phoneme such as *I* (pronoun) or *eye* (noun), pronounced /aɪ/ or *a* (indefinite article), pronounced /ə/, or a combination of phonemes that form the word (cat = k-a-t). A word may be a combination of morphemes (cat+s, teach+er, teach+er+s). *Cats* has two morphemes, one is *cat,* the other is the morphological inflection {-s}, which indicates plurality. *Teacher* has two morphemes, *teach* plus the morphological inflection {-er}, which indicates "one who does"; *teachers* contains three morphemes because the plural is added to *teacher.* By definition, a morpheme is the minimum unit of meaningful speech. It is a unit that cannot be divided, but it is not to be considered the same as a syllable (Gleason, 1961). The morpheme {-s} has meaning. It tells the listener that the speaker is referring to more than one cat and more than one teacher. This inflection can be added to other words, providing information regarding quantity (e.g., hats, caps, and beaks). In contrast, the phoneme /-s/ does not have meaning; rather it helps the listener differentiate between the meaning of two words, for example, *case/Kate, bus-/bug).*

A morpheme may be free in that it can stand alone, such as the word *hat,* which is one morpheme, or the word *cupcake,* which is composed of two free morphemes, each of which can stand alone, *cup* and *cake.* A morpheme is bound if it must be attached to another word, as the {-s} that indicates third person singular in the word *writes.* The plural, third person singular, and possessive morpheme {-s} are identical in appearance but are different in meaning, based on the word that contains them: *books* (plural), *hops* (third person singular), and *Pat's* book (possessive). The production of a particular morphological inflection is determined by its phonetic environment. In a previous example, it was noted that the /b/ contained the +voice distinctive feature, whereas the /p/ contained the −voice distinctive feature. If the plural morpheme is added to the nouns *tab* and *tap* to form *tabs* and *taps* the type of inflection or sound (allomorph) produced depends on the sound preceding it. In *tabs* the {-s} morpheme is pronounced as {-z} because the /b/ is +voice (or voiced as is the /-z/). The inflection or allomorph used in *taps* is {-s} since both the /p/ and /-s/ are −voice (or voiceless). The importance of recognizing phonetic contexts is critical when working on the sound production of a child. One cannot rely on the graphemes (the letters of the alphabet) or the spelling of the words for pronunciation; for example, *fed* and *Fred* rhyme, but *fiend* and *friend* do not. The addition of bound morphemes to other morphemes can add, for example, a time concept to the word (*walked,* past tense; *walking* progressive), a manner concept (*quickly,* adverb), a negative concept (*untold, indecent*), the relative quantity concept (*smaller,* comparative; *smallest* superlative), or the concept of possession (*Judy's coat,* ownership of the coat).

Morphemes are sequenced into syntactic patterns. Children combine two morphemes before they have developed all the phonemes of the language; for example, they may say *hot soup* as *hot toup* because the /s/ sound has not developed. They use syntax or word order before developing all the morphemes of the language. A child may say *want cookies* as *wa cookie* before developing the /-nt/ cluster of consonants in *want* or the {-z} morpheme in *cookies.*

Morphemes are important when determining the linguistic ability of the child. When an author of an article states that a child has mean length of utterance (MLU) of 4.5, the author has calculated the child's MLU by adding the free and bound morphemes, not by just counting the words in the child's utterances. The following is an example of the difference between words and morphemes of a given child:

1. *I want cookies* = three words but four morphemes
   1 1   1 1
   Cookies = cookie + the plural inflection = two morphemes.
2. *John's in the car* = four words but five morphemes
   1   1 1 1
   John's = John + the contraction of the copular verb *is* = two morphemes.
3. *This is Sue's hat* = four words but five morphemes
   1   1 1   1 1
   Sue's = Sue + the posssessive inflection = two morphemes.

Brown (1973, pp. 53–55) has carefully outlined the steps to follow to arrive at the MLU. He stipulated the use of 100 consecutive utterances, but other researchers have reported results based on just 50 utterances. Therefore, the computation given below, which uses just three utterances, is meant to be only an example of the method to follow when computing the MLU:

1. Use 100 consecutive utterances
2. Establish the number of morphemes in each utterance, as indicated above

3. Add the number of morphemes in each utterance, for example, 4 + 5
   + 5 = 14 (using the three utterances in the preceding list)
4. Divide the total by the number of utterances, for example, 14 ÷
   3 = 4.6

Contrast this with the child who says the following:

1. *I want cookie* = three words, three morphemes.
2. *John in car* = three words, three morphemes.
3. *This Sue hat* = three words, three morphemes.

This child produced three utterances with a total of nine morphemes. Add 3 +
3 + 3 = 9, divide the 9 morphemes by 3 utterances, and the calculated MLU is
3.0. Brown organized the linguistic stages of the MLU with an accompanying
chronological age range (Brown, 1973). Not only did he suggest a linguistic age
for the child, but he indicated a hierarchy of 14 grammatical morphemes for
children as they developed through the stages of language development. For
instance, by the end of Stage II (with an MLU of 2.25 morphemes and a chronological age [CA] range of 1 year and 9 months [1-9] to 2 years and 6 months
[2-6]), the three children in his study had developed the use of *in, on,* and the -
ing inflection of the verb indicating present progressive; by Stage III
(MLU 2.75, CA 1.11–3.1), all the children used plurals. Brown contends that
though the age of acquisition of these morphemes may vary, the order of acquisition is relatively constant, indicating that the MLU is a better indicator of
linguistic development than is the CA.

Miller (1981, pp. 55–59) provided a detailed, composite table of Normal
Sequence of Structural Development, relating the Linguistic Age, based on the
MLU; the Cognitive Level, based on Piaget's Sensorimotor Stages (1952);
chronological age; and nonverbal and verbal behaviors with examples and
references to the MLU. The MLU has proved to be sensitive to cognition (e.g.,
temporal, spatial, and quantitative aspects), semantic roles (e.g., agent and object), syntax (e.g., classes of modifiers and levels of questions), and pragmatics
(e.g., request and command). It is said to be a reliable indicator of linguistic
development up to the age of 3 years (Morehead and Ingram, 1973).

Syntax

Syntax is the "domain of linguistics pertaining to organizational rules of morphemes in utterances" (Muma, 1978, p. 378). The ability to judge the grammatical nature of a sentence is in our competence, in the "speaker-hearer's
knowledge of his language" (Chomsky, 1965, p. 4). The accomplished native
speakers of English may not be able to explain why a sentence such as *The boy,
which I spoke to, was hired* is deviant from a standard grammatical sentence, but
they will be able to state that the sentence is not correct. People intrinsically
know the rules of the language, based on linguistic intuition (McNeill, 1970),
though they may not be able to state the organizing principle. In the example

sentence just stated, the +animate, +human noun phrase (The boy) must be modified by the relative pronoun *who*, whereas a +animate (alive), −human noun phrase (e.g., the dog), and a −animate, −human noun phrase (e.g., the curtain), may be modified by *which* or *that*. Competence is necessary for performance, which by theory is divided into two parts: comprehension and production. Performance (comprehension and production) is limited by factors such as memory, fatigue, and ability. Although it is difficult to determine a person's competence, a variety of tests and methods has been devised to aid in quantifying a person's comprehension of language (Carrow-Woolfolk, 1985; DeRenzi and Vignolo, 1962; Dunn and Dunn, 1981) and production of language (Carrow-Woolfolk, 1974; Goldman and Fristoe, 1986; Lee, 1974; Templin and Darley, 1969).

Syntax utilizes a rule system. Chomsky (1957, 1965) revolutionized the field of linguistics when he presented his theory of transformational grammar. Chomsky (1965) believed that a grammar must be able to account for the structure of the infinite number of sentences that are produced by the speaker. Each sentence produced is different and novel. He therefore formulated a finite, or limited, set of rules to describe the unlimited number of sentences that are used. The syntax that he proposed could be divided into three parts: (1) the phrase structure rules, (2) the transformational rules, and (3) the morphological inflection rules.

Phrase structure rules are simply rewrite rules that may govern a simple, declarative sentence, "S → NP ⌒ Aux ⌒ VP, VP → V ⌒ NP, NP → Det ⌒ N" (Chomsky, 1965, p. 68). In the previous sentence, by Chomsky's definitions, *S* is defined as a sentence, *NP* as a noun phrase (e.g., the boy, John, happiness, he), *Aux* as an auxiliary (e.g., is, does, has), (for example) [is] going home, [does] like ice cream, [has] been evident, and *VP* as a verb phrase that can be expressed without the auxiliary verb, for example, goes home, likes ice cream, was evident, ate lunch). Traditionally, the sentence is considered to be a string that is divided into a series of substrings, each with its own grammatical category.

Chomsky acknowledged the phrase-structure rule system, but he was interested in describing the structural rules that showed relationships between sentences. He proposed that the deep structure of a sentence provided the true meaning of the sentence. The **deep structure** of the sentence is the theoretical structure that contains the meaning and the rules of syntax that are to be used in the sentence. The **surface structure** contains the exact words, including appropriate morpheme inflections, placed in the proper sequential order. The surface structure is composed of the exact words the speaker says. If the surface structure of a sentence is ambiguous, as in the sentence, *She fed her dog bones* (Dale 1976), the deep structure could be used to ascertain whether the bones were *dog bones* that were fed to some female or whether *her dog* was *fed bones*. If we examine the sentence, *John was persuaded by Bill to leave* (Chomsky, 1965, p. 70), we note that *John* is the grammatical subject of the sentence but that *Bill* is the logical subject of the sentence (because it is Bill who has persuaded John to leave). *John* is also the "Object-of 'persuade' (to leave) and the Subject-of 'leave' " (Chomsky, 1965, p. 70). This sentence has the same meaning as *Bill persuaded John to leave,* which would be the deep structure of the sentence.

Chomsky stresses the major difference between a grammatical category and a grammatical function. The notion of grammatical categories is indicated by the NP, where the notion of grammatical function is the subject. These rules may generate deviant sentences if the categorical and functional notions are confused.

S → Sincerity (NP) + may (Aux) + frighten (V) + the boy (NP).

This is a perfectly grammatical sentence, but if the functional status is ignored and only the categorical status is applied, the sentence, in this instance, would be deviant

The boy (NP) + may (Aux) + frighten (V) + sincerity (NP)

Thus, the deep structure that recognizes functional notions is different from the surface structure.

In addition to these phrase structure rules, Chomsky (1965) suggested that a set of transformational rules is in operation. Using a transformational rule, linguistic elements may be added, deleted, or permuted. The sentence *Bill* (Noun Phrase 1) *persuaded John* (Noun Phrase 2) *to leave* was transformed to the sentence *John was persuaded by Bill to leave* by the use of transformational rules (Jacobs and Rosenbaum 1968); that is, the sentence was transformed by interchanging, inverting, or permuting the two noun phrases *John* and *Bill;* by adding an auxiliary verb (*was*); by adding an *-ed* on the verb *persuade,* and by adding the word *by* to indicate the agent of the sentence (Quirk et al., 1985). Deletion is another example of a transformational rule and is used in the imperative sentence. The imperative sentence, *Don't go* was derived by deletion of *John* from *John don't go.* Another use can be seen in the example *The girl who is standing there wants her breakfast.* This too is formed by the use of transformational rules. The deep structure has two sentences: (1) *The girl is standing there* and (2) *The girl wants her breakfast.* These sentences are combined by the deletion of the identical NP (the girl), by the addition of a relative pronoun (who), and by permutation of the VP (wants her breakfast).

The use of a morphological inflection may be explained using the third person singular as an example. If the subject NP is *he, she, it, the boy, the girl,* or *the dog,* the syntactic-morphological rules would dictate that there must be an addition to the verb of a morpheme indicating third person singular, for example, *She wants,* or *The man cuts the bread.* The hierarchical order for the development of third person singular morphological inflections in children is {-s} (*hops*), {-z} (*wags*), and {iz} (*matches*) (Berko, 1958).

The tranformational theory of grammar did not explain why language developed or what abilities are necessary to acquire language — beyond suggesting there was a Language Acquistion Device (LAD) (McNeill, 1970) that was the intrinsic ability of human beings to develop a rule system of language when presented with an input of their native language. However the transformational theory did provide a clear and organized framework that has spurred heuristic research and theoretical considerations, involving both the language acquisition patterns of children (Dale, 1976; deVilliers and deVilliers, 1978) and the assessment and intervention plans for children with language disorders (Bloom and Lahey, 1978; Crystal, Fletcher, and Garman, 1982; Cullatta and Horn, 1982; Fey, 1986; Leonard, 1974; Menyuk and Looney, 1972; Miller, 1981; Morehead and Ingram, 1973; Tyack and Gottsleben, 1974).

For a time, the main thrust of research centered on the transformational grammar system proposed by Chomsky, but Chomsky had not accounted for the semantic component of an utterance. In the late 1960s psycholinguists turned to semantics and semantic relationships.

Semantics

As more research was carried out in the area of semantics, it became apparent that, contrary to original thought, the meaning of the deep structure could be altered by some transformations, depending on the words that were used. Although there is no change in meaning in the sentence *The men wash the cows* when it is transformed into the passive sentence *The cows are washed by the men*, transformations can cause a difference in the meanings of sentences when different lexical items or words are used. For example, if the simple declarative sentence *All girls kiss some men* (Bates, 1976, p. 416) is tranformed into a passive sentence by permuting the first noun phrase (All girls) with the second noun phrase (some men), by adding *are* and *by*, and by adding the {-ed} inflection on the verb *kiss*, the sentence becomes *Some men are kissed by all girls*, and the meaning of the original sentence is altered. Linguists are trying to find rules for the exceptions and are looking deeper into the semantic aspect of the sentence because Chomsky's theory did not account for the cognitive, semantic, or perceptual features involved in language (Bates, 1976).

The search for meaning in the deep structure has occupied the thoughts of other researchers. Another major force in the field was Fillmore (1968), whose work was based heavily on the importance of meaning and relationships within a sentence. He recognized, as had Chomsky, that it is not the analysis of the subject or object in the surface structure (spoken sentence) that provides the meaning, but rather, it is necessary to look at the relationships in the deep structure. To do this, Fillmore abstracted a set of universal semantic relationships, which he proposed as his Theory of Case Grammar. *Universal* implies that these features exist across all the languages of the world, and that the concepts presented are innate and probably based on the judgment of human beings. The individual must judge, among other items, who did the action, who or what it happened to, what the action changed, and a subject's expression of needs. The relationship that exists between the verb and the noun phrase is not obvious but rather is covert and can be determined with the use of **case**, which identifies the underlying syntactic-semantic relationship.

Fillmore listed a number of cases that relate to the verb used. In the sentence *John broke the window* (Fillmore, 1968, p. 22), *John* is the agent because John is the animate and is the instigator of the action. In the sentence *A hammer broke the window* (p. 22), *hammer* is the instrument because hammer is an inanimate object that is causally involved in the action. These relationships remain though the sequential order of the words changes, as in the sentence *John broke the window with a hammer* (p. 22). In the (grammatically incorrect) sentence *John and a hammer broke the window* (p. 22), a violation of the system has occurred because the noun phrases that are placed in a compound relationship are not of the same case, that is, either agent or instrument. Brown (1973) applied Fillmore's case form to 202 utterances of his subject, Adam, who was at the Stage I language level. Brown found that though the Case Grammar method did not provide for examination of the categories of imperative, negative, and interrogative, it did provide an effective means of evaluating the deep structure or meaning used by the child. Because of his theory's semantic considerations, it has been criticized by many who did not realize that these considerations are part of the valuable contribution that has made this theory so widely acknowledged.

Traditionally, semantics is one of the subdivisions of language (Muma, 1978) dealing with the relations between signs and their reference (Webster's, 1969); more recently **semantics**, as used in relation to the development of language, refers to semantics as the totality of meaning, whether or not it is coded in vocabulary (Halliday, 1975). In verbal language, a **sign** is a symbol or a word that refers to objects or events or relationships. A **theory of reference** is the meaning of words as they designate a referent or a specific object. A **referent** is the object or event that is being referred to, the **reference** is the meaning, and **verbal symbols** (signs) are used to code the meaning. Olson (1970) argued that the theory of reference does not account for the situation in which one item may have many names (e.g., coach/sofa) or in which the same lexicon (word) may be used to designate a number of items (e.g., light weight, light color, and lightfixture). He stated that our concepts and knowledge of the environment are the central core of semantics. This theme of cognition, concept development, and perception is the basis of many of the prevalent theories. The child must know the meaning of individual words, which make up his lexicon; must know how the words are related to each other, their functions; and must know the structure in which they are used. Recent literature has provided evidence that the child's ability to acquire lexical items depends on nonverbal development, cognitive aspect, and experience in his environment. The child forms a concept based on multiple experiences and uses a word, which is a symbol, to express that concept (Bloom and Lahey, 1978).

Linguistic theorists refer to semantic markers when describing the features or properties of a word. DeVito (1970) suggested that these markers indicate semantic properties that, for instance, might limit the choice of words to be used with a particular word or might designate the type of word to be used. If words such as *man, boy,* and *brother* are used, the pronoun used to denote them is *he.* If words such as *woman, girl,* and *sister* are used, the pronoun used is *she.* The common semantic property of these examples is their maleness or femaleness. These selection restrictions are determined by the semantic properties of the word. Many students of English as a second language commonly say (incorrectly), *He brushed his teeth and washed herself.* Their problem lies in the expression of gender in this language, but not in their native language. Another example is the person who says *He borrowed me the money* rather than *He lent me the money.* That person understands that the common property of the words *to borrow* and *to lend* is to return the item (borrowed or lent) to the original owner but would probably have confused the word that indicates who gives with the word that indicates who receives.

Semantics has also been examined from the feature analysis viewpoint. In the Semantic Feature Model, it is suggested that a set of elementary features specify the meaning of the word. Bierwisch (1970) wrote that these components are based on the human being's ability to develop cognitive and perceptual structures. Clark (1973) explained semantic development using the Semantic Feature Hypothesis, which states that the child notices a perceptual feature or a combination of perceptual features that are then combined to form the meaning of the word; the child identifies the word through some prominent features that the child has singled out. Clark notes that the child's use of words may differ considerably from the adult's use of the same word; the child initially develops a notion of a word by identifying one or two semantic features that may or may not be the important critical features of the word. A child may deviate from the adult use of the word because of an overextension of one or more critical features that compose the word, such as shape, movement, size, sound, taste, and texture (Clark, 1974). If there is an overextension of the critical feature of shape, the sun, the moon, an orange, a green pea, and a ball are all referred to as ball. In this instance, one would have to detail the features to separate the "round" objects. For example, stress the ability to eat an orange or a pea; then stress the color, size, taste, and perhaps the liquid content that differentiate the two "round" items. It is necessary to decide which perceptual features are the critical ones for inclusion of a particular referent (object) in a particular reference (meaning). The child later adds or modifies the number and combination of linguistic features to correspond with the adult meaning of the word. Clark's (1973) famous example is the child's overextension of the word *dog* for many four-legged creatures including cows, sheep, and horses. Gradually, as the child develops cognitively, features are added, deleted, or refined, which leads to the discrimination among the different kinds of animals. Leopold (1948) reported that his calling the last few empty pages in a book *weiss* (white) was greeted with *Schnee? No!* (Snow? No!) (p. 98) by his daughter Hildegard. She was not able to associate the word *weiss* (German for white) with anything but snow. This was an underextension of the color feature. It has been noted that semantic features also develop in a particular order. For instance, in the development of a dimensional adjective (big, little, tall, long, or wide), Clark (1973) noted that in early development, the term *big* may be overextended to *long, high, tall,* and *wide.* The child, who has not developed more refined dimensional terms, uses a global +dimension feature only, later refining this by adding the +vertical feature for the dimension of tall or high. By refinement and addition, the child will slowly develop the adult meaning of the word.

Nelson (1973) used the term *inaccurate generalization,* rather than *overextension,* when a child in her study used *ball* for a light bulb and an orange; the critical feature used was shape. Nelson found that in their first 50 words, children used a higher percentage of nominals: 24 percent specific nominals and 41 percent general nominals in the first ten words, and 9 percent specific nominals and 62 percent general nominals when 41–50 words had been acquired. (A **nominal** refers to things in the world. A **specific nominal** refers to only one example of a particular category [e.g., Mommy and Snoopy], whereas a **general nominal** refers to all members of a category, e.g., objects [chair, doll], animals [cat, dog] [Nelson, 1973]). Nelson stated that in order to learn more about the child's semantic development, it is wise to examine the lexical items that have not been included in the child's repertoire. Using this strategy, Nelson found that the items that were not used by children were items that did not move and did not change, such as sofa, tree, and wall. Children used items that did things and that had recognized movement and interactions, such as roll, run, cry, and fly away. Thus items connected with some change occurred earlier in their semantic development.

Nelson expanded her semantic theory in 1974, suggesting the Functional Core Concept of Semantic development, which contrasted with the Semantic Feature Hypothesis, where the semantic features are developed gradually. In the Functional Core Concept, the child develops the concept not from exposure to the word but from one single instance of the child's interaction with the world and with the object. The whole element takes on the concept that is based on its function or its dynamic relationship. Therefore, it is unnecessary to analyze the whole into parts. When developing a new concept, a child interacts with an object, and a new concept develops out of this interaction. For example, when playing with a ball, the child notes the following "actions or relationships" (p. 277): location of the action, or where the action may occur (in a room); actor, or who handles the object (mother, child); action, or what you do with the object (throw or catch); movement, or what the object is capable of doing (roll or bounce); and location of the object, or where it does this activity (on the floor). In time, this concept generalizes to other objects that have the same functional concept; for example, the ball can be thrown and caught in the playground, or it can be thrown to someone who may hold it or allow it to roll under the fence. In 1986, Nelson continued to stress the conceptual basis for language and the need for dynamic activities to develop this concept. She reiterated in the Functional Core Concept model that language terms are "mapped" onto events and concepts (p. 360), commenting that children will not learn a concept generalized from a picture in a book, but they will learn the concept and be able to generalize it from a single functional example, that is, from using, touching, or even viewing a particular referent or type of referent (e.g., animal includes elephant, lion, rhinoceros).

An additional semantic theory, the Prototypical Complex Theory, was presented by Bowerman in 1978: the best exemplar or prototype is developed by the child from frequent use of the referent by an adult. Other members of the category are included based on the child's view of the referent. For example, in some areas the robin might be the prototype of a bird with the seagull or the sandpiper included in the category as the child fits them into his concept of the bird. The penguin is considered on the periphery of the bird category. The category developed in this instance is a noun category.

Semantics seems to be involved in the development of both noun and verb categories, but inherent differences are seen in the development of these categories. Using data from a number of children who speak different languages — Kaluli, Mandarin Chinese, Japanese, German, English, and Turkish — Gentner (1982) evaluated linguistic variables: word frequency, word order, and morphological transparency, or the ease with which a child may map ideas onto a morpheme. To illustrate the point, note that the noun has few inflections that may be added to it. The noun *boy* is the singular and can be marked for the plural (*boys*) and the possessive (*boy's hat*). The verb has a greater number of inflections that may be joined to it: tense (past — *walked*), number (third person singular — he *gives*), aspect (progressive — *walking*, perfect — *has eaten*). Nonlinguistic variables (the patterns of teaching language to children) were also examined. Gentner proposed the Natural Partitions Hypothesis to explain the consistency of the finding that nouns develop earlier across languages. Objects are seen by humans, even prelinguistic humans (babies), as being stable and coherent, whereas verbs float or move (Gentner, 1982, p. 328). Gentner acknowledged a limitation of the Natural Partitions Hypothesis; it applies to the perceptual level only. Thus a problem exists when carrying the theory to the abstractions, for example, *love, loyalty, and faith*.

The results of Camarata and Schwartz's (1985) study concerning semantic-phonological relationships appear to coincide with the Natural Partitions Hypothesis. They found the accuracy of the production of words (the correct number of sounds produced) was higher when the words were object words (nouns) rather than action words (verbs), providing evidence that a relationship exists between phonology and syntax and between the number of correct sounds produced and the type of grammatical category (noun or verb). A relationship was also found between the number of incorrect sounds and the number of incorrect syntactic structures produced by a child (Hoffnung, 1977, 1981). Macnamara (1972) hypothesized that a relationship exists between syntax and semantics. He stated that syntax is learned based on the semantic development of the child, not as an independent system.

Words written by Fodor and Katz (1964) more than twenty years ago still seem to apply to the field of semantics. They stated, that, as yet, there is no unified accepted theory of semantics, but rather a number of theoretical proposals that have spurred considerable investigation. The systematic evaluation of semantics, which includes semantic-syntactic relationships (e.g., action and possession), is now considered by some researchers as a more basic consideration in the evaluation of children than is the linguistic form (Stockman and Vaughn-Cooke, 1986).

Pragmatics

The examination of meaning has led to the examination of how meaning is expressed (Dore, 1975; Gallagher and Prutting, 1983; Halliday, 1975; Prutting,

1979). They found the inclusion of the extralinguistic context, or environment in which the verbalizations were used, was of major importance. Language is context sensitive and is affected by pragmatics. The context is not only a linguistic one but includes the cognitive and social contexts — a person's knowledge of the physical and social worlds and of the rules for interaction in those worlds. It includes the nonverbal context (e.g., gesture) and paralinguistic context (e.g., stress and pitch change) (Prutting, 1982). Consideration should be given to who said the utterance, under what circumstances, and with what intention. Answering questions concerning the use of language is the component of language called **pragmatics.** The study of pragmatics is the study of "... the rules of governing the use of language in context" (Bates, 1976, p. 420).

Austin (1962) described three kinds of speech acts used by the speaker: the locutionary act, the illocutionary act, and the perlocutionary act. The **locutionary speech act** is the utterance itself, which consists of the formation of sounds and the construction of a proposition, that is, the production of a meaningful sentence. The **proposition** is the internal activity or mental operation of the speaker (Bates, 1976). This mental operation stands for an argument or a relationship in the sentence. The **illocutionary speech act**, or performative act, is the intentional use of some social act for the purpose of communicating to the listener. It expresses the speaker's wish to persuade, plead, urge, order, request, deny, question, or negate. The **perlocutionary speech act** involves the interpretation by the listener of the speaker's verbalization. The listener may or may not interpret the message as intended by the speaker. An example might be the effect that the statement *I love you* might have on the listener. One person might be delighted that these words were finally uttered (planned effect of the speaker who wishes to develop a lasting relationship), whereas another may be dismayed (unplanned effect of the speaker) and seek ways to diplomatically escape from the situation. In another situation, a speaker passing a restaurant may comment, "My, there are so many restaurants in this area." The speaker may intend that the listener recognize that it is well past 1 *p.m.* and, therefore, lunchtime. The listener may hear the locution but may not receive the illocutionary intent of the speaker, interpreting the comment as a statement of information rather than as a suggestion. The desired perlocutionary effect (having the driver stop for lunch) was not successful. Locution requires the onset of verbal speech, whereas the perlocutionary and illocutionary acts do not.

It is the functional linguist who looks at the social interaction and the communicative use of language (Prutting, 1982). Language must be initiated and must be appropriate to the social situation in which it is used. To judge the communication skills of the speaker, Roth and Spekman (1984) suggested adding two levels of analysis to the first level of communicative intentions. The second level would be **presupposition** and the third level **social organization.**

Pragmatic presupposition shows the relationships within the sentence, the context used, and the appropriateness of the sentence used in that context (Bates, 1976). The pragmatic presupposition takes into consideration factors other than the reference alone. It contains concepts of semantic presupposition and psychological presupposition. Semantic presupposition insists that a statement's appropriateness depends on an accurate assertion that a statement is true or false, and this allows us to make inferences from the true or false statements. Bates (1976) gives the example of *John has a sister.* (p. 437). If this is accepted as a true statement, one can infer that John's parents have more than one child. If the first sentence is accepted as true, then one may make a semantic presupposition that *John exists* (p. 435).

Psychological presupposition assumes that some information is shared by both the speaker and the listener and that the speaker and listener are aware of the shared information. Bates (1976) explained that Fred was back from the Orient and that he had brought his new girlfriend, Mai Ling, to the party. When a tall, blonde lady walked into the room and was introduced as Fred's girlfriend, one friend turned to another and said, "She's blonde!" The two friends had the shared information that Fred had returned from the Orient, that his girlfriend's name was Mai Ling, and that all Orientals have dark hair. The speaker and listener had developed a presupposition as a psychological event.

Pragmatics, though believed by many to be separate from semantics and syntax, is still said to have a tremendous effect on all levels of language (Prutting, 1982). The effect on the semantic-syntax level, for example, pronominalization, or the use of pronouns is affected by situation and person (mothers are rarely referred to as *she* by their children). The phonological level is affected by loudness or stress, altering the produced sounds by lengthening the vowel or adding greater aspiration of air to the voiceless consonants /p, t, k/. On the prosodic level, the emotion of anger is produced by major increases in loudness, and when interrogation is taking place, there are appropriate rises and falls of pitch.

Prosody

Prosody is an important factor in conveying meaning, emotions, and nuances. When defining prosody, Minifie, Hixon, and Williams (1973) wrote of the physiological activity or neuromuscular activity required to vary the speech pattern when adding features such as pitch, loudness, duration, and stress (suprasegmental features) to the speech segments. These suprasegments can be added to each syllable, even to an isolated vowel, to vary the intonation contour of the utterance. Quirk and colleagues (1985) speak of analyzing the structure of a sentence for the prosodic units so that their influence on the listener's ability to comprehend the formulated message can be understood. They speak of "tone units" that highlight the information of a sentence by producing one syllable that has a higher pitch level than the other surrounding syllables. Ladefoged (1982) suggests that a "tone group" exists when a single tone pattern extends over a group of words, with a tonic syllable (one syllable in this group) carrying the major pitch change. If the sentence is short, such as *He went home*, it will fall under one tone group, but if it is longer or more complex, a number of tone groups will be combined, as in *He went home, shouting for joy.* The important word in the sentence receives the higher pitch and the louder intensity. The intonation or pitch contour change can signal a difference in the meaning of a sentence or word, the type of sentence, the desired emphasis, or the emotional feelings of the speaker.

There are tone languages in which the changes in meaning are not indicated by a change of a consonant or a vowel phoneme (*bit-bid, bit-bat*) but by changes in the pitch contours or intonations. In Mandarin Chinese, the word *ma* when said with the highest pitch level means "mother"; when said with a high rising pitch, it means "hemp"; and when said with a falling pitch, it means "scold" (Traugott and Pratt, 1980).

The concept of various types of sentences carrying various intonation patterns has long been a concern of researchers. Bellugi (1965) noted that the pitch contour of declarative sentences is a 2-3-1 contour. This could be applied to the sentence: *I am going,* in which the underlined word carries the highest pitch (3), and the pitch drops as the speaker completes the sentence. The intonation contour varies with the type of interrogative structure employed. The earliest evidence of an interrogative form used by a child is the declarative sentence with the question intonation pattern superimposed on it (e.g., *Go home?*), this being similar to the intonation contour of the yes/no question. A yes/no interrogative (a question that may be answered by *yes* or *no,*) such as, *Will you stay for dinner?* or *May I borrow that book?* has a rising intonation contour of 2-3-3 (Bellugi, 1965); the sentence ends with a higher pitch than it began with. The rising pitch level at the end of the sentence is also found in the tag question, for example, *You are coming to dinner, aren't you?* or *He can't take his vacation now, can he?* A *Wh* interrogative sentence uses a *Wh* word interrogative such as *what* (*What did he eat?*) requires a noun in the answer; *What did he do?* requires a a verb in the answer), *where* (*Where is he going?*), *why* (*Why did he do it?*) or *when* (*When will you return?*). This type of sentence has a falling pitch contour, and these contours may signal emotional information as well as syntactic information.

Emotions can be judged (Taylor, Rosegrant, and Meyer, 1980) by the use of pitch changes. Anger, tension, or fear causes a rise in pitch (Taylor, Rosegrant, and Meyer, 1980), whereas mood can be conveyed by a low or loud volume, or by a slow or fast rate. Saying *yes* with a strong voice indicates definiteness, whereas saying *yes* with a falling or rising intonation pattern adds a bit of doubt to the verbalization (Ladefoged, 1982; Taylor, Rosegrant, and Meyer, 1980). Contempt, surprise, disgust, or shades of meaning in utterances can be suggested by varying the intonational patterns (Traugott and Pratt, 1980). The same words uttered with different intonation patterns are said with different intentions by the speaker and are perceived as having different meanings by the listener.

Stress is another way that intent, emotion, meaning, or emphasis can be conveyed to the listener. A stressed sound is usually louder and is usually produced at a higher pitch level than are the surrounding unstressed syllables. This is accomplished by added support of air from the lungs and by adjustments of the vocal folds and of the vocal tract (Ladefoged, 1982). The listener is usually able to detect a longer vowel in the syllable. Stress may indicate emphasis; may be used as a phonemic distinction to signal different syntactic relationships between single words such as the noun *record* and the verb *record* (for which the noun requires the stress to be placed on the first syllable, and the verb requires the stress to be placed on the last syllable of the two-syllable word [Traugott and Pratt, 1980]), and may be used in compounds or two-word phrases, in which stress placed on the first syllable indicates a noun (a put on), but stress placed on both syllables signals a verb (to put on) (Ladefoged, 1982, p. 105).

When said in isolation, words may have stressed and unstressed syllables (story, father), but when combined with other syllables in a sentence, a reduced stress feature may rule some of the individual words. Thus, their stress pattern is subordinated to the total sentence intonation pattern (Ladefoged, 1982). In many sentences in the English language, stress "tends" (p. 109) to occur at regular intervals that may be tapped to the beat of a metronome and that appear to be based on a rule system. People tend to avoid placing stresses next to one another, and there are implicit rules that the speaker obeys without being able to verbalize them, such as placing the stress in front of the first adjective when two adjectives precede the noun (e.g., a big red ball). Traugott and Pratt (1980) provide information concerning rules for stress in groups of words. These rules are based on the number of consonants in the final position, the type of vowels contained in the words, and the number of syllables in the word. For example, collapse and exist (p. 66) have the stress on the last syllable because the last syllable ends with a consonant cluster of two consonants, -ps and -st respectively; whereas exit and cancel (p. 66) have the stress on the penultimate, or next to the last, syllable because a single consonant acts as the last consonant of the word, -t and -l respectively.

As illustrated, relationships exist between prosody and sound, and interrelationships exist among all five of the parameters of language: phonology, morphology, syntax, semantics, and prosody; but other variables, such as cognition, the psychsocial aspect and biological and environmental factors also have a strong effect on language.

LANGUAGE LEARNING AND USE ARE DETERMINED BY THE INTERACTION OF BIOLOGICAL, COGNITIVE, PSYCHOSOCIAL, AND ENVIRONMENTAL FACTORS

Lenneberg (1967) stated that every human creature's unique behavior is determined by biological limits that are species specific. Humans and animals have what seems to be overlapping physical attributes such as a larynx, teeth, muscles of the mouth, and a brain, but there are important anatomical and physiological differences between these seemingly similar structures. He reported the findings of a research project by Nemai and Kelemen (1929), who found that in primates, the large epiglottis, small arytenoid cartilages, and greater calcification throughout the larynx limited the flexibility of movement of the larynx (voice box). The apes were not capable of producing the finely tuned laryngeal movements necessary for the stabilization of sounds.

Humans' facial muscles have undergone differentiation allowing more accuracy and rapidity of oral mobility (movement of the mouth) so that, for example, the lips can be compressed and tightly held momentarily and then immediately released for the production of the plosives [b, p] or released more gradually for the production of the nasal [m]. In addition, humans do not have the protruding canine or eye teeth common to the apes (Lenneberg, 1967). In humans, the central and lateral incisors (front teeth) and the canine teeth have an evenness of height in the maxillary arch (upper part of the mouth that holds the teeth) and in the mandibular arch (jaw portion that holds the teeth). This meeting of the upper (maxillary) and lower (mandibular) incisors allows for the production of the fricative sounds (f, v, s, z, sh [shoe], zh [beige]). To form these sounds, there must be air produced over a surface at a particular angle and rate of speech (Chomsky and Halle, 1968). The stridency of air noisiness, which is modified by the tongue as it passes over the articulators (teeth), causes the frictionlike sounds called fricatives. For the /f, v/ the air must be passed between the upper teeth and the lower lip; for the /s, z, sh, zh/ the air is sent over the tongue and between the teeth. The modification, or changing, of the tongue and lips during the expulsion of air causes the differentiation of sound. The comparative studies of the brains of humans and of primates are interesting. Humans and apes each have a brain, but the fissures of the human brain are deeper and more extensive than those of the primate brain, creating an area for the increase of cortical matter. Visually, the human brain appears to have more hills and valleys on its surface than does the primate brain; for example, the chimp's brain is smoother and less undulating in appearance (Lenneberg, 1967). These differences lead to important neurological differences. The SLPs studying aphasia have long recognized the importance of understanding the neurological bases of speech disorders. The need to understand the defective underlying neural mechanism responsible for the speech and language problem is an important factor for the SLP when assessing a child or an adult. By assessing the symmetry, the movements, and the interrelationships of the articulators, it is possible to judge the type of dysarthria present (e.g., flaccid, lower motor neuron lesion; spastic, upper motor neuron lesion; ataxic, cerebellum lesion; hypokinetic, extrapyramidal lesion; and hyperkinetic, basal ganglion lesion [Aronson, 1981]). By utilizing the Point-Place System, it is possible to judge the problem location(s) important to the motor speech system. Seven crucial areas are specified in their line drawing: (1) muscles and structures of respiration, (2) larynx, (3) soft palate, (4) tongue blade, (5) tongue tip, (6) lips, and (7) mandible. For example, if there is faulty valving or closure of area 3, velopharyngeal closure would be inadequate. The velum or soft palate enables one to separate the oral and nasal cavities and thus reduce unwanted hyper-nasality by elevating the velum and having it make contact with the pharyngeal wall (back of the throat) and, with the assistance of the pharyngeal wall, separate the oral cavity (mouth) from the nasal cavity (nose). If closure does not occur, then a resonance problem or hypernasality will exist. By utilizing the Point-Place System and by analyzing initiation and consistency of muscle movements, it is possible to judge the existence of dysarthria versus apraxia of speech (e.g., paralysis or paresis of the volitional movements versus problems with the programming of muscle movements [LaPointe, 1986; Rosenbek and

LaPointe (1978)]). The exact pinpointing of neurological defects is still under the purview of the neurologists, but it is incumbent on the members of our profession to understand the neurological factors, the neurological theories, and their ramifications on diagnosis and intervention procedures (Love and Webb, 1986).

With the development of greater anatomical, neurological, and physiological differentiation combined with cognitive diversification and social needs, language was created. Prior cognition is suggested as a basic requirement for the development of language; the unanswered question is how cognition relates to language. The Functional Core Concept of semantic development (Nelson, 1974), the Semantic Feature Hypothesis (Clark, 1974), the development of the rule system for Case Grammar (Fillmore, 1968), the ability to use a rising intonation to ask a question (Bellugi, 1965), and the ability to develop hierarchy of structure for embedding sentences (Chomsky, 1968), all suggest an active participation of a cognitive system. A child speaks about his nonlinguistic knowledge of the world, but there are researchers who believe that, in addition to general knowledge, the child must possess a language-specific knowledge, and it is this knowledge that provides the development of language. Rice (1983) presents six viewpoints of the relation of cognition to language, from the strong cognitive hypothesis of language, which states that cognition is developed first and accounts for language development, to the hypothesis that there are some areas of language that are not dependent on cognition. Questions are raised concerning the development of cognition and language from a common root, relevant to what cognitive factors are necessary for what language competences and pertaining to the weak hypothesis of cognition (Cromer, 1978), which suggests that cognition is necessary but not sufficient for language development. The child must develop linguistic capabilities to express wants, needs, questions, and knowledge of the world. Environment plays a part in the language learned, in the dialect spoken (e.g., Southern, General American), and in the beginning, in the basic vocabulary learned that allows one to function well in the environment.

EFFECTIVE USE OF LANGUAGE OR COMMUNICATION REQUIRES A BROAD UNDERSTANDING OF HUMAN INTERACTION INCLUDING SUCH ASSOCIATED FACTORS AS NONVERBAL CUES, MOTIVATION, AND SOCIOCULTURAL ROLES

Emerick and Haynes (1986) and Hall (1959) have outlined some of the nonverbal body language cues that provide sensitive information: grooming, body posture, shifts in body position, the way one walks (which is copied from models in the environment), and the distance required between two people who are holding a conversation. A greater distance is required in a formal situation or among strangers, whereas the distance decreases as the degree of intimacy increases. The equal distance that separates people of the American culture when queuing up to wait for service (to get a ticket for the theatre or to board a bus) is said to reflect the ideology that all people are alike; a rich person gets no preference in this situation. Other countries find this too subdued, and in some of those countries, the behavior that is prevalent is what Americans consider "pushiness" or lack of consideration for others. Americans stand closer in a crowded place and further apart in a less crowded place. If this unwritten rule of space is violated, we feel uncomfortable and may find ourselves moving away to establish the accustomed distance. Other nonverbal cues are the time that one arrives for an appointment, the loudness of voice, and the eye contact that is made. Cultural patterns are learned very young, therefore it is imperative for us to realize that the behavior of children of different cultures will vary from our expectations.

Trifonovitch (1980) listed four stages of cultural adjustment in a person new to a particular culture. The first is the honeymoon stage; everything is new, exciting, and acceptable. People may go out of their way to help the person who is new to their environment. But when the honeymoon is over, people expect the newcomer to behave as others in that environment. Nevertheless, the old customs are not forgotten, and the new language, English, is still difficult and awkward. In the second stage, hostility may appear. The teacher, classmates, and other people in the environment are not as helpful, and the new member of the community starts to withdraw. With time, depending on the environment and the new person's ability to adjust, the third, or humor, stage will appear. Incidents that caused grief are recalled as funny, and some lightheartedness is present. The fourth and last stage is the home stage; the new environment feels like home, but the person is still able to retain some customs from and some allegiance to the native culture. The person will use the new and still-difficult second language and, though biculturalization has occurred, will revert to the native language, which is less demanding in effort and concentration, when at home with friends and family. Language is a prime factor in maintaining a subculture within a culture, and as in the Canadian province of Quebec, can be the cause of hostility, economic hardship, discrimination, and separation from the larger culture.

The adjustment factor should be considered when assessing and working with a bicultural child. The examiner's physical appearance, dress, and manner may be totally alien to the child. Tests may be failed, not because of academic incompetencies but for non-test-related reasons (Omark, 1981) such as tension, shyness, strangeness to the environment, and language.

CONCLUSION

Language is the behavior that separates humans from all other living creatures. It helps us subtly modify our behaviors, think, abstract, become educated, and use our intelligence on a level that does not have to deal with the here and now, the visibly present, the concrete. It aids us in planning and in executing our plans with accuracy, detail, and sophistication; it fosters our social patterns, allowing us to comfort and support other human beings; it helps us hold on to our history and, we hope, learn from the past; it provides the tools for joking with each other, but these same tools may be used for lying. It adds a special skill that allows each individual to reach his or her full potential.

REFERENCES

ASHA, Committee on Language (1983). Definition of language. *ASHA, 25,* 6, 44.
Aronson, J. (1981). Dysarthria. In T. Hixon, T. Shriberg, D. Lawrence, and J. Saxman (Eds.), *Introduction to communicative disorders* (pp. 407–447). Englewood Cliffs, NJ: Prentice-Hall.
Austin, J. (1962). *How to do things with words.* New York: Oxford University Press.
Bates, E. (1976). Pragmatics and sociolinguistics in child language. In D. Morehead and A. Morehead (Eds.), *Normal and deficient child language* (pp. 411–463). Baltimore: University Park Press.
Bellugi, U. (1965). The development of interrogative structures in children's speech. In K. Riegal (Ed.), *The development of language functions* (Report No. 8). Ann Arbor, MI: The National Institute of Child Health and Human Development.
Berko, J. (1958). The child's learning of English morphology. *Word, 14,* 150–177.
Bierswisch, M. (1970). Semantics. In J. Lyon (Ed.), *New horizons in linguistics.* Baltimore: Penguin Books.
Bloom, L., and Lahey, M. (1978). *Language development and language disorders.* New York: Wiley.
Bowerman, M. (1978). The acquisition of word meaning: An investigation of some current conflicts. In N. Waterson and C. Snow (Eds.), *The development of communication* (pp. 263–286). New York: Wiley.
Brown, R. (1973). *A first language.* Cambridge, MA: Harvard University Press.
Camarata, S., and Gandour, J. (1985). Rule invention in the acquisition of morphology by a language-impaired child. *Journal of Speech and Hearing Disorders, 50,* 40–45.
Camarata, S. M., and Schwartz, R. G. (1985). Production of object words: Evidence for a relationship between phonology and semantics. *Journal of Speech and Hearing Research, 28,* 320–330.
Carrow, E. (1973). *Test of Auditory Comprehension of Language.* Austin, TX: Learning Concepts.
Carrow-Woolfolk, E. (1974). *Carrow Elicited Language Inventory.* Austin, TX: Learning Concepts.
Carrow-Woolfolk, E. (1985). *Test of Auditory Comprehension of Language,* Revised. Allen, TX: DLM Teaching Resources.
Chomsky, N. (1957). *Syntactic structures.* The Hague: Mouton and Company.
Chomsky, N. (1965). *Aspects of the theory of syntax.* Cambridge, MA: The MIT Press.
Chomsky, N., and Halle, M. (1968). *The sound pattern of English.* New York: Harper & Row.
Clark, E. (1973). What's in a word? On the child's acquisition semantics in his first language. In T. Moore (Ed.), *Cognitive development and the acquisition of language* (pp. 65–110). New York: Academic Press.
Clark, E. (1974). Some aspects of the conceptual basis for first language acquisition. In R. Schiefelbusch and L. Lloyd (Eds.), *Language perspectives — acquisition, retardation, and intervention* (pp. 105–128). Baltimore: University Park Press.
Compton, A. J. (1970). Generative studies of children's phonological disorders. *Journal of Speech and Hearing Disorders, 35,* 315–339.
Costello, J., and Onstine, J. (1976). The modification of multiple articulation errors based on Distinctive Feature Theory. *Journal of Speech and Hearing Disorders, 41,* 199–216.
Cromer, R. F. (1981). Reconceptualizing language acquisition and cognitive development. In R. L. Schiefelbusch and D. Bricker (Eds.), *Early language: Acquisition and intervention* (pp. 51–137). Baltimore: University Park Press.
Crystal, D., Fletcher, P., and Garman, M. (1982). *The grammatical analysis of language disability.* Baltimore: Edward Arnold.
Cullatta, B., and Horn, D. (1982). Program for achieving generalization of grammatical rules to spontaneous discourse. *Journal of Speech and Hearing Disorders, 47,* 174–180.
Dale, P. (1976). *Language development.* New York: Holt, Rinehart, & Winston.

DeRenzi, E., and Vignolo, L. A. (1962). The Token Test: A sensitive test to detect receptive disturbances in aphasia. *Brain, 85,* 665–678.

de Villiers, J., and de Villiers, P. (1978). *Language acquisition.* Cambridge, MA: Harvard University Press.

DeVito, J. (1970). *The psychology of speech and language.* New York: Random House.

Dillard, J. L. (1972). *Black English.* New York: Random House.

Dore, J. (1975). Holophrases, speech acts, and language universals. *Journal of Child Language, 2,* 21–40.

Dunn, L. M., and Dunn, L. M. (1981). *Peabody Picture Vocabulary Test — Revised.* Circle Pines, MN: American Guidance Service.

Edwards, M., and Shriberg, L. (1983). *Phonology applications in communicative disorders.* Boston: College-Hill Press.

Emerick, L., and Haynes, J. (1986). *Diagnosis and evaluation in speech pathology.* Englewood Cliffs, NJ: Prentice-Hall.

Fey, M. (1986). *Language intervention with young children.* Boston: College-Hill Press.

Fillmore, C. (1968). The case for case. In E. Bach and R. Harmes (Eds.), *Universals in linguistic theory* (pp. 1–87). New York: Holt, Rinehart & Winston.

Fodor, J. A., and Katz, J. J. (Eds.). (1964). *The structure of language.* Englewood Cliffs, NJ: Prentice-Hall.

Gallagher, T., and Prutting, C. (Eds.). (1983). *Pragmatic assessment and intervention issues in language.* Boston: College-Hill Press.

Gentner, D. (1982). Why nouns are learned before verbs: Linguistic relativity versus natural partitioning. In S. Kuczaj (Ed.), *Language development* (pp. 301–334). Hillsdale, MN: Erlbaum Associates.

Gleason, H. A. (1961). *An introduction to descriptive linguistics.* New York: Holt, Rinehart & Winston.

Goldman, R., and Fristoe, M. (1986). *Goldman-Fristoe Test of Articulation.* Circle Pines, MN: American Guidance Service.

Grunwell, P. (1982). *Clinical phonology.* Rockville, MD: Aspen Systems.

Hall, E. (1959). *The silent language.* New York: Fawcett World Library.

Halle, M. (1964). On the basis of phonology. In J. Fodor and J. Katz (Eds.), *The structure of language* (pp. 324–333). Englewood Cliffs, NJ: Prentice-Hall.

Halliday, M. A. K. (1975). *Learning how to mean: Explorations in the development of language.* New York: Elsevier/North-Holland.

Hodson, B. W. (1980). *The assessment of phonological processes.* Danville, IL: The Interstate Printers Publishers.

Hodson, B., and Paden, E. (1983). *Targeting intelligible speech: A phonological approach to remediation.* Boston: College-Hill Press.

Hoffnung, A. S. (1977). An analysis of the language performance of the negative structure in children with normal and deviant articulation. In M. S. Burns and J. R. Andrews (Eds.), *Selected papers in language and phonology* (Vol. 1, pp. 18–30). Evanston, IL: Institute for Continuing Professional Education.

Hoffnung, A. S. (1981). Judging cognition during language assessment. *Topics in Language Disorders, 1,* 47–58.

Jacobs, R., and Rosenbaum, P. (1968). *English transformational grammar.* Waltham, MA: Blaisdell Publishing.

Jakobson, R., Fant, C. G., and Halle, M. (1967). *Preliminaries to speech analysis.* Cambridge, MA: The MIT Press.

Labov, W. (1970). The logic of nonstandard English. In F. Williams (Ed.), *Language and poverty: Perspective on a theme* (pp. 153–189). Chicago: Markham Publishing.

Labov, W. (1972). *Language in the inner city* (2nd ed.). Philadelphia: University of Pennsylvania Press.

Ladefoged, P. (1982). *A course in phonetics.* New York: Harcourt Brace Jovanovich.

LaPointe, L. L. (1986). Neurogenic disorders of speech. In G. Shames and E. Wigg (Eds.), *Human communication disorders* (2nd ed., pp. 495–530). Columbus, OH: Merrill.

Lee, L. (1974). *Development sentence analysis: A grammatical assessment procedure for speech and language clinicians.* Evanston, IL: Northwestern University Press.

Lenneberg, E. (1967). *Biological foundations of language.* New York: Wiley.

Leopold, W. F. (1948). Semantic learning in infant language. *Word, 4,* 173–180.

Leonard, L. (1974). A preliminary view of generalization in language training. *Journal of Speech and Hearing Disorders, 39,* 429–436.

Locke, J. (1980). The inference of speech perception in the phonologically disordered child. Part I: A rationale, some criteria, the conventional tests. *Journal of Speech and Hearing Disorders, 45,* 431–444.

Locke, J. (1983). Clinical phonology: The explanation and treatment of speech sound disorders. *Journal of Speech and Hearing Disorders, 48,* 339–341.

Love, R., and Webb, W. (1986). *Neurology for the speech-language pathologist.* Boston: Butterworths.

Macnamara, J. (1972). Cognitive basis of language learning in infants. *Psychological Review, 79,* 1–13.

McNeill, D. (1970). *The acquisition of language.* New York: Harper & Row.

McReynolds, L., and Bennett, S. (1972). Distinctive feature generalization in articulation training. *Journal of Speech and Hearing Disorders, 37,* 462–470.

McReynolds, L., and Engmann, D. (1975). *Distinctive feature analysis of misarticulations.* Baltimore: University Park Press.

McReynolds, L., and Huston, K. (1971). A distinctive feature analysis of children's misarticulation. *Journal of Speech and Hearing Disorders, 36,* 155–166.

McWilliams, B. J., Morris, H. L., and Shelton, R. L. (1984). *Cleft palate speech.* St. Louis: Mosby.

Menyuk, P., and Looney, P. (1972). A problem of language disorder: Length versus structure. *Journal of Speech and Hearing Research, 15,* 264–279.

Miller, J. F. (1981). *Assessing language production in children.* Baltimore: University Park Press.

Minifie, F., Hixon, T., and Williams, F. (1973). *Normal aspects of speech, hearing and language.* Englewood Cliffs, NJ: Prentice-Hall.

Morehead, D., and Ingram, D. (1973). The development of base structure in normal and linguistically deviant children. *Journal of Speech and Hearing Research, 16,* 330–352.

Muma, J. (1978). *Language handbook — Concepts, assessment, intervention.* Englewood Cliffs, NJ: Prentice-Hall.

Nelson, K. (1973). Structure and strategy in learning to talk. *Monographs: The Society for Research in Child Development, 38,* (Serial No. 149).

Nelson, K. (1974). Concept, word and sentence: Interrelations in acquisition and development. *Psychological Review, 81,* 267–285.

Nemai, J., and Kelemen, G. (1929). Das stimmorganden orang-ustan, z. *Anat. Eng. w. Gesch., 88,* 697–709.

Olson, D. R. (1970). Language and thought: Aspects of a cognitive theory of semantics. *Psychological Review, 77,* 257–273 (in *TLD,* September 1986).

Omark, D. (1981). Pragmatics and ethological techniques for the observational assessment of children's communicative abilities. In J. Erickson and D. Omark (Eds.), *Communication assessment of the bilingual bicultural child* (pp. 249–284). Baltimore: University Park Press.

Piaget, J. (1952). *The origins of intelligence in children.* New York: International Universities Press.

Pollack, E., and Rees, N. (1972). Disorders of articulation: Some clinical applications of distinctive feature theory. *Journal of Speech and Hearing Disorders, 37,* 451–461.

Poole, I. (1934). Genetic development of articulation of consonant sounds in speech. *Elementary English Review, 11,* 159–161.

Prutting, C. (1979). Process /'pra, s s/n: The action of moving forward progressively from one point to another on the way to completion. *Journal of Speech and Hearing Disorders, 44,* 3–30.

Prutting, C. (1982). Pragmatics as social competence. *Journal of Speech and Hearing Disorders, 47,* 123–134.

Quirk, R., Greenbaum, S., Leech, G., and Svartvik, J. (1985). *A comprehensive grammar of the English language.* New York: Longman.

Rees, N. (1980). Learning to talk and understand. In T. Hixon, L. Shriberg, and L. Saxman

(Eds.), *Introduction to communication disorders* (pp. 1–41). Englewood Cliffs, NJ: Prentice-Hall.

Rice, M. (1983). Contemporary accounts of the cognition/language relationship: Implications for speech language clinicians. *Journal of Speech and Hearing Disorders, 48,* 347–359.

Rosenbek, J. C., and LaPointe, L. L. (1978). The dysarthrias: Description, diagnosis, and treatment. In D. F. Johns (Ed.), *Clinical management of neurogenic communication disorders* (pp. 251–310). Boston: Little, Brown.

Roth, F., and Spekman, N. (1984). Assessing the pragmatic abilities of children: Part 2. Guidelines and considerations, and specific evaluation procedures. *Journal of Speech and Hearing Disorders, 49,* 12–17.

Sander, E. (1972). When are speech sounds learned? *Journal of Speech and Hearing Disorders, 37,* 55–63.

Shriberg, L., and Kwiatowski, J. (1985). Continuous speech sampling for phonological analysis of speech-delayed children. *Journal of Speech and Hearing Disorders, 50,* 322–334.

Stockman, I. J., and Vaughn-Cooke, F. B. (1986). Implication of semantic category research for language assessment of nonstandard speakers. *Topics in Language Disorders, 6,* 15–26.

Taylor, A., Rosegrant, T., Meyer, A., and Samples, B. (1980). *Communicating.* Englewood Cliffs, NJ: Prentice-Hall.

Templin, M. (1957). *Certain language skills in children.* Minneapolis: University of Minnesota Press.

Templin, M. C., and Darley, F. L. (1969). *Templin-Darley Test of Articulation.* Iowa City, IA: Bureau of Educational Research and Service, University of Iowa.

Traugott, E., and Pratt, M. (1980). *Linguistics for students of literature.* New York: Harcourt Brace Jovanovich.

Trifonovitch, G. (1980). Culture learning/Culture teaching. In K. Croft (Ed.), *Readings on English as a second language* (pp. 550–558). Cambridge, MA: Winthrop Publishers.

Tyack, D., and Gottsleben, R. (1974). *Language sampling, analysis, and training: A handbook for teachers and clinicians.* Palo Alto, CA: Consulting Psychologists Press.

Webster's Seventh New Collegiate Dictionary. (1969). Springfield, MA: Merriam.

Wepman, J. (1958). *Auditory Discrimination Test.* Chicago: Language Research Associates.

CHAPTER 4

The Development
of Oral Language

AUDREY SMITH HOFFNUNG

As noted in Chapter 3, the parameters of language (phonology, morphology, syntax, semantics, and pragmatics) overlap. The development of nonverbal communication, comprehension, sounds, words, sequences of words, and uses of words are interrelated. Traditional discussions of development stress the productive and receptive aspects of language. In production, the reflexive birth cry occurs first, followed by cooing, or vowel-like sounds, at 1 to 2 months; by babbling, or the playful production of vowel and consonant sounds, from 3 to 6 months; by echolalia, or the production of the sounds heard in the environment, at approximately 9 months; and by true speech, or the use of meaningful words not just playful sounds, around 12 months of age. Running parallel in receptive aspects, the child responds to a loud sound with a Moro reflex (extension of the arms and legs) at birth, can localize a sound by 2 weeks of age, and can recognize familiar and unfamiliar voices by 4 months of age. At 4 months, a child can also differentiate between the voiced and voiceless sounds _ba_/_pa_ (Eimas, Siqueland, Jusczyk, and Vigorito, 1971) when they are piped into the crib area, as well as distinguishing between sound differences caused by changes in the place of articulation, between _da_/_ga_, a tongue-tip sound versus a tongue-back, or velar, sound (Moffitt, 1968). The child comprehends simple words and phrases starting at 9 months (e.g., *Where's mommy?* and *Make bye bye*).

Current discussions of the development of language involve a good deal more of the early nonverbal aspects of communication. Considered are the child's intent to communicate long before the child structures the sounds to form the words of the language, the child's cognitive ability that underlies the development of communication, the child's affect or interpersonal relationships, and the rule-governed productive and receptive aspects of the language, which require cognitive development but which are considered by many (Cromer, 1974, 1981; Moore and Meltzoff, 1978) to be a separate and independent system.

PRAGMATICS

How do cognition, social contact, affect, and the need to communicate fit into the total picture? Communication begins long before the first word is established. Bruner (1975) noted that, as early as 2 months, the mother and child have a "line of regard." Together, they react to the same item in the environment when they both focus on that item. First, there must be a recognition of the object by the child, which must be followed by an interaction between the child and another person, which must be followed by an interaction with the environment. As the child develops physically and mentally, the child can recognize an object at rest (0–4 months); the object in motion, when moving from a stopped position (5–8 months); and the object's appearance and disappearance either in motion or at rest (9–18 months) (Moore and Meltzoff, 1978).

Bates, Camaioni, and Volterra (1975) were interested in determining which items in cognitive development occurred before the onset of symbolic referential speech; that is, which nonverbal acts performed by the children occurred prior to verbal acts. They believed that the nonverbal acts children perform will later be paralleled by verbal acts or speech acts. Their subjects were three children whose ages at the onset of the study were 2 months, 6 months, and 12 months. The children were followed until they were approximately 16 months of age in order to judge what the researchers considered to be the nonverbal prerequisites of verbalization. Bates and colleagues reported the results of their study by using Austin's Speech Acts: perlocution (how the communication is interpreted by the recipient of the communication), illocution (the intent of the person communicating), and locution (the sounds formed into verbally meaningful communication) (see Chapter 3). For the purpose of their study, Bates and colleagues decided to concentrate on only two of the performative, or illocutionary, states of language development: imperative and declarative. Though the illocutionary stage was stressed, it is important to note the perlocutionary and locutionary involvement. Their findings are discussed later in the chapter where cognition and communicative intent are jointly considered.

SPEECH ACTS

As indicated in Chapter 3, a perlocutionary act, whether verbal or nonverbal, creates a planned or an unplanned effect on the listener or the recipient of the action. For example, when you tap someone on the shoulder to get that person's attention, the recipient turns around. Your intention, or illocutionary act, is to get the person's attention. The effect that has been created, or the perlocutionary act, turns out as you planned when the person turns around. An unplanned perlocutionary act might be when a baby cries and the caretaker comes running. At an early stage of development, crying is not planned, but the effect on the listener is the same as if it had been. The signalling occurs prior to the time when children can intentionally communicate their needs (Bates et al., 1975). This nonplanned communication, or onset of the perlocutionary stage of communication, occurs from birth. During the early period of development, at around 1 month, the baby has not reached the point at which he or she is requesting help, nor does the baby use objects to get the adult's attention. The child is not an intentional sender of messages, though the baby's cries are interpreted as messages by the caretaker as cries for help. The child will gradually learn to cry with the intention of conveying his message to the adult. When crying with intention, the child is in the nonverbal illocutionary stage.

COGNITION: PIAGET'S SENSORIMOTOR STAGES

At 4 months (Piaget's Stage 2), though the child smiles and coos and there is a mutual imitation of sound between the child and the adult, there is still no specific intention to communicate (Ginsburg and Opper, 1969). At this point the child tries to imitate the adult's vocalization, or to turn-take (Bruner, 1975), but is only able to imitate the sounds that are within his or her own repertoire. This imitation increases at 5 or 6 months, and the child is able to imitate the intonation patterns of the language, developing suprasegmental features such as stress and pitch change (Sinclair, 1971). Weir (1966) studied infants who were brought up in homes where English or Chinese was spoken. Naive listeners could classify the language of the household of these 6-month-old infants by listening to the children's vocalizations on tapes. The infants babbled the intonation patterns of the Chinese or English speakers of their environment, and the prosodic features or suprasegmental features used by the Chinese and American infants varied with great enough significance for the differences to be recognized by the naive listeners.

At 5 months (Piaget's Stage 3), the child reaches to make contact with the adult by touching or mouthing, but it is not until 10 months (Piaget's Stage 4) that the child intentionally uses an adult as an object or agent to attain a desired goal. Intentional communication begins before speech begins, as a gesture, as eye contact, or as a prelinguistic vocalization. At 10 months there is an intentional use of the imperative and declarative. From 10 to 12 months, the child also develops a means-end behavior, at which time the child uses various unfamiliar, or new, means to attain an object.

A number of the following paragraphs refer to behaviors that develop at the specific stages described by Piaget. Because some researchers attribute slightly different age spans to the six stages of Piaget's sensorimotor period, the age table utilized by Muma (1978) has been chosen as the point of reference: Stage 1, 0–1 months; Stage 2, 1–4 months; Stage 3, 4–6 months; Stage 4, 6–10 months; Stage 5, 10–18 months; and Stage 6, 18–24 months. At about this time, the development of the locutionary stage begins. At first the child produces a word-like signal that has no obvious referent; that is, the signal does not refer to an object. Bates and colleagues (1975) reported that Marta (a child in their study) used *mm* as a preverbal signal indicating a demand for something. The pitch was high when she was demanding something but was low if the adult had not guessed the correct item desired. At this illocutionary phase, the child begins to understand that she could have an effect on the listener and that the listener could serve in the role as an agent, or the one who will do things for her (Bates et al., 1975).

At this time the child will also "show" an object but not "give" it (Piaget's Stage 5). The child will first only show the object being held; later, by 13 months, the child will look for an object to show it. At this time "giving" becomes separate from "showing" and "pointing" and is now used for communication. This act of pointing, called a deictic act, is said to indicate that the child understands the difference between self and object (Werner and Kaplan, 1963).

The protoimperative, or command, is used before the development of speech utterances, and it is used to cause the listener to follow the directions of the child. *Proto* means "first in time" or "first or lowest in a series" (Webster's, 1969) and in linguistics indicates that the action mentioned occurred before the development of oral language. Gestures such as pointing may be used to say, "I demand" or "I indicate" (Gruber, 1973, p. 443). A declarative differs from an imperative in the responses expected from the listener. When using a proto-declarative, the child indicates an event or object to the listener in order to share the experience with the listener or to get the listener's attention, smile, comment, or chuckle. The child might point, give, or show something to the listener as a social experience but at this stage does not speak.

Bates and colleagues (1975) suggested that cognitive development to the level of Piaget's Stage 5 (10–18 months) is essential for the development of language because the child must develop cognitively to the means-end stage, at which time objects are used to obtain and operate on other objects. The children's use of actions to communicate precedes the use of words. There is a hierarchy in the development of verbalization: the child vocalizes, uses vocalization as a signal, uses words as signals, and then uses words with a symbolic value, that is, the words symbolize some specific referent. The use of referential speech, or symbolic speech, occurs at Piaget's Stage 6. Bates and colleagues (1975) believe that symbolic play and referential speech develop together. Rice (1983) states that they both stem "from a common deeper underlying system."

Though parallelisms are found in the sensorimotor stage and in language development, no direct relationship between the two has been determined (Muma, 1986). It has not been proven that object permanence or a means-end relationship must occur before the development of speech. In earlier literature, many writers stressed the need for preverbal development of means-end or symbolic play as a base for referential speech, but recent studies have reported that children in the one-word stage, although using a means-end scheme (e.g., using a stick to get an object), may not have engaged in symbolic play (e.g., using a block as a cup). Thus, the exact relationship between linguistic abilities and preverbal behavior or between sensorimotor development and cognition has not been established (Folger and Leonard, 1978).

SUGGESTIONS

Recognize and start at the child's level. If there is no verbal language, perhaps start with (1) the Line of Regard (Bruner, 1975) by looking at an item (a doll, a train) and talking about it while looking from the child to the item, or with (2) babbling by playing with the formation of sounds just for the fun of it. If the Continuity Theory is correct, these babbled sounds are the foundation for the formation of the true speech sounds. Just say, "ma,ma,ma,ma," and wait, or say, "ba,ba,ba," and play with the changes of pitch, saying one syllable high and the other low. Or you may want to start with (3) stimulation for the development of the symbols of language by choosing various items. For example, say, "Which one shall we play with? The baby!" (sing "Rock-a-bye Baby" and sway, or "the car!" (make a car noise and move the car), or "the ball!" (play catch; throw the ball; roll the ball; bounce the ball). Repeat the name, take the child's hand and place it on the object (have the child feel it) while saying the name. Use simple one- or two-syllable words that contain the basic sounds. Or you might start with (4) stimulation of turn-taking in vocalization. Talk to the child in short phrases about the immediate environment and then wait for some sound, any sound, and accept this as the child's turn in the conversation; for example, "Did you eat? Yes?" (wait); "What did you eat? Bread? No? Cereal? No? Cookie? Yes?" Change your pitch and intonation. Be sensitive to the child's vocalization, intonation, eyes, and facial expression. Is the child using a rising intonation for a question, a falling intonation for agreement, a stronger sound for a demand or for rejection? Is the child looking in a particular direction, turning his or her body, stretching out a hand? Respond to the child's body movements and verbalize, "John wants the ball . . . ball?" Then give the ball to the child if he or she smiles, looks, vocalizes, or reaches. Respond to the child's desire to share or stimulate the desire to share, by saying, "You want to show me your new book . . . this book?" or "Show me your new shoes." Then *share in the child's delight;* use gestures to point and facial expressions to show pleasure. Let the child use you as an object to get what is wanted.

While involved in these activities, you are playing with stress and intonation patterns, developing a "Play-ese" behavior, and developing the concept of turn-taking. The objects of the lesson are production of sound and the very basic requirement for the development of conversation, that is, the ability to participate in dialogue.

COGNITIVE HYPOTHESES

How does one develop the linguistic knowledge necessary to relate nonlinguistic knowledge? The Strong Cognition Hypothesis suggests that cognition precedes language and is responsible for language acquisition, but this hypothesis has been challenged and modified by a number of investigators. Cromer (1974, 1976, 1981) and Miller (1981) defined the Weak Hypothesis of Cognition, suggesting that cognition is necessary but not sufficient for language development. Cromer contended that cognitive abilities cannot explain linguistic capabilities. The present perfect tense (as in *The lamp has fallen* [1976, p. 300]) indicates that the action has happened in the past but that the lamp has still not been righted. Although children may not be able to express the present perfect tense until the age of 4 or 5, when they are cognitively aware of temporal relationships, they must have developed an auxiliary system for using a form of the verb *have* and for placing the inflection {-en} on the verb *fallen.* There may be correlations between the development of cognition and language, but no cause or effect has been established. Linguistic knowledge requires its own competencies.

The child must have knowledge of the world, but knowledge of the world and knowledge of language and its use are not synonymous. The desire to communicate and the mental and physical abilities to communicate are required, as are the linguistic skills with which to communicate. In her comprehensive article, Rice (1983) summarized six varying cognitive-linguistic hypotheses that attempt to explain, clarify, and support six developmental systems (see Chapter 3).

SUGGESTIONS

Stimulate the development of comprehension by using items, people, or events that provide pleasure or fun.

"Look who's coming to take you out ... Daddy!"
"What can we do now? Paint? Build?" (guide or hold the child's hand, if necessary, while doing the action)
"Guess what we're going to eat? A cookie? An apple?"
"Let's push the train ... yes, you push it."
"Let's catch the ball. Catch! Hold out your hand. Catch!" (use a large ball)
"Let's wash the baby."
"Let's wash the baby's face ... yes, her mouth, her nose, her cheek."
"Let's wash the baby's hands." (use the possessive *baby's* and the plural *hands*)
"Let's build a house ... a big house!" (emphasize the adjective *big*)
"Let's knock it down!" (hold child's hand, if necessary, and knock it down; then build it up again)

Stress nouns and verbs. Even though you, as the stimulator, use the function words (articles such as *and,* and prepositions such as *of*), the noun and verb words will be acquired first. Just keep talking, and reinforce the child with smiles, laughter, hugs, and a positive feeling. The teacher, parent, and caretaker must be alive, vital, and interested.

Use the environment for your stimuli. The child may not recognize a picture at first, especially a black-and-white picture, so use the real object or toy. When pictures are used, they should be large and colorful. Photos are great, but abstract schematic drawings may not be recognized as the intended object.

Use small sentences or phrases, and use lots of repetition. Say the sentences a little more slowly than usual, but retain the prosodic features (i.e., the pitch and stress). Retain the inflections on the words, for example, Two cookies, you have two cookies. We are building ... building a house.

Stimulate the concept of quantity as functionally as possible. Have each child

"Beat the drum one time. Do it one time."
"Jump one time, one time. Do it one time."
"Turn one time, one time. Do it one time."

The child may learn *one* and *one time* but not generalize to *Do it once.* Have each child

"Take two blocks."
"Throw two darts."
"Place two pegs."

The child may learn the word *two* but not generalize to *Do it twice.*

Give each child two cookies, one for each hand, and count, "one, two." Repeat with two pretzels, two socks, and two shoes. Emphasize the number and

and the last sound of the word to indicate the plural (e.g., two shoe<u>s</u>). Ask the child, "Do you want one cookie or two cookies? You want <u>two</u> cookie<u>s</u>, one, two."

The child must be able to use the final sound (mou<u>s</u>e, bu<u>zz</u>) if he or she is to produce the plural. The absence of production does not mean the absence of comprehension. Be sensitive to the child's comprehension of quantity terms such as *more;* two, three, four, and so on; *less;* and *a few.* Carrow (1973) states that 75 percent of the children know *two and more* by 4 years of age, *many* and *four* by 5 years of age, *a few* by 5.6 years of age, *some* and *half* by 6 years of age, and *pair* by 7 years of age. As we can see, even though the child understands *two* by 4 years of age, the concept of the same two items matched identically and presented as a *pair* (the concept is different and a new label is added) is not comprehended until 7 years of age or older. In addition, the *Boehm Test of Basic Concepts* (Boehm, 1967), which is administered to children from kindergarten through second grade, tests *most, several, zero, third,* and *least.*

Care should be taken to teach concepts and not just words or numbers. The child may count from 1 to 10 and have no idea of the meaning of the numbers just recited. Teach the concept of *one* and then the concept of *more.* Then teach *two* in contrast to *one.* The child must understand *more than two* before being able to select *a few* or *several.* Teach the positive *more* before the negative *less,* and teach *most* before *least.*

Stimulate the concept of time by using the child as an active participant in the activity. The {-ing} morpheme is usually present when the child is using an MLU of 2.5. At this point, the child has developed the concept of continuing activity. Have the child *do* the activity while saying the verb + *ing;* for example, have the child paint or eat or jump, and ask, "What are you doing?" The answer must be "Painting or eating, jumping, writing, or running." Accept any evidence of a two syllable word that you can in any way relate to the desired target word (e.g., /pā i/ for *painting,* /wə i/ for *running*). The child does not have to have accurate sound production to demonstrate the concept of progressing time.

The concept of time in the past (past tense) may be verbalized by some children at 27 months but not until 48 months by other children. To use the past tense morpheme with meaning, the child must understand time in the past. Some children memorize irregular past tense forms that they have heard repeatedly (*ate, ran*) and later incorrectly develop the {-ed} inflection for them (eated, runned). The child must be able to produce the final sound in order to be able to produce the regular past tense (e.g., *owe, owed* [ō, ōd]) but most verbs have a consonant for the final sound (fi<u>sh</u>, ca<u>ll</u>), and for those verbs, a consonant cluster is formed when the past tense morpheme is added (*fish, fished* [fish, fisht]; call, called [/kȯl, kȯld/]). The consonant clusters are /-sht/ and /-ld/ respectively. These are difficult productions for many children. If the regular past tense ends in {-id} (hunte<u>d</u>), then the child may produce the past tense by using just a vowel (/h ə nti/). The irregular past tense may be expressesd with just one final consonant because, in many words, a vowel change signals the change of time (eat, ate [/ēt, āt/]; run, ran [/rən, ran/]; hide, hid [/hīd, hid/]; get, got [/get, gät/]). The regular past tense depends on learning the past tense rule (add {-d, -t, -id}), but each irregular past-tense form of the verb must be memorized separately. When teaching the past tense, have the child *do* the action; for example, have the child wash his or her face and then stop washing. Ask, "What did you do?" The answer should be, "I washed." Have the child walk across the room (if possible). Ask, "What did you do?" The answer should be, "I walked." Children with language impairment who have difficulty with the morphological markers of past tense (Jansky, 1975; Moran and Byrne, 1977; Vogel, 1977) may omit the marker (*He wash yesterday*), may use a redundant marker (*He jumpted*), or may use *did* plus the uninflected verb (*He did wash*) rather than use the {-d, -t, -id}.

Stimulate the concept of spatial relationships. Again, have the child involved as an active participant. Using the *Test for Auditory Comprehension of Language* (Carrow, 1973) as a guide, it was determined that 75 percent of the children succeed in comprehending *up* and *in* by 3 years of age; *between, side of, middle,* and *in front of* by 4 years of age; and *under* by 5.6 years of age. First stimulate the concept of enclosure, or *in*, followed by the concept of *up*, or spatial direction. Have the child put items "into the box," and ask, "Where's the horse?" (answer: "In the box.") "Where's the truck?" (answer: "In the box.") Have the child climb into the box, or place the child in the box, and ask, "Where are you?" (answer: "In the box.") For spatial direction, have the child hold a hand up, look up (at the sky, at the plane, at the shelf), and climb up (onto the chair, the desk).

Have the child place items on the chair, on the shelf, on the floor, and on his or her head. Be careful; one of our children learned *on* but did not comprehend when his therapist varied the stimulus and asked the child to "Put the pencil on top of the book" rather than to "put the pencil on the book." Brown (1973) states that the range of productive acquisition for *on* is 21–34 months of age, with an MLU of 2.25. Playing Simon Says with these spatial terms can be fun (e.g., "Put your hands on your head," "Put your hands in your pocket," "Hold your hands up," "Look up").

As indicated, the terms *between, side of,* and *middle* (indicating positions between two items) were understood by 75 percent of the children at 4 years of age (Carrow, 1967). If you were to tell the child to place the *block* between the *cars*, the child would be required to know the name of the two referents (block and car) plus the concept of quantity (more than one). If you asked the child to place the *block* between the *car* and the *truck*, the child would have to be able to identify the label attached to each object. Therefore, when teaching the concept of *between*, it is important to verify the child's knowledge concerning all other elements of the sentence. Before attempting to develop comprehension of *between*, use the comprehension hierarchy and ascertain whether the child understands the spatial terms *up, in,* and *on*. Have the child "Put this (hand the child the object) in the box, put this on the box (use a box with a cover, a closed box), and put your hands up."

When teaching *between*, start with two identical items (e.g., trains) and have the child put the *boy* between the *trains*, then between the *dogs*, and then between the *cups* so that the relational concept is established. Later the two items may be dissimilar. Line up three or four items and be sure the child can select each item from a verbal cue. Then have the child place the block between the *car* and the *bed,* or between the *boy* and the *crayon.* If there is any difficulty, take the child's hand and model the behavior. If the child succeeds with two similar items (two cars) but not with two dissimilar items (car, truck), the problem may not be the concept *between* but short-term memory or naming difficulties. Please realize the many variables that you are placing in the sentence. *Between, side of,* and *middle* may be stimulated when painting a picture, selecting ingredients for cookie baking, playing with the doll house, or placing seeds in the garden. Try to use the concepts and terms in as many situations as possible.

Stimulate the concept of dimension. According to Carrow (1968), 75 percent of the children learn *little* by three years of age, *big* by 3.6 years of age, and *tall* by 4.6 years of age.

When teaching size, it is important to realize that *big* and *little* are general, or global, terms for overall size, whereas *tall* is a term describing vertical dimension only and therefore is learned at a much later age. *Big* and *little* are learned before *long* and *short,* which in turn are learned before *wide* and *narrow.* The negative global term *little* is learned before the positive term *big,* just as *short* is learned before *long,* and *narrow* is learned before *wide* (Eilers, Oller, and Ellington, 1974). As children develop, they may change their interpretation of the word *big* (at around 4 or 5 years of age) and use it as a synonym for *long* (related to height) (Marastos, 1973).

When teaching *big* and *little,* give the children two similar objects that vary only in global size and have them choose the one they want, indicating, "Yes, you can have the big cookie (the big piece of cake), and I will have the little one." If they are selecting the "big" crayon, they are probably selecting the "longer" one (one dimension), whereas the "little" crayon is the shorter one (again, just a single dimension, length).

When stimulating the concept of color, what are our goals?

To develop perception and discrimination (can the child match two red blocks? Develop comprehension of the color name? Select the red block when shown a red block and a blue block?)
To develop comprehension of the color name applying to other objects that are the same color (i.e., a red book, a red bow, a red hat)

To develop production of the color name, start with red. It is a primary color, it is bright, and it is learned by 75 percent of the children by 3 years, whereas black and yellow are learned by 3.6 years of age (Carrow, 1967). Orange is learned early by some children because they associate it with fruit. To stimulate the color red, have the child match the red block to a line of three red blocks. Have a line of three blue blocks as the decoy. Pick up the red block and ask the child to put it with the block that looks just like it (with the red block). Guide the child's hand, if necessary, and do this same activity for the blue block. Have the child build a tower with red blocks or select the red block from a number of blocks of different colors. Have the child paint or color an apple red, a cherry red. Bring in an apple and a cherry. Point to the red light on the street corner when walking or driving. Wait for the red light to change to green; then walk or drive across the street. Play a red-light game; the child must stop what he or she is doing when the red light appears and can start again when a green appears.

When you stimulate a child to develop any concept, you may work on a number of different areas at once, if they are not too similar. That is, working on *in* and *on* at the same time may confuse some children, but it is possible to work on *in* while working on the concept of possession (John's hat). For example, you might say, "Put Tom's pencil in the drawer. Put Sue's coat in the closet. Put Bill's lunch in his desk." For carry-over, use these (or similar) directions every day in connection with school experiences. Combine your work on concepts with stimulation of syntax (e.g., adjective + noun). Say, "Give me the red doll (the red house)," or "Cut out the blue dog (the green cat)." Ask, "What should I do?" and have the child give you directions.

HALLIDAY — LEARNING HOW TO MEAN

Halliday (1975) believed that when a child is in the process of developing language, he or she behaves cognitively and is actively (as compared to passively) involved in that process. Halliday also believed that a child has a communication system before being able to use words and that an interaction with human beings and with the environment must be present for a child to develop a personal linguistic system. It is from these interactions that the child develops a functional need to communicate. Halliday's orientation toward a sociolinguistic approach, rather than the more traditional linguistic approach, stimulated a different method for analyzing the emerging language of children. He selected six functions that he believed were expressed by his son Nigel's vocalizations and intonation patterns during Phase I (10½–18 months) of Nigel's linguistic development: (1) the instrumental function, or instrumental use of language, enables a child to obtain what he or she wants, for example, Want juice, (2) the regulatory function is used to get someone to get something for the child, for example, *ball*, and so control or regulate someone's behavior; (3) the interpersonal function of language helps the child interact with others in his or her environment by saying, "Hello, hi, or goodbye" or by calling the persons being addressed by their proper names; (4) the personal function allows the child to express his or her own individuality, for example, pleasure ("Tickle") or displeasure ("No tickle," or "Stop it") and so allows the child to indicate his separateness from the environment; (5) the heuristic function is the "tell me why" stage, when the child questions and asks for the names of items; and (6) the imaginative funtion, which Halliday calls the "let's pretend" function, lets the child pretend or create his or her own world. A seventh function occurred at 22 months of age when the child was able to provide the listener with information.

Halliday evaluated his son's earliest use of a vocal system as being the beginning of the development of his linguistic system when, at 10½ months, Nigel used an utterance to demand that the adult give him a specific item. The similarity between this report and the observation of Bates and others (1975) and Gruber (1973) is obvious. Again, it must be stressed that the child is not using an advanced sound system to relay these wishes but is using his or her own sounds and an intonation system of tones that are rising, falling, falling-rising, or rising-falling or that are at a low, medium, or high level. That the adult interprets and reinforces the child's use of this preverbal communication system is evident. Halliday reported a use of intonation similar to the one reported by Bates and colleagues (1975). When Nigel was about 13 months, he used a high-level tone of *yiyiyi* to respond affirmatively when questioned about whether he wanted an object. He used a high, rise-fall intonation when indicating that he wanted a person to do what he had suggested, for example, putting on a record. These two intonation patterns were seen as serving both the instrumental and regulatory functions. Sounds and tones were used as an interactional function to greet a person, to initiate an interaction or respond to an individual (e.g., to say "Hello"), and to indicate a desire to do something with someone (e.g., "Let's go") as early as 10 months, but the frequency of use does not increase until about 16 months. An early use of the personal function (10½ months) was found in the production of a sound that Nigel made naturally when going to sleep (e.g., sucking), which later became a part of his linguistic system to express a desire to go to sleep. This personal function expresses Nigel's awareness of himself as an individual separate from his environment; that is, he can express his own feelings and his own wishes to be involved or to be left alone.

The heuristic function starts to emerge at around 16½–18 months and with it the beginning of dialogue. Vocabulary increases as the child begins to recognize the need to understand more of the environment and is interested in knowing "why?" and "what's that?" At this point, the child relates well, is involved, and asks questions.

The imaginative function of language is a "let's pretend" stage, in which the child uses language for make believe. Though listed as occurring twice in 29 utterances at 13 months and four times in 52 utterances at 6 months, this type of function does not develop until the child can create an imaginary environment. An increasing vocabulary and phonology accompanies the use of these functions. Initially, a sound or intonation may compose a child's total linguistic system, but this system develops and expands to become more like the adult linguistic system.

Halliday differentiates between the pragmatic function of language and the mathetic function of language. The mathetic system is built on the personal, heuristic, and interactional functions of the pragmatic stage. Halliday reported that his son Nigel recognized the difference between the pragmatic and mathetic functions when communicating pragmatic information such as, *Do this for me* by using a falling tone and by using a rising tone to impart his observations of his environment such as *black cat* and *bubbles round-and-round* (p. 29).

The mathetic function in language development in Halliday's Phase II (approximately 16½–24 months) is seen as a spurt of ideational development.

The child observes his environment and is interested in items that are not pragmatically oriented, such as an eyelid, bubbles, and toy stars. Dialogue or conversation is begun, and the child in his role either of an addressor or of an addressee is able to adapt to varying social demands. The child shows an ability to differentiate between a declarative and interrogative sentence and comprehends verbalizations addressed to him such as commands, statements or *Wh* types of question ("What are you eating?" or "Where are you going?"). Nigel used the declarative sentence to impart information that he knew the speaker knew, and he used the interrogative to impart information unknown to the speaker. The child's vocabulary has increased, an understanding of grammatical structure has begun, and the child wants to relay information. This stage cannot exist without the development of language. At the end of Phase II (22½–24 months), the child has come to realize that the function of language and the use of the linguistic system are separate; the vocabulary, sound system, and structure have increased in their development.

SUGGESTIONS

Use objects functionally. When you are stimulating language, try to use the items as they are actually used in everyday life. Further, recognize that the semantic relationships (Fillmore, 1968) being expressed may be different, even though you are using just two- or three-word phrases (Table 4-1).

Table 4-1. EXAMPLES OF CASE GRAMMAR

Child's utterance	Meaning	Case relations
John push.	John is pushing the train.	Agent (John) + action (push)
Push train.	Push the train.	Action (push) + object (train)
John train.	John has the train.	Dative (John) + object (train) Dative, in this instance, indicates possession.
Train floor.	The train is on the floor.	Object (train) + locative (floor) Locative indicates location.
I made train.	I made the train.	Agent (I) + action (made) + factitive (train) Factitive indicates something that was created from the action.
John train.	John sees the train.	Experiencer (John) + object (train)
John train.	John wants the train.	Experiencer (John) + object (train) Experiencer indicates an experience or mental disposition of the animate subject.

To teach relations, you might want to start with action + object. For example, use one action and change the object. During lunch, ask, "What are you doing?" "Yes, you're eating bread (or a cookie, or soup)." During clean-up in the bathroom, ask, "What are you doing?" "You're washing your hands (or your face, or the doll)." Next, add agent + object. Help the child do the appropriate action, and show the appropriate object. "John (shows) the picture," "John (drinks) the milk," "John (bangs) the nail." Next, add agent + action. Take the child's hand and do the motions. "John push (the train)," "John throw (the ball)," or "John paint (the picture)." Finally, combine all three relationships. Change the subject: "John (or Sue or Bill) reads the book." Change the action: "Sue gives (or cleans or drives) the car." Change the object: "Bill drives the car (or the truck, or the tractor). With older children, you might want to build categories. Play, "I'm going on a trip" by saying the other person's word and then adding your own. "I'm going on a trip. I will bring (all nouns) a hat, a toothbrush, a book." "I'm going to the zoo. I will see (all animals) a lion, a giraffe, a zebra." You might also want to stimulate various specific categories. "I will wear (clothing); I will eat (food); I will see (color, different types of occupations); I'm going outside to play, I will (all verbs) hop, dig, jump, run, swim."

Teach location. When getting dressed, ask, "Where is your coat?" (In the closet, on the chair). When getting ready to read, ask, "Where is the book?" (In the drawer, on the shelf.)

Teach possession. Ask, "Whose coat is this?" (Hold up the coat so that the referent is visible.) Answer, "John's. Yes, John's coat." (Give the coat to John to show that it belongs to him.) Ask, "Whose lunch is this?" (Hold up the lunch so that the referent is visible.) Answer, "Mary's. Yes, Mary's lunch." (Give the lunch to Mary to show that it belongs to her.) When stimulating the concept of possession, colorforms that contain different figures or perhaps two types or sizes of doll might be helpful.

Teaching possession when it relates to kinships or family relationships is a harder task; although the two referents may be present (e.g., Mary and Daddy), the relationship concept is more abstract. *Mary's daddy* and *Mary's mommy* can be taught using pictures from a storybook, photos of the child's family, or wooden family figures. Perhaps *Mary's grandma* and *Mary's grandpa* may be understood, but teaching that Grandma is *Mary's mother's mother* or that Aunt Joan is *Mary's mother's sister* is much more difficult. The child has to keep a number of referents in mind (Snyder, 1984) and understand abstract relationships.

The possessive pronouns may also pose a problem in teaching because they change, depending on who is speaking. When I say to you, "This is *your* book," you would answer, "Yes, it's *my* book," and if the noun *book* were not included, you would say, "It's mine." Use familiar words (e.g., chair, hat, coat) when teaching possessive pronouns so that the child does not have to learn two bits of information in order to succeed. For example, sit around the table and ask the child to select the color of bead he or she likes. Then have the child pick up the *red* bead (his or her choice), saying, "My bead." The stimulator then picks up the yellow bead, saying, "My bead." Once this has been established, select a red bead and ask, "Is this your bead?" Select the yellow bead and ask, "Is this your bead?" Be sure the child can differentiate red and yellow before you start; if this is not possible, then use apples and chairs or blocks and play dishes or any available items.

PRIMITIVE SPEECH ACTS

Dore (1974) studied what he called the primitive speech act of two children, CA 1.3–1.7, who were in the single-word stage, defined as using a single-word or a single-prosodic (intonation) pattern to present an intention. Dore observed that at the one-word stage, the child was able to label, repeat, answer, request action, request answer, call, greet, and protest. These primitive speech acts occurred in the early preverbalization stages. At a later multiword stage, CA 2.10–2.30, the child can request information or action, respond to requests, make statements, and regulate interpersonal conversation (e.g., by initiating or terminating conversations) (Dore, 1975, 1977, 1986). Roth and Spekman (1984a, 1984b) listed communicative intentions from the preverbalization period through one-word to multiword development. Children with language disorders may differ in their functional communication and in their linguistic ability (the use of structure in language). To communicate, a person must intend to communicate and must presuppose or have the ability to estimate the amount of knowledge the listener has or the amount that must be provided (Halliday and Hasan, 1976). These are important factors in the maintenance of the cohesiveness of a conversation or in the narration of a story (Roth, 1986). For conversation, a heuristic period of behavior, a child must be able to initiate the conversation; initiate a topic; and maintain, repair, and terminate a conversation. To repair a conversation that breaks down because of misunderstanding, a child must revise his statements and be able to understand the questions asked of him by the speaker (Spekman and Roth, 1982). To converse, the child develops at varying rates in various areas of language, integrating all the components at a later date. Specific knowledge is required to analyze each area of the child's competence or incompetence; therefore, it is necessary to discuss each area separately — sounds of language, syntax, conversational acts, and narrative skills — so that a firm understanding of the conversational foundations is acquired.

SOUNDS OF LANGUAGE

PHONES

Intelligibility in speaking is based on the development of the sound system of the language. Initially, the words the child uses are monosyllabic and are used to represent items and actions in the present, thus allowing their limited sound system to be adequate for their communicative purposes. As the ideas represented discuss different time periods (past and future) and different environmental settings, the development of a more advanced sound system is essential to ensure the listener's comprehension.

The study of children's acquisition of the sound system is based on their ability to use their articulators (tongue, lips, palate, jaw, and vocal cords) to form a sound and then on their ability to develop the phoneme sound system of the language. The phylogenetic development of human articulatory structures has evolved slowly. The term *speech disorder,* when attributed to persons who have some difficulty with their articulators, is used to describe individuals who have dysarthria, for example, or who have a speech problem based on a neural mechanism disorder such as cerebral palsy (Netsell, 1984) or who have a structural disorder such as a facial-cranial problem or cleft palate (McWilliams, Morris, and Shelton, 1984). Problems can be noted in the direction, strength, and coodination of muscular movement and in the loss of automatic movements (Darley, Aronson, and Brown, 1975). The development of the phoneme is based on the development of the rule system language and is independent of motor coordination.

Lenneberg (1967) compared the phylogeny of development of the articulators in the chimpanzee and in other primate families related to man. He found that humans and gorillas, chimpanzees, and monkeys have structures that are labeled the same (that is, the brain, tongue, jaw, and vocal cords), but there is a vast difference in their structures and in their use. For example, humans have greater differentiation of muscles in the region of the mouth; have a difference in the ratio of the height, length, and width of the mouth; have different angles of closure for the teeth; are capable of more rapid muscle movement of the lips, have a larger brain, and have a different size and configuration of the larynx (voice box). A child's articulators are not just smaller versions of the adult articulators. A child's articulators (Zemlin, 1968) continue to change from birth in both position and size. The child's larynx differs from the adult's in shape and in neck placement, and it is not only smaller than the adult larynx at birth but is proportionately smaller than the other articulators. Ontogenetic changes occur as children grow. The size of the structures increases, the position relative to other structures alters, and there is an increase in the rapidity of production for alternating movements of the tongue and lips. A child of 6 years can produce twenty syllable repetitions of [pə]* in 4.8 seconds and twenty syllable repetitions of [kə] in 5.5 seconds. A 13-year-old requires only 3.3 seconds and 3.7 seconds, respectively, to produce the same number of syllable repetitions (Fletcher, 1978).

To have expressive verbal language, the child must be able to produce the sounds, or the phones, of the language. The development of the phoneme that is part of the rule system of the language requires more than just the ability to produce sounds. The phoneme is on the phonological level of language and requires the ability to develop and use sounds meaningfully in intentional communication.

PHONEMES

A child coos until around 4 months old with sounds that are mainly vowel-like in quality. The child then goes on to babble phones (consonants plus vowel

---

* Merriam-Webster Pronunciation Symbols, Webster's (1969).

combinations) at about 6 months of age. In this stage, the child plays with sounds and can initiate sounds produced by others if they are within the sound repertoire that the child can spontaneously produce. The question of whether these sounds continue on to become phonemes of the language (Continuity Theory) or whether there is a break in development between the babbled sounds and the sounds used as phonemes in true speech (Discontinuity Theory) (Jakobson, 1968) is still being probed. Research is favoring the Continuity Theory, for the sounds heard in babbling are more like the sounds in the child's environment, and these sounds continue on to become the sounds produced in a child's early words (Locke, 1983). Oller, Wieman, Doyle, and Russ (1974) studied the sounds produced in babbling and found that the children in their study used the same type of processes for babbling that they used in their true language, or their meaningful use of words. A child will use a reduction of a consonant cluster (e.g., *tar* for *star*) and a final consonant deletion (e.g., *ka*, for *cat*) in meaningful speech and will also use these same processes with the sounds they babble. Oller and colleagues believe that the same ability will be used by the child when babbling or when producing phonological strings. The relationship between the child's preferences for specific processes used in babbling is stressed, and they maintain that these will be the child's production preferences when words are used. Their findings support the Continuity Theory and give credence to the claims made by mothers of language-impaired children that their child did not babble or that their child was silent.

The speech-language pathologist is interested in the sequence of normal sound development, in the rules that are needed to acquire these sounds, and in the phonological processes the child uses when spontaneously producing the sounds to form words, phrases, and sentences. Templin (1957) was one of the earliest investigators of sound development. Using 480 subjects, she noted among other items, the three positions of sound development (initial, *seat*; medial, *myself*; and final, *mouse*) and the type of sound: nasal (m, n, ng), plosive (p, b, t, d, k, g), fricative (f, v, s, z, sh, zh, th), semivowels (r, l, h, w, y) single sounds (k as in *cards*), double consonants (sk as in *skate*, and -sk as in *ask*), triple consonants (str as in *string*, and kst as in *next*), the gender of her subjects (male or female), and their socioeconomic level (high or low). She did not examine the phonological context or the sounds preceding or following the target sounds, which is a highly regarded element of analysis today. When considering the mean percentile of correct utterances, the order of acquisition of the sounds was nasals, plosives, fricatives, semivowels, and combinations. The initial sounds were produced earlier in development, followed by the medial, and then the final. She found no significant differences in the scores obtained by boys and girls, with girls producing slightly higher scores at an earlier age. This trend disappeared at 7 or 8 years, with both sexes scoring slightly superior at varying times. There were significant differences between the upper and lower socioeconomic groups, with differences becoming statistically significant after 4 years of age. (The production of the high socioeconomic group was significantly better.) The groups listed in order from simple to more difficult were the single, double, and triple consonants. The order of acquisition of individual sounds in all three positions with 75 percent accuracy for an upper age evaluation was as follows:

at 3 years: m, n, ng, p, w, h, f
at 3.5 years: y (yellow)
at 4 years: b, d, k, g, r
at 4.5 years: s, sh, ch
at 6 years: t, th (thinner), v, l
at 7 years: th (those), z, zh (pleasure), j (jumped)

Other researcher's findings have differed slightly from the above findings. The problem arises with respect to the acceptable criteria for stating that the sound is within the child's ability. Many tables quote upper age limits and require that the sound be produced in all three positions; thus the /t/ in Templin's study had to be produced in the initial position (*toes*, *table*), in the medial position (*skating* for 3- to 5-year-olds, and *outing* for 6- to 8-year-olds) and in the final position (*bat* and *skate*). If only the initial and final positions of the /t/ sound were included, the /t/ would have been placed at the 3-year-old level. The /s/ was produced in the three positions by more than half of the 3-year-old children. After examining Templin's results and reanalyzing the information presented by Templin (1957) and by Wellman, Case, Mengert, and Bradbury (1931), who included 2-year-old children in their study, Sander (1972) created a table indicating acquisition of the sound when 51 percent or more of the children used the sounds in two of the three positions. He considered that the criteria included information on the customary production or the average age of production of the sounds. In addition, Sander felt that the variability among children must be recognized and so included a range in development, listing age not only when at least 51 percent of the children used the sound but also when 90 percent of the children mastered the sound. (The following list was adapted from Sander, 1972, p. 62.)

51% of the children have mastered the sound in two of three positions		*90% of the children have mastered the sound in two of three positions*	
Before 2 years:	p, m, h, n, w, b		
at 2 years:	t, d, k, g, ng (sing)		
at 2½ years:	f, y (yellow)		
at 3 years:	r, l, s	at 3 years:	p, m, h, n, w
at 3½ years:	ch, sh, z		
at 4 years:	j (jump), v	at 4 years:	b, d, k, g, f, y
at 4½ years:	th (think)		
at 5 years:	th (those)		
at 6 years:	zh (pleasure)	at 6 years:	t, ng, r, l
		at 7 years:	ch, sh, j, th
		at 8 years:	s, z, v, th
		at 8½ years:	zh

Note the variability between the average age of production and the acquisition of sound by 90 percent of the children.

Other researchers currently view the development of sounds or the use of sounds from a different perspective. Ingram (1976) stressed looking for the rules the child uses and the development of the phonology of language in comparison to other developmental systems. When producing words, a child develops a consonant-vowel syllable (CV syllable — *ba* for *bottle*) or a CVCV word (*nana* for *banana*). The developmental hierarchy agreed on is that lip sounds occur first in a single syllable (ma or ba) and then in a reduplicated syllable (mama or baba). These are followed by tongue sounds when the tip of the tongue raises to the roof of the mouth (n, d, and t) and later when the tongue is pulled back and elevated (ng, g, or k). The progression is from front to back sounds. The order of acquisition of the various types of sound is vowels, nasals, stops (plosives), and then fricatives and affricatives (Ingram, 1976). The exact time of their development differs slightly from child to child, but the order is consistent. The sounds are organized into words and the words into phrases and sentences.

SUGGESTIONS

Persons working with and caring for the child should produce sounds clearly when speaking to the child, should speak slowly, should speak in simple sentences, should use a variety of short sentences and phrases, and should use words that the child needs in his or her environment (e.g., out, up, car, milk, apple, mommy). At first, provide words that contain the earlier sounds in development so that the child may choose to say what he is capable of saying. Later, more advanced words may be used to enlarge the child's vocabulary.

Accept the child's production as you stimulate for more advanced productions. Children simplify their expressions or use phonological errors, even though they have knowledge about the sound; that is, they have the underlying representation for the sound. For example, they know the difference between *tea* and *team* and between *top* and *stop*, even if they cannot produce the final sound in the word *team* or the s in the /s/ cluster of *stop*.

It is important to look for a *pattern* of errors because errors usually do not occur randomly; rather, it is hypothesized that the productions are based on the rule system of the child, now called by many the phonological processes (Edwards and Shriberg, 1983; Hodson and Paden, 1983; Shriberg and Kwiatowski, 1980). (See also Table 3-2).

If a child deletes the final sound, the process may occur in *all* instances where a final sound should be present (e.g., *hop* [p-plosive], *hat* [t-plosive], *home* [m-nasal], *fun* [n-nasal], *cough* [f-fricative], *race* [s-fricative], *match* [ch-affricative], and *school* [l-liquid], or it may occur only for specific sound categories (e.g., only for plosives such as *pop* [p-plosive], *tub* [b-plosive], *hot* [t-plosive], *sad* [d-plosive], *sick* [k-plosive], *bug* [g-plosive], but not for nasals such as *arm* [m-nasal], *pan* [ŋ-nasal], *ring* [n-nasal], or other sound categories). Because of the final deletion process, try to provide the child with words that have different final sounds (e.g., pea/peep, tie/tight, hi/hike).

The following paragraphs provide some suggestions for stimulating the development of distinctive features that have not matured and for reducing some of the phonological processes that are used as strategies for production by the child.

The ±voice-distinctive feature is important for the production of the cognates (sounds that are similar except for voicing such as /b, p; t, d; k, g; s, z; sh [Asher], zh [azure]; ch [choice]; j [Joyce]; th [thigh], th [thy]/). If a child uses the prevocalic voicing phonological process, the word *pea* will be produced as *bee*, and the word *card* will be produced as *guard*. This child also has a problem with the −voice-distinctive feature. As indicated previously, the /p/ and /b/ are mastered in words in two positions by 50 percent of the children by 2 years of age; therefore, it can be said that they have developed the ±voice-distinctive feature. If this early feature has not developed to differentiate the various cognates, it would be wise to stimulate this feature.

Start with the differentiation of the production of [p] and [b]. It is assumed that the child can close his or her lips, can produce the [m], and can combine the *m* with a vowel for a consonant vowel construction (e.g., *ma* for ma, man, and more). Listen to what the child can produce. Can he or she imitate the [p] easily? [b] easily? It is up to you, the stimulator, to decide which sound is easier for the child to produce; that is, which sound is more stimulable. To stimulate the [p], have the child explode the air from closed lips. Hold the lips together for a moment and then release them. Have the child blow on a tissue, gently flicker a flame, and feel the air that is exploded from your lips; then have the child produce the air from his or her own lips.

Combine the [p] with a vowel for a CV construction that produces a word. In a play situation, you can chug down the street in a make-believe car saying "pa-pa-pa," or you can stimulate *pop* with the toy Jack-in-the-box that goes "pop." In an informal or formal situation, you can stimulate *pop* for lollypop, *pop* for ice cream pop, *pa* for grandpa, *pea* when you bring in some green peas, *pot* and *pan* when playing house, and *pail* and *pie* when playing in the sand box. Try to make the words meaningful so that the child is learning a phoneme and not just producing sounds (phones). This type of production will also stimulate the production of the plosive (stop) sounds (−continuant-distinctive feature).

Contrast the +voice /b/ with the −voice /p/. Say *ba* when banging the table hard with the palm of your hand to get a strong sound. Stamp your feet on the floor and again say *ba*. Contrast the softness and the air of the voiceless /p/ with the louder sound (activation of the vocal cords) for the voiced /b/. Have the child say *bye* and wave bye-bye, make the noise of a sheep when shown the object or the picture or when taken to the zoo, and say *ba* when giving the baby the bottle (*baba* can refer to the baby).

A song can be used to stimulate /m/, /b/, and /p/ use in words. Sing the song to the child so that he or she is familiar with it, and then sing it leaving out words and waiting for the child to fill them in. If the child does not fill them in, do it and try again. Be sure to decide which word you want, and wait for that word. Start with only one or two words:

- Row, row, row your _____ (boat)
  Gently down the stream.
- Patty cake _____ (Patty) cake,
  Baker _____ (man)

- Bake me a _____ (bun)
  As fast as you can,

- We'll roll it, (use gesture) and _____ (pat) it, (use gesture)
  and mark it with a _____ (B),

- And put it in the oven,
  For _____ (baby) and me. (Later: For _____ [baby] and
  _____ [me].)

The song or poem should be appropriate to the age and interests of the child.

At this point, check the child's ability to discriminate the sound as meaningful to the differentiation of words. Draw a picture of a pea, or better yet, bring in some peas and have the child eat one and feel one. Draw a picture of a bee. Place the two pictures side by side and ask the child to point to the bee and the pea when they are presented verbally by you in random order. If the child can accurately point to five pictures that have been randomly named, it is believed that the child has made the ±voice distinction in meaningful words. At this point, ask the child to say words so that you can point to the appropriate picture. If you find that you are not pointing to the picture the child believes he or she is saying, then review the production again. When the child can produce and discriminate between meaningful words (bat/pat, back/pack), it is hypothesized that the child has the ±voice-distinctive feature and will eliminate the prevocalic voicing phonological process. It is hoped that this ± voice feature will generalize to the production of other cognates containing the feature (e.g., /t,d/[time, dime]; /k,g/ [coat, goat]; /s,z/ [see, Z]).

The +continuant-distinctive feature might also require your attention. Producing the +continuant-distinctive feature (or eliminating the phonological process of stopping for fricatives) is necessary for the production of /f,v; s,z; sh,zh; th,th/. In addition to developing the proper voicing feature, these eight sounds require a constant flow of air that must be modified by the lips or teeth. The /f/, the earliest acquired fricative, is visible because the lower lip is placed slightly under the top teeth, and frication is produced by releasing the air between the lower lip and the top teeth. The /f/ is easy to produce for some; for others, though, the *shshsh* sound that is made when the baby is sleeping (use a baby doll or a book with a picture of a baby) or the *ssss* sound of the steam radiator or of a tire going flat might be easier. Bring the lips forward for the *shshsh*, and retract the lips in a smile for the *ssss*. The consonants must be combined with a vowel and with meaning for the production of a word. The /f/ is used in the number *four*, which children use when counting before they have the number concept or know what it means to have four apples and four cookies. The /f/ can also be used in *foot* or *finger*, in *fat* as a descriptor or an adjective, and in *fun*. The /s/ is produced in a wide variety of words (e.g., *soup* [eatable], *soap, sink* [bath or washing activity], *sit, sing* [action], *sun* [part of nature's environment], *suit* [daddy's clothing], *sunsuit* [baby's clothing], *juice* [popular beverage], *house* [living quarters], *bus* [vehicle that takes sister to school], and *face* [part of the body]).

SYNTAX

With syntactic development or the sequential use of parts of the language, a child's formation of two-word phrases depends on the child's knowledge of grammatical relations (Bloom, 1971), that is, on the child's intrinsic knowledge of the rules of the language. The child is not able to explain the rules but is able to use the rules. *My shoe* (possessive pronoun plus noun) expresses a genitive relationship. *Mommy shoe* (noun plus noun) might express a possessive relationship (Mommy's shoe), but could express a subject-object relationship, if the sentence is interpreted as *Mommy give me the shoe.* The phrase *red shoe* (adjective plus noun) expresses an attributive relationship. When producing these sentences, the child utilizes three rules to produce a word before the noun *shoe.* As the child's MLU increases, as additional concepts develop, and as knowledge of the grammatical system of the language expands, the child is able to combine these structures to produce longer and more complex utterances. The child is then able to produce, *My red shoe or Mommy's red shoe.* The following are examples of rule use (modification of Chomsky, 1965):

- S   → NP + VP   (a sentence is rewritten as a noun phrase + a verb phrase)

- NP → The boy   (article [*the*] + noun [*boy*])
        The big boy   (article + adjective + noun)
        He   (pronoun)
        James   (proper noun)

- VP → V + P   (a verb phrase is written as a verb + noun phrase)

- V   → V1   (intransitive verb requires no object; e.g., cry — *The boy cried*)
        V2   (transitive verb requires a direct object; e.g., open — *The boy opened the door*)
        V3   (transitive verb may have both a direct and an indirect object in any order; e.g., give — *The boy gave the book to her* or *The boy gave her a book*)

The following are examples of sentences:

1. *I eat.* Noun phrase + verb phrase.
2. *He eats.* The {-s} ending is added to the verb to indicate the third person singular. The sentence may be modified by the use of transformations (i.e., by adding to, deleting from, or changing the order of the items in the sentence). The third person singular was present in all 48 of the children (CA 3.1) in Menyuk's study (1963).

3. *The boy is eating.* noun phrase (*the boy*) + auxiliary (*be* + *ing*) + verb (*eat*). The auxiliary *be* is added and changed to *is* for subject-verb agreement. The use of *be* in the present progressive mandates the addition of the {-ing} inflection on the verb. The {-ing} is then permuted (order changed) and attached to the verb *eat*. These sentences are used by the stimulator and are repeatedly modeled for the children, but they should not be explicitly taught. The present progressive tense is used to indicate ongoing activity.

4. *The boy has washed; The boy has eaten.* The present perfect tense is used to indicate action that has occurred in the past (perhaps a number of times) and that will probably occur again; that is, *He has eaten in that restaurant and he will probably eat there again.* noun phrase + auxiliary (*have* + *-ed* or *-en*, depending on the verb) + verb. In this tense, the auxiliary *has/have* mandates addition of the {-ed} or {-en} to the verb. Again, the sentence was changed by adding and permuting various morphemes.

BROWN'S STAGES

Brown (1973) studied the language development of three children. He used the MLU as a guide to linguistic development rather than as a guide to chronological age, and he indicated the order of development of a number of morphemes. In this study, a child at Stage I of language development has an MLU ranging from 1.01 to 1.99 morphemes and an age ranging from 1.6 years to 2.3 years of age. Most 2-year-old children are using two-word phrases. As the MLU increases, the child proceeds to the next language stage, using longer and more advanced production. At Stage II, when MLU = 2.25 and CA = 1.9–2.10, all three children in his study used *on, in,* and *-ing* in their utterances (e.g., *on table* = two morphemes, *in box* = two morphemes, and *Boy going* = three morphemes for a total of three utterances and seven morphemes, or an MLU of 2.33). At Stage III, when MLU = 2.75 and CA = 1.11–3.1, all the children could use the plural morpheme with the noun (e.g., blue shoe<u>s</u>).

Although two children could produce the uncontractible copula (e.g., Here I a<u>m</u>), the youngest child, who was 1.11, was not able to do so. This child was able to use as many morphemes in an utterance as the other two children were but was not able to use the same syntactic complexity. Stage IV, when MLU = 3.50 and CA = 2.2–3.2, all children could produce the possessive morpheme with the noun (e.g., mommy'<u>s</u> hat).

It was not until Stage V, when MLU = 4.0 and CA = 2.3–4.0, that all the children used articles (<u>the</u> book), past tense regular (wash<u>ed</u>), past tense irregular (<u>ate</u>), uncontractible copula (There he <u>is</u>), uncontractible auxiliary (They <u>were</u> writing), third person singular regular (he write<u>s</u>), third person singular irregular (she goe<u>s</u>), contractible copula (He'<u>s</u> big), and contractible auxiliary (He'<u>s</u> riding). The copula is the *to be* verb used, for example, with a predicate adjective (She'<u>s</u> <u>happy</u>, He'<u>s</u> <u>serious</u>), predicate noun (He'<u>s</u> the <u>mayor</u>), or a locative (I a<u>m</u> <u>here</u>). The contractible auxiliary is the *to be* verb used an an auxiliary or helping verb in the presence of a main verb (I'<u>m</u> singing, She'<u>s</u> washing,

We're jumping, They're hopping). The use of the *to have* auxiliary verb, which is used with a main verb or the perfect tenses (have written, has walked) was not included because it was rarely used by children at Stage V in Brown's study. The use of the perfect tense indicates that the action has occurred in the past and may occur in the future; for example, *I have eaten in that restaurant many times* contrasts with *I ate in that restaurant.* The latter sentence is in the past tense and indicates an action completed in the past.

It is important to realize that before the child can use the {-ing} morpheme progressive inflection on the verb, the child must have a concept of an ongoing activity such as flying, drinking, or driving. Each of the syntactic forms used by the child, unless memorized, has a cognitive base plus the linguistic formation. The use of the plural inflection (hats, bags, bushes) requires that the child have the concept of quantity (one and more than one), the use of the possessive inflection (Pat's glove, John's shirt, Mitch's car) requires that the child understand ownership, and the use of the past tense regular (pushed, hugged, hunted) or irregular (drank, slept, ran) requires that the child understand the concept of time in the past and indicates a completed action.

The child may understand plural, possessive, and past tense but may not be able to use them because of an inability to use a final sound at the end of words; instead the child uses the phonological process of final consonant deletion to produce a CV word (e.g., ha for hats, pi for pig's, ma for mapped). The child, then, will not be able to form a plural or a past tense because his or her production strategy does not provide for inclusion of a final sound. If the child does not say *hat* or *nap,* he or she will not be able to say *hats* or *napped* when an additional sound must be added after the final sound. It is possible for the child to say *bu i* for *buses,* expressing the plural through the use of the vowel. This demonstrates knowledge of the concept of plurality. The development of the other 14 morphemes designated by Brown requires a greater understanding of the grammar of the language. For example, if the English sentence *He walks to school* is marked for number and for tense, the {-s} ending indicates the present tense and also that the subject is *he, she,* or *it* (e.g., *The boy runs, She eats,* and *It rains*). The copula *to be* is considered a state-of-being verb, or linking verb, which describes an attribute, condition, or state of a person or object (e.g., *He is hungry,* and *She is angry*) (Quirk et al., 1985). The use of the stages, age ranges, and morphemes are helpful in analyzing the linguistic development of children.

PAUL'S ASSIGNMENT STRUCTURAL STAGES

Paul (1981) analyzed some syntactic productions of children using five MLU stages. Her general conclusion was that the MLU is a better indicator of syntactic development than of chronological age and that, as the MLU increases, so will the syntactic complexity of the utterances. Different syntactic constructions were reported to appear at different levels of MLU. The information reported here includes suggestions for the Assignment Structural Stage (ASS) method of analysis of children's language as developed by Paul.

At early Stage IV, when MLU = 3.0–3.5 and at approximately 3 years of age, children start to use complex sentences. The syntactic productions listed are used at least once by 50–90 percent of the children studied by Paul at the specific MLU stage quoted. At early Stage IV, the children used (1) the cantenatives — gonna, wanna, gotta, hafta, let's, and let me, which were combined with another verb (e.g., I gotta go home); (2) an infinitive clause using the same subject (e.g., He wants to paint); (3) a sentence containing a "full propositional complement" (p. 67), for which the main verb is usually *think, guess, wish, wonder, know, hope* (e.g., I hope [that] he comes); (4) a sentence with a *Wh* clause introduced by what, where, why, how, or when that does not use an infinitive (e.g., I forget where it goes); and (5) a sentence using the conjunction *and* to join two clauses (I colored a picture and he painted a car).

At late Stage IV and early Stage V, when MLU = 3.51–4.00 and at a little below 3½ years of age, the children used (1) embedding (e.g., The boy hasta run to find the ball) and (2) embedding and conjoining together in one sentence (e.g., I told the boy to make it and I want to eat it).

At early Stage V, when MLU = 4.01–4.50 and at a little over 3.9 years, the children used (1) a sentence with an infinitive clause, but in this case, the subject differed from the subject in the main sentence (e.g., I want him to go = I want and he will go); (2) sentences containing a relative clause (e.g., I know what we can do); and (3) the conjunction *if* (e.g., We can go to the party if we are not sick).

At late Stage V, when MLU = 4.51–5.00 and at approximately 4 years and older, the children included the production of (1) the gerund (e.g., Swimming is fun) and (2) the conjunction *because* (e.g., The tower fell 'cause he pushed it). At an MLU of 5.01 and up, the children included conjunctions *when* and *so* (e.g., He should stay home when it's cold).

NEGATIVES

The development of negatives and interrogatives are added to verbalizations even in a two-word combination. The children use *not car* and *no truck* as well as *a car?* and *that truck?* (Trantham and Pedersen, 1976, p. 6).

An identical production of a negative phrase may not carry the same message (Bloom, 1970). A child may use *no car* to indicate nonexistence, that the car is not there or does not exist; rejection, that the car is not wanted; or denial, that the object being held or being pointed to is not a car. The utterance *no car* therefore utilizes the same negative + noun construction but is used to express various concepts of the negative. The syntactic complexity of the negative sentence increases as the child is able to use longer sentences, but it was found that greater syntactic complexity is used with the simpler negative concept; that is, nonexistence was expressed with greater syntactic complexity than were the concepts of rejection or denial. The modals *can* and *will* are used in a negative sentence as *can't* and *won't* before they appear alone in a declarative sentence.

At this stage, *can't* and *won't* are thought to be learned as one morpheme to indicate negation, not as two morphemes (can + not). It is only after *can* and *will* are correctly used in a declarative sentence (e.g., *He can swim* and *He will sleep*) that they can be counted as two morphemes in a negative sentence (e.g., *He can't jump*) and are produced correctly in questions (e.g., *Can he swim?* and *Will he sleep?*) (Trantham and Pedersen, 1976).

The use of *can* and *will* implies that the child has acquired additional concepts that are expressed with the addition of specific words. The modal *can* implies the ability to do something; the modal *will* implies that something will take place in the future. Other modals (*may, must, could, would, shall, should*) also carry specific meanings.

The auxiliary verb *do* was added to a verb and used as a negative imperative (*Don't!*) by children 18 months–1.6 years of age, probably as a memorized term. The emphatic *do* (*I do want it*) is not a common production. The negative *don't* (e.g., *I don't like that*) was used by children from 1.6 to 2.6 years, and the interrogative *do* (e.g., *Do you want this?*) was used at an overall correctness from 71 to 94 percent by children ranging in age from 2.3 to 3.0 years. At this point it was used as a separate element. The use of *does* (third person singular) and *did* (past tense) were not developed as early. The auxiliaries *does* and *did* were first used by children in Trantham and Pedersen's study at ages ranging from 1.11 to 2.7 years and from 1.8 to 3.0 years, respectively. *Isn't* and *couldn't* appeared by 2.6–3 years, but *wouldn't* and *wasn't* were rarely in existence at 3 years.

INTERROGATIVES

Studies of interrogative forms have shown a steady development of comprehension abilities in children. Bellugi (1965) has shown that for children of approximately 2 years (the age range of the children in her study was 18 months to 28 months), the understanding of interrogatives (*what* + *do* + object or *what* + *do* + verb or *what* + progressive) was poor (e.g., "What did you hit?" Answer: "Hit."; "What did you do?" Answer: "Head"; "What are you writing?" Answer: "Arm.") (p. 177). By 32 months, children understand *what* + *do* + object (e.g., "What do you hear?" Answer: "Hear a duck."; "What do you need?" Answer: "Need some chocolate.") (p. 120). By 38 months, children understand *Wh* questions that are more complex in linguistic and conceptual requirements (e.g., "What d'you need a rifle for?" Answer: "I wanna shoot."; "Then what will you do for milk?" Answer: "I gonna buy some more cows.") (p. 124). Of course, understanding here, while dependent on the comprehension of the key *Wh* interrogative word, is also dependent on the child's comprehension vocabulary and understanding of the world. Ervin-Tripp (1970) studied hierarchy of interrogative development in children and found the locative *where* and the *what* request of a nonanimate object (e.g., ball) were understood by all five of her subjects in the CA range 1.9–2.5 (in early development, some children confuse *what* for *where* and will answer a *what* + *do* question as if the interrogative word were *where*.) *Whose* requires the concept of animate possession or ownership (e.g., daddy's car, dog's bone) and was acquired by CA 2.3. About one quarter of the children answered a *who* + object question at CA 3.0 (e.g., "Who is this?" Answer: "Dolly.") (p. 85), but confusion existed for many between a *who* + subject question ("Who is reading?") and a *who* + object question. Some children confused the types of *who* questions even at CA 3.0. Various children used different strategies to answer questions. If the child always uses a human noun to answer a *who* question (e.g., man, girl) then he or she will use the subject to answer all *who* questions (e.g., "Who is playing?" Answer: "The boy."). If the child uses a nonhuman noun to answer the *who* question, he or she may then answer all *who* questions with an object (e.g., "Who is playing?" Answer: "Truck.").

Other studies (Cairns and Hsu, 1978) found that *who* + object questions are not more difficult than *who* + subject questions if the *who* + object sentence contains a *do* construction (e.g., Who did the girl see?). Therefore, it is important to look at the exact construction and the surrounding context before judging the child's ability to comprehend a question or other utterances.

Why is answered as *what* before CA 3.2. *How* and *when* questions were answered as *why* questions around this period. Comprehension of *when* is usually the last interrogative to be acquired because it requires a time concept; that is, a concept of events that occur in periods other than the present. The event may have occurred an hour ago, yesterday, or some other time in the past, or it may occur later, that is, when daddy comes home or some other time in the future.

In other studies, there was a general agreement as to the hierarchical order of the development of *Wh* interrogatives (*where, what, whose, who* + object with *do, who* + subject, *who* + object with progressive, *why, when*) (Ervin-Tripp, 1970; Tyack and Ingram, 1977; Cairns and Hsu, 1978).

Comprehension of interrogatives has been viewed from other perspectives by other researchers (Hooper, 1971; Leach, 1972; Parnell and Amerman, 1983). Hooper was interested in the "communicative demand" of the question. Could it be answered with a yes or no response (e.g., Is this a spoon?), or did it require a label for "use" (e.g., What do you do with a spoon?), an explanation (e.g., Why do we eat with a spoon?), or an open-ended response (e.g., How do you eat with a spoon?). The yes/no and the label-use questions were answered with fewer mistakes than were the explanation or open-ended questions by the 3- and 4-year-olds, with the 4-year-olds performing significantly better than the 3-year-olds. The label-use question requires a semantic response and comprehension of the function of the object, whereas the yes/no question can be answered with a nod of the head or other nonlinguistic response. The explanation and open-ended questions required greater use of linguistics in choice of words and sentence structure. Leach (1972) stressed the need for the child to be sensitive to linguistic cues (e.g., a singular, nonhuman question, *What is this?* in contrast to a singular, human question, *Who is this?*). Children's responses to questions depend on the interaction of their knowledge of the world and their level of language development.

Parnell and Amerman (1983) were interested in the information available to and used by the child when comprehending a question, as well as in whether the child's verbal expression revealed comprehension and in what ways. Was there a difference in the response if the referent was immediately visible (picture) in the environment (Type I question: "What is this?"), if the referent was visible in the vicinity but additional knowledge was necessary (Type II question: "Why are the leaves falling off the trees?"), or if the referent was not available in the environment at all (Type III question: "When do you brush your teeth?"). They analyzed the questions by combining the children's responses with the level of the question type, noting how functionally appropriate or functionally accurate the child's responses were. Functionally appropriate responses are responses that use the correct category or kind of information, whereas functionally accurate responses additionally provide more logical and factual information. For instance, one response to the Type II question *Why are the leaves falling off the trees?* was *Because the wind blowed them,* which was considered functionally appropriate and functionally accurate; whereas the response *Because it's spring* was considered functionally appropriate but not functionally accurate. The response *On the ground* was considered inadequate in both of these areas. This area of functional communication is fertile for future investigation.

REQUESTS

Negatives and interrogatives are frequently used when making a request. This type of communication is often difficult for a child to acquire, but this more subtle aspect of communication must be learned by the child in order for the child to communicate effectively. An example of this is the need for the child to understand direct and indirect requests when engaged in conversation. Using videotapes as stimuli, Leonard, Wilcox, Fulmer, and Davis (1978) found that, by the age of four, a child can recognize indirect requests that use *can* and *will* in the affirmative (e.g., "Can you open the door?") and in the negative (e.g., "Won't you answer the phone?") above the 50 percent-level of chance. For these children, the negatives were not found to be more difficult than the affirmatives. There was a statistically significant improvement in the responses of five-year-olds and again for six-year-olds. In a second experiment, again using videotapes for stimuli, Leonard and colleagues (1978) found that four- and five-year-olds did not understand an indirect request that changed the activity mentioned in the predicate of the sentence when *must* and *should* were used (e.g., "Must you tap the pencil?" "Should you erase the blackboard?") (p. 533). In these last two sentences, the action requested was different from the act that was expressed in the predicate of the sentence. For example, for the first sentence, the child watched a man on the videotape who was supposed to stop tapping the pencil; for the second sentence, the man was supposed to stop erasing the blackboard. The authors suggested possible reasons for this difficulty: (1) it might be more difficult for a child to need to change or modify the behavior in the predicate of the sentence, and (2) when using *Should you?*, you are requesting that the person stop the act, whereas when using *Shouldn't you?*, you are really indirectly requesting the performance of the act (e.g., "You should erase the blackboard, shouldn't you?"). The four- and five-year-olds did not perform above the level of chance, but the six-year-olds were able to make judgments when *must* and *should* were used, although their errors exceeded those produced for *can* and *will*.

Children engage in conversation even though their sounds of the language are not fully developed, their sentence structure is not totally accurate (by adult standards), and their understanding of the speaker's verbalizations is faulty, in other words, with less than perfect comprehension and production skills.

Suggestions

Negation. Children may use the morpheme {no} + a noun or a verb to indicate nonexistence, rejection, or denial (Bloom, 1970). To ensure comprehension of the negative by the child, it is suggested that negation be taught in this hierarchical order.

1. When no pencil (or bear or coat) is in sight (therefore the item is nonexistent), ask, "Do you see your pencil? (your bear? your coat?) No, no coat. No, no hat. Oh, we found it! Yes, we have your pencil." You are teaching the concept of nonexistence as well as the basic negative syntactic structure of *no* + noun. Accept a frown, a shake of the head, or some vocalization as an indication that the child understands.

2. When you know the child does not want an item or does not want to do something, teach the concept of rejection using the basic *no* + noun, *no* + verb, or *no* + adjective. Ask the following:

* Do you want carrots?

  Answer: "No, no carrots." (and provide the more advanced modal, "No, you don't want carrots.")

* Do you want to go inside?

  Answer: "No, no go inside." (and provide the more advanced modal, " I don't want to go inside.")

* Do you want the yellow?

  Answer: "No, no yellow. You don't want the yellow. You want the red. I don't want the yellow. I want the green."

3. When the child wants to deny that something has occurred or wants to state that something is different, stimulate the concept of denial by denying one element and by stating why you have denied it. Ask the following:

* Did you go swimming yesterday?

  Answer: "No, no swimming" (Reason) "It was too cold."

* Is this *your* hat?

  Answer: "No, it's not *your* hat. It's Jimmy's hat."

- Is that a dog?   Answer: "No, that's not a dog, that's an elephant."

To deny, the child must know what the element is and, therefore, what the element is not.

More advanced negation requires the use of auxiliaries and modals. The *can't* in *I can't* may be a memorized term, but if you hear *can* used in an affirmative declarative sentence, it is assumed that the child has mastered the modal *can.* In the sentence *The boy can eat,* the *can* indicates an ability to do something. In the sentence, *The boy can't eat,* the *can't* indicates an inability to do something. The negative morpheme *not* is attached to the modal *can,* and a contraction rule is used to form *can't.*

Each modal (e.g., can, may, will, shall, could, might, would, should, must) expresses a different meaning or perhaps a number of different meanings. *I may* suggests possibility, whereas *May I?* asks for permission. *I will* indicates action at some future date. *I shall* expresses determination, whereas *You shall* suggests a command. *I could* expresses ability but is weaker or perhaps a more polite form than *I may. I might* indicates possibility or may be used as a more polite form of *may. I should* expresses obligation or responsibility. *I must* suggests an urgency or compusion (Webster's, 1969). The negatives *can't, don't,* and *won't* occur early in development.

Interrogatives. The sequence for the modals and auxiliaries applies to interrogatives as well as to negatives. Children ask a question using a rising intonation pattern before they are able to utilize a complex syntactical structure. They ask permission ("Cookie?" [May I take a cookie?]), ownership ("Doll?" [Is this my doll?]), and information ("Out?" [Are we going out?]). The person working with the child may want to ask questions first in a more basic form and then in a more advanced form. They could ask

"Mommy?"   "Is Mommy calling for you?"
"New hat?"   "Is this your new hat?"
"Look at your book?" "May I look at your book?"

The intonation pattern is an important feature of the yes/no question. The child may gradually expand a two-morpheme verbal production to include additional morphemes and more advanced structures. The child may say, "My doll? This my doll. This is my doll. Is this my doll?" Each of these utterances adds a new element: (1) the possessive pronoun *my* was added to the noun *doll,* (2) the demonstrative pronoun *this* was added, (3) the copula *is* was added, and finally (4) the permutation rule was used to change the order of *this* and *is,* as required for an interrogative structure.

The following are examples of syntactic formations:

1. *The boy is big.*   *Is* is the copula, expressing state of being

2. *The boy is eating*	*Is* is the auxiliary
	Eat is the main verb
	Ing is the inflection on the main verb
3. *Is the boy big?*	Yes/no question
	The copula *is* and the NP *the boy* are permuted
4. *Is the boy eating?*	Yes/no question
	The auxiliary verb *is* is permuted with the NP *the boy*
5. *Where the boy is eating?*	*Wh* interrogative pronoun + sentence (*where* + *the boy is eating.*)
	According to Bellugi (1965), this rule occurs in normal language development before the child is able to use the permutation rule
	The auxiliary is included
	Permutation for the question (the NP and the auxiliary verb is) has not occurred
	Location is requested
6. *Where is the boy eating?*	Permutation has occurred
	The NP *the boy* has been permuted with the auxiliary verb *is*
7. *Where this goes?*	*Wh* interrogative + sentence (Bellugi, 1965)
	S → NP + VP
	NP *This* (Demonstrative pronoun)
	VP *goes* is marked for third person singular
8. *Where does this go?*	*Does* is the auxiliary verb
	Does is marked for third person singular because the auxiliary carries the number and tense
	The main verb *go* is not marked

CONVERSATIONAL ACTS

Dore (1977) organized and defined a list of communicative intentions used by children, CA 2.10–3.30. The main categories were requests, responses, descriptions, statements, conversational devices, and performatives. In 1978, Dore, Gearhart, and Newman developed a model of conversation for the analyses of seven 3-year-old middle-class children in a nursery school setting. They stipulated in their grammar-illocutionary-interactional model that certain skills must be possessed by the child in order for a conversation to take place. The child must know the grammar structure of the language, including the ability to express content using appropriate lexical items; must have communicative intent; must be goal oriented; must interact with someone so that speaking turns occur; and in a coherent conversational sequence, must provide appropriate responses. These types of behavior are distinct but interrelated. Dore, Gearhart, and Newman (1978) divided a list of conversational acts (C-acts) into three primary functions: providing content (initiating and responding to), regulating conversations, and expressing attitudes. These functions were divided into six classes: requestives, assertives, performatives, responsives, regulatives, and expressives. The list was later revised by Dore (1986) to include four main classes: "requestives, assertives, responsives, and organizational devices" (p. 38).

Based on Dore's list (1986, pp. 39–40), the C-acts of Evan (male, CA 2.2) and Alison (female, CA 5.6) were analyzed by this author. Evan's use of the C-act included communication intention and content, but it did not include the use of complete syntactical form or phonological accuracy. The C-acts he did *not* use are preceded by an asterisk (*) and are not followed by an example. Examples of these C-acts are provided when discussing Alison's use of them.

I. Requestives
  A. Questions
    1. Choice Questions
       Evan said, "Daddy?" to question who was entering the house.
    2. Product Questions
       Evan said, "Poppy?" to question where Poppy was.
    3. Process Question*
       Speaker would request elaboration of a description or explanation.
  B. Requests
    1. Action Requests
       "Get up," "More back ride."
    2. Permission Requests
       "Out?" to ask, "May I go out?"
    3. Suggestions
       Evan said, "Come on," when he wanted someone to accompany him or to participate in an activity with him.
II. Assertives
  A. Reports
    1. Identification
       Evan said, "Doggie," to show a dog passing by
    2. Description
       "Blue car," "Fall down."
    3. Internal Report
       Evan said, "Ear hurt," and "Diaper wet," to express a feeling or state of being.
  B. Evaluations (when the speaker judges the situation)
    1. Judgments
       "Taste good," "No good," "No, don't like."

2. Attributions*
Speaker would state beliefs about another person's feelings.
3. Explanation*
Speaker would use to provide reasons or to make predictions about the future.
C. Declarations*
1. Procedurals
Speaker would use to indicate rules or procedures as they are used in a game or in a situation.
2. Claims
Evan said, "Mine." to assert that the blocks belonged to him.
III. Responsives (Speaker uses to provide information for requestives or assertives)
A. Answers (When the speaker provides information)
1. Choices
a. Yes/No.
Q: "Do you want broccoli?" Evan: "Uh huh."
b. not B
Q: "Do you want apple juice or orange juice?" Evan: "Apple."
2. Products (Information is provided when a *Wh* question is asked)
Q: "Where's Ali?" Evan: "TV," (to indicate that Alison was watching television).
Q: "What do you want to eat?" Evan: "Steak."
3. Processes
Evan said, "Broke," to explain that the toy dog would not move because it was broken.
4. Clarifications
"No," "No." (Repeat utterance to clarify position.)
5. Compliances
Q: "Let's take a nap?" Evan: "No nap."
Q: "Let's go to the pool?" Evan: "Uh huh." (Evan agreed or disagreed with the request.)
B. Replies (When the speaker provides the information without being asked)
1. Qualifications*
Speaker adds information to expand or to change the previous statement.
2. Agreement
(Evan agreed with the information just presented to him.) Information: "Let's play with your ball." Evan: "My ball."
3. Acknowledgements*
Speaker acknowledges previous statements.
IV. Organizational Devices (These are used to regulate conversation.)
A. Attention Getters
Evan said, "Mama," to show the tower he had just built.
B. Speaker Selections*
The speaker would indicate the person to speak after him.

C. Rhetorical Question*
The speaker is using a question that he will answer so as to continue as speaker in that conversation.
D. Clarification Questions
Evan: "That's thunder. Why thunder?"
E. Boundary Markers
Evan says, "Hello," when someone enters the room or, "ByeBye," when he wants to terminate the phone conversation.
F. Politeness Markers
"I want juice please." (The use of "please" was very tenaciously taught.)
G. Exclamation
Evan says, "Oh boy," to express his pleasure at receiving two cars from his aunt and uncle.
H. Repetitions*
Speaker repeats part of previous statements as an organizational device.

Dore's (1977) organization of communicative intentions listed a number of items that were not specifically mentioned in 1986. They included (1) indication of possession ("Boy bike."), (2) indication of an event ("Eat steak," as he was eating a hamburger), (3) indication of location ("Plane up."), and (4) protest ("No tickle!"). Evan answered questions, but did not carry on a conversation because there was no continuation of the subject after a listener responded to his verbalization.

Alison (Ali), who was 5.6 years old, utilized all the conversational acts listed by Dore and used complete, well-formed utterances. Examples of the C-acts (Dore, 1986) used by Alison but *not* employed by Evan are listed below.

I. Requestives
   A. Questions
      3. Process questions
         Ali used "Why?" "How come?" and other questions to seek additional information or explanations. "Why can't I go swimming now?" "How come Uncle Serge didn't come with Aunt Tami?" "What about Evan? Will he come?"
II. Assertives
   B. Evaluation
      1. Judgments
         Ali was able to identify the concept of good and evil and form a judgment: "Here comes the wicked witch."
      2. Attributions
         Ali expressed her belief regarding the reason for Evan's screams: "He wants to go with daddy."
      3. Explanation
         Ali was able to reason from cause to effect: "If you pull that way, it will fall." And Ali was able to make predictions: "If it rains tomorrow, we won't go swimming."

C. Declarations
   1. Procedurals
      "You're not allowed to jump in," said Ali to a little girl who had never been at the pool before. "First you spin, and it tells you how many (spaces) to move," said Ali to her friend when playing *Chutes and Ladders*. (The use of these statements indicates a recognition of rules or procedures established for a specific situation or for a specific game.)
III. Responsives
   B. Replies
      1. Qualifications
         Statement: "Oh, you played at the beach with Jessica." Ali: "Yes, and I'm going to the beach again." Statement: "We just got Ali a new comforter." Ali: "If one side gets dirty, you have the other."
      3. Acknowledgements
         Ongoing conversation: "Would you like to come and visit grandma and poppy next week?" Ali: "Without mommy and daddy and Evan?" Answer: "Yes, all by yourself." Ali: "Yes, but I go to camp."
IV. Organizational Devices
   B. Speaker Selection
      Ali was able to turn to the person she wanted to answer her question or to fulfill her request. "Who will come with me? Mommy will you come?"
   C. Rhetorical Questions
      Ali: "Do you know what I did yesterday?" Having received a negative response from the listener, Ali was then able to continue as speaker in the conversation and tell about the Walt Disney movie she had seen the previous day.
   D. Clarification Questions
      Ali: "Why do you want to stop at the store?" This question asks for clarification of the reason for an extra stop made on the way home. (This was used marginally by Evan.)
   F. Politeness Markers
      Though Evan used tutored politeness markers (Please and Thank you), Ali not only used those, but was able to judge a situation and alter her approach. For example, in a situation where a direct request was not socially acceptable, she used an indirect request to obtain her desired goal. "Do you have ice cream in your freezer?"
   H. Repetitions
      Part of the previous statement was used by Ali to organize her response. Statement: "What did you do in swimming instruction?" Ali: "In swimming instruction, I put my head under the water."

Based on Dore (1977), in addition to the above C-acts, Ali was able to (1) role-play (She was able to establish an imaginary world of a doll family with a mother, father, and children), (2) joke (Ali rhymed words, producing sound combinations that were not true words and then laughed about them: "Hug, rug, mug, kug."), (3) use game-markers to start or to end a game ("I'll hide first and you have to find me."), (4) make claims (In this situation, claims give her the right to do something: "I'm first."), (5) warn ("Look at the puddle."), and (6) tease ("This is my bedroom," when she is sleeping in her Aunt Tami's room, or "I didn't make my bed," when she really had.).

As far as conversation devices are concerned, Ali was able to maintain a conversation in person (when facial expression, gestures, and props can be used) or on the phone (when one must convey the message through verbal means alone). She opened and closed conversations, filled in pauses, called attention to items she considered to be of importance, and corrected an inaccurate interpretation of her message. In addition, Ali told a story about events that happened in the past or about fairy tales that she had been told.

SUGGESTIONS

Projects or outings or just doing things together are good ways to stimulate C-acts. Think of how you can phrase questions or make comments to stimulate the desired C-act that is not in the child's repertoire.

1. Requestives
   Choice: "Do you want to build with
                                blocks or play in the sand?"
                                "Do you want juice or milk?"

   Product: "What shall I make?"
                                "What will you make? a house,
                                a cow?"

   Requests   "What do you need? a shovel?"
                                "What do I need? a pail?"

2. Assertives
   Description: "Tell me what happened. Car
                                broke? Scott fell?"

   Inner feeling: "How do you feel? Good? Sick?
                                Sad? Happy?"
                                "How does your baby feel?"

   Possession: "Whose picture is this? Yours?
                                His?"
                                "This one is mine. Yes, this one
                                is yours. Your picture."
                                "This is Jim's picture. His picture."

3. Answers to provide information
                                "What do you have for lunch?
                                Peanut butter? Hamburger?"
                                "What do you have for lunch?
                                Tell me."

4. Clarification

"Did you want the big one or
the small one? I'm not sure."

A game such as Animal Domino is fun and will help you engage in C-acts. Have the children state what they need (a horse, a parrot, a cat), whether they have the desired picture, what they should do if they don't have it, what they should do if they do have it, where they will place it, why they will place it there, what you need, and what you should do.

Whether you are making clay people for the house, pasting styroforms for snow, coloring objects in a park scene, playing house, playing dress-up, playing garage mechanic, or building a plane, continually ask the children what they want to do; which order of materials or events they wish, in other words, what comes next; and the specifics as far as color, shape, size, number, or item. Ask, "What shall we paste? The black hat? Paste the black hat on the snowman. What now? Give him eyes. How many? Where shall we put them? Anything else?" Use materials, wait for the children to answer, help them initiate, and respond to every attempt.

NARRATIVE SKILLS

Recent researchers have suggested that the development of children's cognition and memory is dependent on their own organization of the narrative, or the "scripts," rather than on the development of categories that have been ascribed to them by psychologists (Sutton-Smith, 1986).

During the infant's developmental stages, parents provide sound and prosodic stimulation and are involved in what is called "mother-ese" when they play with sound, use wide variations in pitch and loudness, play with stress and intonation, slow their rate, and use exaggerated facial and body postures. "Playese" behavior is used with Peek-a-Boo and This Little Pig. As the child grows older, the parents provide more of a theater dialogue situation, playing the parts of director, actor, and audience (Sutton-Smith, 1986).

Initially, the young child also plays with sound, using pitch and loudness variation, changes in rate, and exaggeration of stress to tell a story, the prosodic elements overshadowing informative content. The prosodic elements (Sutton-Smith, 1986) used by a young child between the ages of 2 and 3 years include items such as repetition of words ("The cookie went on the carousel. The cookie went on the puzzle. The cookie went on the doggie." [p. 4]), alliteration, or rhyming. The children used pauses and variations in intonation patterns that provided a prosodic gestalt or wholeness that did not include semantic information or syntactic structure found in adult language. In addition, early stories of two-year-olds involve "disequilibrating" factors or events in their lives such as falling or biting someone (Sutton-Smith, 1986). Sutton-Smith classified as metaphors the child's use of "a cat biting a bird," when in reality the child was the biter, or "choo choo falling out of the sky," when the child fell down (p. 6). In such early types of stories, called vectors, the children use vivid disequilibrating circumstances of problems existing in their lives and present them using more prosody than semantics and syntax. At this point the child uses no introduction, explorations, or ending statements in the story being narrated.

At 3 years, children still devise their own line structure, using rhyme and alliteration (use of the same sound in neighboring words), but now they have a main fictional character who did things in the past; have a beginning, or initial, marker and an ending, or terminal, marker; at times provide an evaluative statement such as something is good or bad or long; and are capable of using longer and more complex syntactic structures such as conjunctions (and, then) and locatives (in, over, up) (Sutton-Smith, 1986). From 3–7 years, the characters in their stories become more constant and are able to perform different actions, and with the development of causal statements, children are able to use some appropriate time sequence. By 7 years, children are capable of telling a story with a plot and with characters who are beginning to resolve issues of good and evil. From 8 to 12 years children develop the ability to solve problems that arise from the content of a story. Children at this age have ". . . all the verbal devices of turn-taking, argumentation, teasing, rebuttal, introductions, asides, giving background, summaries, morals, scandalous content, evaluations, dramatizations and prosody" (p. 9) necessary to hold the attention of their audience.

NARRATIVE STRUCTURES

Stein and Glenn (1979) presented a structure to explain the child's organization of a story. They found that the information recalled even by a child as young as 5 years was not random but was organized in a logical manner. The children remembered major settings, characters, and activities. The following list is an example of the structure developed by Stein and Glenn to analyze the narrative ability of Alison, CA 5.5 (The quotes listed below are from Alison's rendition of Cinderella. She had been told the story many times.)

Rule 1. Setting or Character
  "Once upon a time (opening) there was a little girl whose name was Cinderella (main character). Her stepsisters (additional characters) made her work very hard (activity)."
Rule 2. Episode: Initiating Event
  (Then) "One day a letter came to the house. The king is having a ball. Every girl in the kingdom must go."
Rule 3. Episode: Internal Response
  "Cinderella said, 'That means I can go.' "
Rule 4. Episode: Plan Sequence
  " 'The dress just needs a little mending,' said Cinderella."
Rule 5. Attempt
  (The stepsisters, in this version of the story, had thrown away a sash and a necklace). "Cinderella picked up the sash and necklace."

Rule 6. Direct Consequence

> (When Cinderella came down with her dress and their sash and beads, the step-sisters were angry). " 'My sash,' 'My beads,' said the stepsisters, and they ripped them off." (Alison changed her voice, using stress and intonation to present the different characters. Garnham [1983] believes that the prosodic features of stress and intonation are used to provide additional information.)

Rule 7. Reaction

> "Cinderella ran into the garden, 'Oh, how I did wish to go to the party, but it's no use.' "

The story continued with the introduction of another main character, the fairy godmother, and with another episode.

In their studies of the narrative ability of children in the first and fifth grades, Stein and Glenn (1979) found that children remembered the story. Of the following elements, items 1–4 were used most frequently in their text (1) the major setting or characters, (2) the initiating events, (3) direct consequences, and (4) attempt; older children were able to use (5) reaction, (6) internal response, and (7) minor settings. The fifth graders recalled more of each type of information, using connective terms (causality: *because, so that, in order to;* temporal: *and then*), which were rarely used by first graders.

NARRATIVE COHESION

Garnham (1983) stated that there are two major principles that should be used when telling a story. He refers to them as "referential continuity" and "plausibility" (p. 150).

Referential continuity exists if the sentences in a story refer to the same set of items and the "anaphoric references" are easy to infer. (An anaphoric reference provides cohesion to a story; for example, the pronoun used refers to a previously used noun so that the first and second sentences are combined to form a text [Halliday and Hasan, 1976]). In Alison's telling of the story of Cinderella, Cinderella said, "Oh, wishes don't come true." This was responded to by the fairy godmother who said, "Oh, don't they?" A relationship exists between *wishes* and *they* that is easy for the listener to follow, for the item *wishes* was expressed first, followed by the referring item *they*. The lexicon item *wishes* does not have to be expressed again because *they* is the anaphoric reference to them.

Plausibility exists when certain events are more likely to occur than others, thus enabling the listener to understand the message more easily (Garnham, 1983). At the end of the story of Cinderella, "the grand duke said, 'Are there any other girls in the house?' Just then Cinderella walked downstairs," (plausible expected action). The listener anticipates the discovery of Cinderella as the prince's true love, so her entrance at this time is plausible. (Discussions of additional skills needed for conversation and for narration are found in Chapter 10).

SUGGESTIONS

To be able to tell a story, children must have varied experiences in different settings and must have an understanding of how and why events occur. Take children to as many places as possible (e.g., to the store, to the playground, to the
city, to the country, on a train, on a bus, to the zoo, on a visit). Talk to them about
the places they visit, give them the words they need, and provide ideas for them
to think about. Supplement this with books about the places you have visited.

Read to the children; tell them stories. It may not be possible at first to read all
the words in the text. The text accompanying the pictures may be too long, too
detailed, or filled with words the child does not understand. Start by reading
slowly; accompany your words with gestures and appropriate changes in your
voice to highlight meaning; point to the items in the book as you talk about
them. Very young children may require a book with only one picture per page,
whereas slightly older or more developmentally mature children might respond
well to action pictures or pictures portraying various events that help narrate the
story. The A. H. Rey *Curious George* books are an excellent example of a fun set of
books. In the first book of the series, the reader can ask questions; answer them,
if necessary; and stimulate the child's answers.

"What's George doing?"	"Yes, he's swinging."
"Where does he live?"	"Yes, in the jungle. There are lots of trees there."
"What's he eating?"	"Yes, a banana."
"What is he?"	"Yes, a monkey."

The reader can now read the text about the monkey who lives in the jungle
and who is very curious, explaining that a curious person or monkey wants to
know everything. Then turn the page.

"Who's this?"	"A man"
"Yes, it's a special man because he has — what?"	"Yes, a hat."
"A special hat, what color is it?"	"Yes, a yellow hat. That's the man in the yellow hat."
"What is he doing?"	"Looking at George."
"What do you *think* he will do?"	"Catch George."
"Where will he put him?"	(various guesses)
"Where did he put him?"	"In the bag."
"If I had a bag over my head, what would happen?" (Cover the child's eyes with his or her hands.) "What happened?"	"You couldn't see. That's what happened to George. He couldn't see." (Try it again. Try to get cause and effect.)

Continue the story, asking questions, answering questions, reviewing, making it exciting — especially when George gets into mischief; let the child suggest what will happen and what George should do.

Develop cohesion (the ability to put the story together). If you use a pronoun, be sure the children know to whom it refers. If you delete part of the sentence, make sure the children have the information and are aware that they have the information so that they can fill it in for themselves (e.g., *They went there.* Who is *they* and where is *there?*).

Later on in the story, when George is watching the birds fly, ask for opinions about the plausibility of George being able to fly. Do the children think George can fly? Do they think George thinks he can fly? Develop inference. What does the child think will happen if George tries to fly? Proceed in small steps. Start with a book that has lots of different pictures and many different events.

CONCLUSION

It is extremely important for the educator working with the preverbal child to understand preverbal communication and to recognize the child's methods, systems, and levels of communication so that stimulation can be provided to aid in developing the next level. It is important to be aware of pragmatic function: in the use of body language, facial expressions, and gestures; in the use of the primitive linguistic system; and in the use of intonation patterns as they are superimposed on the sounds that convey the child's intention. It is important to be able to analyze the type, extent, and appropriateness of use of the phonological, semantic, and syntactic components of the language. It is important to be cognizant of the various levels and purposes of conversational acts and to recognize the skills that are present or absent. It is important to recognize the items included in the narrative and to make the child aware of items that should be included when they are not present. It is important for the evaluator to look at the complete manner of communication in every part of the environment.

CHAPTER APPENDIX

Chronological Development of
Nonverbal and Verbal Behaviors

Table 4-2 contains a compilation of infant and toddler developmental milestones that are achieved chronologically, beginning at 2 months of age and
extending to 48 months of age. The nonverbal and verbal behaviors were based
on the following:

Piaget's (1952) Stages

Stage 1	0–1 month
Stage 2	1–4 months
Stage 3	4–6 months
Stage 4	6–10 months
Stage 5	10–18 months
Stage 6	18–24 months

Brown's (1973) Stages	*MLU (mean)*	*Age*
Stage I	1.75	18–27 months
Stage II	2.25	21–34 months
Stage III	2.75	23–37 months
Stage IV	3.5	26–38 months
Stage V	4.0	27–48 months

Poole (1934) Upper
Chronological Age Limit for the
Development of Sounds

3½	p, b, m, w, h
4½	t, d, n, k, g, ŋ, y
5½	f
6½	v, th, sh, zh, l
7½	s, z, th, r,

* Merriam-Webster Pronunciation
Symbols used.

The table was designed to display the order, the approximate time periods of
occurrence or co-occurence, and the development of behaviors over time. In
an attempt to maintain the hierarchy of development, items acquired earlier
in each period are listed first, whereas items acquired toward the end of a
period are listed last. The information in the table is detailed in Chapters 3, 4,
and 10.

The exact time of acquisition of behaviors varies among children because
children develop at various rates. Therefore, these stages should be viewed as
approximate time ranges in which certain behaviors are expected to occur.

Table 4-2. CHRONOLOGICAL DEVELOPMENT OF NONVERBAL AND VERBAL BEHAVIORS

Age/MLU	Behavior concepts and language use	Speech and language
2 mo.	Line of regard between child and caretaker	Child initiates sound
4 mo.	Recognizes object at rest Smiles Touches adult for contact	Discriminates voicing /b-p/, /d-g/ Coos Turn-takes Changes pitch Follows sound
6 mo.	Sits	Babbles Uses intonation pattern of native language
10–18 mo.	Uses an adult as an object to get something Uses an object to get an object Shows before giving (e.g., I indicate) Points before giving (e.g., I demand)	Uses protoimperative, preverbal signal (e.g., to demand) Uses protodeclarative (e.g., to indicate) Uses rising and falling intonation to indicate intent Develops comprehension of frequently used words Recognizes that specific sounds are related to specific objects Associates items with referents (e.g., bottle, ball)
	Beginning of object permanence Beginning of means-end Beginning of symbolic play	True words start to develop Sounds are used to differentiate meaning First sound: m, b, p, w and h; lips sounds; nasals; plosives Develops CV pattern (consonant-vowel) (e.g., ma [mom, more], ba [bye, bottle], pa [Grandpa, pop]) Uses words or sounds to regular the behavior of others, to develop relationships, to express his own individuality, to question why, to pretend (Halliday, 1975)
18–27 mo. MLU 1.50	Gives information Uses declaratives Comments on the environment (e.g., what he sees, items of interest)	The next group of sounds developed are t, d, n; nasal; and plosives The tongue tip is elevated to the roof of the mouth. Examples of words: nō (no), nana (banana) (reduplication), da (down), dada (daddy)

(continued)

Table 4-2. *(continued)*

Age/MLU	Behavior concepts and language use	Speech and language
18-27 mo. *(cont.)*	At the one-word stage, the child can label, repeat, answer, request, call, greet, protest (Dore, 1974)	The child may use the phonological process of stopping for the fricative and use the same phone [d] for *there* (location) and for *that* (demonstrative pronoun) The order for the development of vowels is usually /a/ as in father, /ē/ as in me and feet, /ü/ as in boo and shoe. The back sounds are developed next: k, g, n; nasals; and plosives (e.g., ka [car, cup] kúkē [cookie], gō [go], baŋ [bang])
	Negative concept: Nonexistence Rejection (20–27 mo.)	No car (negative + noun) No; no milk (negative + noun); no wash (negative + verb), also protest; no more
18–32 mo.	Emphatic rejection	Don't, don't like that (probably learned as one word for the expression of negation and not as *do* + *not* + contraction)
21–34 mo. MLU 2.5	Language use (Dore 1977, 1978)	Uses two-word phrases that vary in structure, categories of language, lexicon, phonology, cognitive content and use.
	Reports	Fall down
	Evaluates	No good
	Claims-possession	Mine, boy bike
	Provides information: choices	(Do you want broccoli?)) No (Do you want apple or orange juice?) Apple (noun)
	clarification	Broke (explained why toy would not work)
	Answers questions	(What do you want?) cookie (noun) (What happened?) broke (verb) (Where is it?) truck (noun) (Who came?) daddy (noun)
	Protest	No tickle (negative rejection)
	Agrees	Uh-huh
	Disagrees	No
	Attention getters	Hi
	Boundary markers	Bye
	Indication of event	Daddy go
	Indication of location	Plane up (May use *p* for *pl*, a cluster reduction of liquid /l/)

Age/MLU	Behavior concepts and language use	Speech and language
21–34 mo. *(cont.)*	Specific concepts: Spatial (These also indicate location)	In box (preposition + noun); on box (preposition + noun); plane up (noun + preposition)
	Ongoing activity (continuous)	Going (verb + *ing*)
	Comprehension of questions: Who (name) (18–21 mo.) Where (place) (18–21 mo.) What (requiring a noun phrase) (27 mo.) What that?	
18–28 mo.	Questions	Baby? (asks a question with a rising intonation [Bellugi, 1965]) Who? (asks about a person) Where? (asks about a place) Where daddy? (asks about a place + a person) Where bat? (asks about a place + an object) What's that? (This utterance may be memorized because the copula *is* + contraction does not develop until 27–48 months.) What cat doing? (What [NP] doing? This question requires a verb in the answer.) The production hierarchy correlates to a great extent to the research findings regarding comprehension.
23–37 mo. MLU 2.75	Specific concepts: Quantity (more than one)	Cookies (noun plus plural inflection)
	Color	Blue shoes (adjective + noun + plural inflection). The child may say /bu/ and use the liquid cluster reduction phonological process.
	Special concepts: Negative-denial (Bloom, 1970) (developed later than nonexistence	No (similar construction to nonexistence and rejection negatives), no truck (*no* + noun), no run (*no* + verb), no hot (*no* + adjective)

(continued)

Table 4-2. *(continued)*

Age/MLU	Behavior concepts and language use	Speech and language
23–27 mo. *(cont.)*	or rejection negatives. The child must know what the item is before he or she can say what it is not, that is, before he or she can deny that it is a truck or that the water is hot.)	
	Possession, ownership Dative case	My shoe (possessive pronoun + noun) Mommy shoe (possessive relationship; at this stage the child may not always add the possessive inflection) Mommy's shoe (noun + possessive inflection + noun) The child may have the concepts of quantity, time, and possession but may not be able to express these concepts because the child does not use the final consonant (e.g., plural — eye<u>s</u>, past tense — play<u>ed</u>, possessives — Joe'<u>s</u>, copula + contraction — He'<u>s</u>, I'<u>m</u>)
	Comprehension of *Wh* interrogative pronoun Whose (possessive)	Whose book?
	Use of past tense irregular indicating time in the past Does not use the rule for regular past tense verbs	Ate, ran, caught. The early irregular verbs are considered to be based on memorization and not on the development of the past tense rule (e.g., add {-ed} inflection to the verb.)
	Wishes, needs, and desires are expressed	Beginning of the development of compound and complex sentences. Use of cantenatives: hafta, gonna, wanna, gotta (e.g., "I gotta go.") These are precursors to the structural formation of the infinitive (e.g., "I want to paint.")
	Expresses addition	Table and chairs (the use of the conjunction *and* to express addition)

Age/MLU	Behavior concepts and language use	Speech and language
23–27 mo. (cont.)	Beginning of the narrative: Describes a fact or event.	Fall, break, go
	Comprehension of "What do" question	What do you want? What do you see? (Example of the comprehension question.)
26–38 mo. MLU 3.5+	Concept: Inability to do something	He can't. (The negative is memorized whole at first. It is counted as one morpheme unless the modal *can* is used by the child in a declarative sentence. The *can't* may be used before the *can*; the *don't* may be used before the *do*.)
	Ability to do something	He can. (The child can use the modal *can* as a separate element. Auxiliaries are usually not used by the child unless he is capable of producing an MLU of 3.5+.)
	Concept of state of being or existence.	Here he is. Here I am. (uncontractible copula). (The contractible copula would be ungrammatical in these sentences, e.g., Here he's.)
	Emphasis concerning the present	I do write. (The *do* is an auxiliary in a declarative sentence.)
	Emphatic statement concerning the past	He did go. (The *did* serves as an auxiliary.)
	Relationship or joining of two ideas	I know why it works. (subject + verb + *Wh* clause. The child can use two subjects in a sentence.)
27–48 mo. MLU 4.0	Concept: Question using *do* Action at some future time	Do you want this? (yes/no question) He will go. (modal *will*)

(continued)

Table 4-2. *(continued)*

Age/MLU	Behavior concepts and language use	Speech and language
27–48 mo. *(cont.)*	Concepts: Inability to take action at some future time	It won't run. (modal + negative + contraction)
	State or existence	I'm big (contractible copula). The *I'm* is formed by the contraction of the copula *am* and the nominative pronoun *I*. The child is able to use the copula at an earlier stage [MLU 3.5] but is not able to use it with the contraction rule.)
	Item or state does not exist	He isn't happy. (copula + negative + contraction)
	Continuing action using more advanced syntactic construction	Is he going? (uncontractible auxiliary *is;* yes/no question) You are going. You're going (contractible auxiliary *are*)
	Temporal concept of past tense: Uses the past tense rule for regular verbs irregular verb	Washed (add the {-ed} inflection to the verb) Ate, slept (Each word has to be memorized separately. There is no rule that can be learned for the irregular verb.)
	Syntactic redundancy: when *he, she, it* is the subject, add {-s} inflection to the verb	He writes (third person singular, regular) This formation is based on a rule. He goes, He does, He has (third person singular, irregular)
	Obligation exists	I should do it (declarative sentence, modal *should*) Where should I put it? (the child may not use an inversion of the modal and the subject: Where should I put it?)
	Joining and relating two ideas	The lady gotta hurry to catch the bus. (use of embedding: hurry) I cut the bread to eat it and I want to have it (use of embedding and conjunction)

Age/MLU	Behavior concepts and language use	Speech and language
27–48 mo. (cont.)	Joining of two ideas but with different subjects performing different actions	I want her to eat. (subject one wants, but subject two will do the eating.)
	Addition of a relative clause pronoun that introduces a new idea	I forgot what we can eat. (object) I know who we can ask. (person) (Subject + verb + a relative clause — the relative pronoun + subject + modal + verb. The relative clause can ask "who" for a person, "whose" for possession, "which" for the selection of an item, "what" for an indication of an item.)
	Comprehension of question — why (causality)	Why? (the *why* is a popular *Wh* interrogative pronoun that may exist in a precausality period, e.g., intention before the true causality period [age 7 and 8] develops)
	Explanation or procedure — how? (22–38 months)	How do you work that?
	Reason — how come?	How come you like that?
	Temporal — when? (38–48 months)	When you come? When will you come? (This occurs late in development. The child must have a time concept.)
	Elaborate on a narrative: Has a main character The character does things in the past. Evaluates events and people as good or bad.	Uses the concepts and constructions developed up to this time.
	Locates events	Spatial (up, over, down)
	Adds items	Uses *and,* plurals
	Sequences events	Uses then (conjunction, time in the past and the future

(continued)

Table 4-2. *(continued)*

Age/MLU	Behavior concepts and language use	Speech and language
34–48 mo.	Multiword stage Uses language in a syntactically more complex way (Dore, 1977, 1986; Dore, Gearhart, and Newman, 1978) Request information Request action Respond to statements Make statements Regulate interperson conversation (e.g., initiate greetings, terminate conversations)	The first fricative sound /f/ starts to develop. This is an important development because it leads to the development of many other fricative and affricative sounds. Other fricative sounds start to develop /s, z, sh, zh/. See page 80. The /s/ is particularly important because the /s/ cluster development depends on this sound (e.g., st-store, sp-speak, sm-small, sk-school, sn-sneeze, and later the clusters using the liquids /l, r/, e.g., str-stream, spr-spread, spl-splash).
48 mo.+ MLU 4.0+	The ability to use one word to function as a noun (the subject of sentence) and the verb (the action of the sentence)	Playing is fun. (gerund = verb + ing) (Paul, 1981)
	Use of reason or cause to connect the main part and the subordinate part of the sentence. Child can state the event and the cause.	The train crashed 'cause the track broke (subordinating conjunction *because*)
	Use of time to connect the main part and the subordinate part of the sentence. Child can state event in relation to a particular period of time.	He can come when he's finished. (subordinating conjunction *when*)

Age/MLU	Behavior concepts and language use	Speech and language
48 mo.+ *(cont.)*	Use of purpose or result to connect the main part and the subordinate part of the sentence. Child can state the event and the result.	He ran so he wasn't late (subordinating conjunction *so*)

Source: Adapted from Bates (1976); Bates, Camaioni, and Volterra (1975); Bellugi (1965); Bloom (1970); Brown (1973); Bruner (1975); Dore (1974, 1977, 1986); Dore, Gearhart, and Newman (1978); Eimas, Siqueland, Jusczyk, and Vigorito (1971); Meltzoff (1978); Fillmore (1968); Gruber (1973); Halliday (1976); Hoffnung (1974); More and Meltzoff (1978); Paul (1981); Piaget (1952); Poole (1934); Quirk (1985); Sander (1972); Sutton-Smith (1986); Templin (1957); and Trantham and Pedersen (1976).

Clearly, the language used during later stages is based on the behavioral development of earlier stages. Initially, eyes, gestures, and vocalization of sounds communicate intent. Later, verbalization, or words, supplement the nonverbal communication and become more dominant. It is interesting to note that Piaget's Stage 6, the Means-End and Object Permanence Stage, coincides with Brown's Stage I, MLU 1.01–1.99.

REFERENCES

Austin, J. (1962). *How to do things with words*. London: Oxford University Press.

Bates, E., Camaioni, L., and Volterra, V. (1975). The acquisition of performatives prior to speech. *Merrill-Palmer Quarterly, 21*, 205–266.

Bates, E. (1976). Pragmatics and sociolinguistics in child language. In D. Morehead and A. Morehead (Eds.), *Normal and deficient child language* (pp. 411–463). Baltimore: University Park Press.

Bellugi, U. (1965). The development of interrogative structures in children's speech. In K. F. Riegel (Ed.), *The development of language functions* (Report No. 8, pp. 103–137). Ann Arbor, MI: University of Michigan.

Bloom, L. (1970). *Language development: Form and function in emerging grammars*. Cambridge, MA: MIT Press.

Bloom, L. (1971). Why not pivot grammar? *Journal of Speech and Hearing Disorders, 36*, 40–50.

Boehm, A. (1967). *Boehm Test of Basic Concepts*. New York: The Psychological Corporation.

Brown, R. (1973). *A first language*. Cambridge,MA: Harvard University Press.

Bruner, J. S. (1975a). From communication to language — a psychological perspective. *Cognition, 3*, 255–288.

Bruner, J. (1975b). The ontogenesis of speech acts. *Journal of Child Language, 2*, 1–19.

Cairns, H. S., and Hsu, J. R. (1978). Who, why, when and how: A development study. *Journal of Child Language, 5*, 478–488.

Carrow, E. (1973). *Test for Auditory Comprehension of Language*. New York: Teaching Resources.

Carrow, M. A. (1968). The development of auditory comprehension of language structure in children. *Journal of Speech and Hearing Disorders, 33*, 99–111.

Chomsky, N. (1965). *Aspects of the theory of syntax*. Cambridge, MA: MIT Press.

Cromer, R. F. (1974). The development of language and cognition: The cognition hypothesis. In B. Foss (Ed.), *New perspectives in child development* (pp. 184–252). Harmondsworth, Middlesex: Penguin Books.

Cromer, R. F. (1976). The cognitive hypothesis of language acquisition and its implications for child language deficiency. In D. Morehead and A. Morehead (Eds.), *Normal and deficient child language* (pp. 283–333). Baltimore: University Park Press.

Cromer, R. F. (1981). Reconceptualizing language acquisition and cognitive development. In R. L. Schiefelbusch and D. Bricker (Eds.), *Early language acquisition and intervention* (pp. 51–137). Baltimore: University Park Press.

Darley, F. L., Aronson, A. E., and Brown, J. R. (1975). *Motor speech disorders*. Philadelphia: Saunders.

Dore, J. (1974). A pragmatic description of early language development. *Journal of Psycholinguistic Research, 4*, 343–350.

Dore, J. (1975). Holophrases, speech acts, and language universals. *Journal of Child Language, 2*, 21–40.

Dore, J. (1977). "Oh them sheriff": A pragmatic analysis of children's responses. In S. Ervin-Tripp and C. Mitchell-Kernan (Eds.), *Child discourse* (pp. 139–164). New York: Academic Press.

Dore, J. (1986). The development of conversational competence. In R. L. Schiefelbusch (Ed.), *Language competence: Assessment and intervention* (pp. 3–60). Boston: College-Hill Press.

Dore, J., Gearhart, M., and Newman, D. (1978). The structure of nursery school conversation. In K. Nelson (Ed.), *Children's language* (Vol. 1). New York: Wiley.

Edwards, M., and Shriberg, L. (1983). *Phonology: Applications in comunicative disorders*. Boston: College-Hill Press.

Eilers, R., Oller, D., and Ellington, J. (1974). The acquisition of word-meaning for dimensional adjectives: The long and short of it. *Journal of Child Language, 1*, 195–204.

Eimas, P. D., Siqueland, E. R., Jusczyk, P., and Vigorito, J. (1971). Speech perception in infants. *Science, 171*, 303–306.

Ervin-Tripp, S. (1970). Discourse agreement: How children answer questions. In J. Hayes (Ed.), *Cognition and the development of language* (pp. 79–107). New York: Wiley.

Fillmore, C. (1968). The case for case. In E. Bach and R. Harmas (Eds.), *Universals in linguistic theory* (pp. 1–88). New York: Holt, Rinehart, & Winston.

Fletcher, P. (1978). *The Fletcher Time-by-Count Test of Diadochokinetic Syllable Rate.* Tigard, OR: C.C. Publications.

Folger, M. K., and Leonard, L. B. (1978). Language and sensorimotor development during the early period of referential speech. *Journal of Speech and Hearing Research, 21,* 519–527.

Garnham, A. (1983). What's wrong with story grammar. *Cognition, 15,* 145–154.

Ginsberg, H., and Opper, S. (1969). *Piaget's theory of intellectual development.* Englewood Cliffs, NJ: Prentice-Hall.

Gruber, J. (1973). Correlations between syntactic constructions of the child and of the adult. In C. A. Ferguson and D. I. Slobin (Eds.), *Studies of child language development* (pp. 440–445). New York: Holt, Rinehart, & Winston.

Halliday, M. A. K. (1975) *Learning how to mean.* New York: Elsevier.

Halliday, M. A. K., and Hasan, R. (1976). *Cohesion in English.* London: Longman.

Hodson, B. (1980). *The assessment of phonological processes.* Danville, IL: The Interstate Printers & Publishers.

Hodson, B., and Paden, E. (1983). *Targeting intelligible speech: A phonological approach to remediation.* Boston: College-Hill Press.

Hoffnung, A. (1974). An analysis of the syntactic structures of children with deviant articulation, Ph.D. dissertation, City University of New York, New York.

Hooper, R. (1971). Communicative development and children's responses to questions. *Speech Monographs, 38,* 2–9.

Ingram, D. (1976). *Phonological disability in children.* London: Edward Arnold.

Jakobson, R. (1968). *Child language, aphasia, and phonological universals.* The Hague: Mouton (Original work published 1941)

Leach, E. (1972). Interrogation: A model and some implications. *Journal of Speech and Hearing Disorders, 37,* 33–46.

Lenneberg, E. (1967). *Biological foundations of language.* New York: Wiley.

Leonard, L., Wilcox, M. J., Fulmer, K., and Davis, G. A. (1978). Understanding indirect requests: An investigation of children's comprehension of pragmatic meanings. *Journal of Speech and Hearing Research, 21,* 528–537.

Locke, J. (1983). Clinical phonology: The explanation and treatment of speech sound disorders. *Journal of Speech and Hearing Disorders, 48,* 339–341.

Maratsos, M. (1973). Decrease in the understanding of the word "big" in preschool children. *Child Development, 44,* 747–752.

McWilliams, B. J., Morris, H., and Shelton, R. L. (1984). *Cleft palate speech.* St. Louis: Mosby.

Menyuk, P. (1963). Syntactic structures in the language of children. *Child Development, 34,* 407–422.

Miller, J. (1981). Early psycholinguistic acquisition. In R. L. Schiefelbusch and D. Bricker (Eds.), *Early language: Acquisition and intervention* (pp. 330–337). Baltimore: University Park Press.

Moffitt, A. R. (1968). Speech perception by infants. Unpublished doctoral dissertation. Minneapolis: University of Minnesota. Reported in Clark, E. (1974). Some aspects of the conceptual basis for first language acquisition. In R. Schiefelbusch and L. L. Lloyd (Eds.), *Language perspectives — Acquisition, retardation, and intervention* (pp. 105–128). Baltimore: University Park Press.

Moore, M., and Meltzoff, A. (1978). Imitation, object permanence and language development in infancy. In F. Minifie and L. Lloyd (Eds.), *Communicative and cognitive abilities: Early behavior assessment* (pp. 151–184). Austin, TX: PRO-ED.

Muma, J. (1978). *Language handbook.* Englewood Cliffs, NJ: Prentice-Hall.

Muma, J. (1986). *Language acquisition: A functionalist perspective.* Austin, TX: PRO-ED.

Nelson, L., Kamhi, A., and Apel, K. (1987). Cognitive strengths and weaknesses in language-impaired children: One more look. *Journal of Speech and Hearing Disorders, 52,* 36–43.

Netsell, R. (1984). A neurobiologic view of the dysarthrias. In M. R. McNeil, J. C. Rosenbek, and A. E. Aronson (Eds.), *The dysarthrias: Physiology, acoustics, perception, management* (pp. 1–36). Boston: College-Hill Press.

Oller, D., Wieman, L., Doyle, W., and Ross, C. (1974). Child speech, babbling and phonological universals. *Papers and Reports on Child Language Development, 8,* 33–41.

Parnell, M., and Amerman, J. (1983). Answers to Wh-questions: Research and application. In T. Gallagher and C. Prutting (Eds.), *Assessment and intervention issues in language* (pp. 129–150). Boston: College-Hill Press.

Paul, R. (1981). Analyzing complex sentence development. In J. Miller (Ed.), *Assessing language production in children* (pp. 36–40, 67–71). Baltimore: University Park Press.

Piaget, J. (1952). *The origins of intelligence in children.* New York: International Universities Press.

Poole, I. (1934). Genetic development of articulation of consonant sounds in speech. *Elementary English Review, 2,* 159–161.

Quirk, R., Greenbaum, S., Leech, G., and Svartvik, J. (1985). *A comprehensive grammar of the English language.* New York: Longman.

Rice, M. (1983). Contemporary accounts of the cognition/language relationship: Implications for speech language clinicians. *Journal of Speech and Hearing Disorders, 48,* 347–359.

Roth, F. (1986). Oral narrative abilities of learning-disabled students. *Topics in Language Disorders, 7,* 21–30.

Roth, F., and Spekman, N. (1984a). Assessing the pragmatic abilities of children: Part 1. Organization framework and assessment parameters. *Journal of Speech and Hearing Disorders, 49,* 2–11.

Roth, F., and Spekman, N. (1984b). Assessing the pragmatic abilities of children: Part 2. Guidelines, considerations, and specific evaluation procedure. *Journal of Speech and Hearing Disorders, 49*(1), 12–17.

Sander, E. (1972). When are speech sounds learned? *Journal of Speech and Hearing Disorders, 37,* 55–63.

Shriberg, L., and Kwiatowski, J. (1980). *Natural process analysis (NPA): A procedure for analysis of continuous speech samples.* New York: Wiley.

Sinclair, H. (1971). Sensorimotor action patterns as a condition for the acquisition of syntax. In R. Huxley and E. Ingram (Eds.), *Language acquisition: Models and methods* (pp. 121–135). London: Academic Press.

Snyder, L. (1984). Development language disorders: Elementary school age. In A. Holland (Ed.), *Language disorders in children* (pp. 129–158). Boston: College-Hill Press.

Spekman, N., and Roth, F. (1982). An intervention framework for learning disabled children with communication disorders. *Learning Disability Quarterly, 5,* 429–437.

Stein, N., and Glenn, C. (1979). An analysis of story comprehension in elementary school children. In R. O. Freedle (Ed.), *New directions in discourse processing* (pp. 53–120). Norward, NJ: Ablex Publishing.

Sutton-Smith, B. (1986). The development of fictional narrative performances. *Topics in Language Disorders, 7,* 1–10.

Templin, M. (1957). *Certain language skills in children.* Minneapolis: The University of Minnesota Press.

Trantham, C., and Pedersen, J. (1976). *Normal language development.* Baltimore: Willliams & Wilkins.

Tyack, D., and Ingram, D. (1977). Children's production and comprehension of questions. *Journal of Child Language, 4,* 211–224.

Webster's Seventh New Collegiate Dictionary (1969). Springfield, MA: Merriam.

Weir, R. (1966). Some questions on the child's learning of phonology. In F. Smith and G. A. Miller (Eds.), *The genesis of language* (pp. 153–168). Cambridge, MA: The MIT Press.

Wellman, B., Case, I., Mengert, I., and Bradbury, D. (1931). Speech sounds of young children. *University of Iowa Studies Child Welfare, 5,* 1–82.

Werner, H., and Kaplan, B. (1963). *Symbol formation.* New York: Wiley.

Zemlin, W. (1968). *Speech and hearing science.* Englewood Cliffs, NJ: Prentice-Hall.

CHAPTER 5

The Nature and Development of Nonverbal Communication

PETER J. VALLETUTTI

The nature of the communication process cannot be explored, nor communication problems be discussed, nor communication skills be developed without considering the total communication act, including nonverbal as well as verbal elements. However, little pedagogical attention has been directed to the perception and expression of nonverbal communication. This situation is indeed unfortunate because a substantial amount of beginning communication with young children is of a nonverbal nature, and for many children with severe handicaps, some variety of gesture language may be the only possible means of communication.

FACIAL EXPRESSIONS AND BODY LANGUAGE

The ability to comprehend and to express oneself through facial expressions, gestures, and other body-language cues is critical to interpersonal communication from birth and is essential to the functional life of people of all ages as they operate in the diverse social contexts of their lives (Spignesi and Shor, 1981). The science of **social kinesics** deals with the role and meaning of various body movements in a social context (Devito, 1978). Ekman and Friesen (1969) identified five types of nonverbal bodily movements based on the origin, function, and coding of the specific behavior: emblems, illustrators, affect displays, regulators, and adaptors. **Emblems** are those gestures that directly translate words and other communication units into a physical representation, that is, a motor abstraction of the underlying concept. Emblems are natural gestures that are endemic to a culture and that are used frequently and universally, or at least, that are understood. Examples of emblems or natural getures include pointing, the goodbye wave (however, there are cultural differences in this emblem, e.g., the direction of the Italian goodbye wave is different from that of the American.), the "give me" gesture, the "come here" gesture, and the "be quiet" gesture, which is usually paired with a shushing sound (Valletutti and Bender, 1985). **Illustrators** accompany and clarify the verbal message, for example, when someone illustrates the smallness of an object being described with an accompanying and appropriate size gesture. **Affect displays** refer to those facial movements that communicate and illuminate the emotional content of the message. **Regulators** control the speech of others by signalling the listener's response to the message, whereas **adaptors** are those movements that serve the speaker's basic communicative needs.

THE VOCALIZATION PROCESS

The ability to interpret and to express appropriately the nonword elements of the vocalization process is yet another key nonverbal element in the total communicative process. The term **paralanguage** is used to describe the communication of meaning through vocal tone, emphasis, and inflection. Young children, on the average, respond to vocal tone, especially friendly and angry voices, much earlier than they respond to the spoken word (Weiss and Lilly-white, 1981). It is clear that the same words can be uttered in a variety of ways to express various emotional content or speaker intent. The paralinguistic component, then, is the primary element of a communication unit, for example, in the parental comment *You're my little angel.* This comment can be rendered with differing vocal emphases, pauses, tones, and inflections and can thus be an expression of love, joy, resignation, displeasure, or sarcasm — and woe to the child who misinterprets the vocal message and expects love when there is displeasure. Egolf and Chester (1973) postulated that up to 93 percent of a message's content is communicated nonverbally, whereas Kraus, Apple, Morency, Wenzel, and Winton (1981) disagreed. Their study of judgments of affect found no support for the belief that nonverbal elements of the communication act form the primary basis for the communication of affect. This apparent disagreement may be merely a function of the degree of implicitness; that is, the greater the ambiguity of the message, the greater attention is paid to nonverbal elements.

PROXEMICS AND EYE CONTACT

Nonverbal communication includes distance between speakers. **Proxemics** refers to the space created by the positions taken by two people engaged in conversation. The amount of space between the two parties is shaped not only by their attitude toward each other but by the content of the communication itself and the cultural perception of appropriate distancing (Minskoff, 1980b). Students with handicaps, especially those with learning disabilities, often do not learn the culturally acceptable proxemic pattern and disturb others by invading their space. Closely related to proxemics is the role of eye contact in the communicative act. Both the failure to make eye contact and the maintenance of a prolonged gaze interfere with communication because the listener is likely to be made uncomfortable and thus become distracted and fail to listen to the speaker's message.

ARTIFACTUAL CLUES

Artifactual clues are the clothes and jewels worn, the makeup used, and the physical attributes; they are also part of nonverbal communication (Minskoff, 1980b). What person has not made judgments about the temperament and personality of others based on their dress? A television or movie scene can paint a rapid picture of an unsavory section of a city or town and the "profession" of the women on the street by their stereotypic dress and body language. Body language and artifactual clues can send an explicit message to viewers with no need for dialogue or narrative explanations. A prime example of the communicative strength of physical attributes is the "halo" effect, in which people make automatic decisions about the intelligence of speakers by their conformity to societal norms of attractiveness; the better looking the individual, the smarter he or she is. The negative halo effect, unfortunately, does damage to many students with facial stigmata and physical anomalies who are automatically believed to be intellectually restricted. It is clear that people develop implicit theories of human behavior to evaluate others rapidly. For example, most people are more wary of a disheveled, unconventionally dressed individual than they are of a well-groomed, conventionally dressed, baby-faced killer. Social intelligence, to a large extent, is a function of how well behavioral stereotypes are incorporated into the functional judgments of people. Intuitive evaluations incorporate a wide range of human characteristics, to which personality, temperament, and behavioral correlates are assigned. Unfortunately, unprincipled people who manipulate others understand the communicative power of both nonverbal and verbal clues and emit neither verbal nor nonverbal clues in their deceptions. A judgment of a manipulative person's Machiavellian nature may have to be based on the cognitive processing of the words expressed, the speaker's credentials, an analysis of manipulative techniques, and an evaluation of the relative likelihood that the speaker's message is fact and not fantasy. The skilled perceiver must often disregard nonverbal clues that crafty speakers have learned to manipulate to their advantage, especially those of an artifactual nature (Valletutti, 1987). It is interesting to note that a person's speech is probably the most powerful clue to that individual's social-class membership. Judgments of an individual's intelligence and value in society are often based on that person's grammatical and syntactical conformity and on patterns of pronunciation, articulation, and word usage.

INSTRUCTIONAL PROGRAMMING IN NONVERBAL COMMUNICATION SKILLS

Instructional programming designed to facilitate the development of nonverbal communication skills has received scant attention in both teacher preparation programs and in school curricula. A possible reason for this de-emphasis is undoubtedly due to the relative ease of programming in the traditional academic areas. Instruction in academics is less demanding and more familiar than, for example, working on the perception of paralinguistic and body-language clues. Minskoff (1982) decried the fact that something is missing in the education of students with learning disabilities and recommended training in social information, verbal social skills, and nonverbal social skills. She indicated that individuals with learning disabilities must become aware of the effect of their behavior on others and of the effect of others' behavior on them. Siegel and Gold (1982) cited the high degree of gullibility frequently manifested by students with learning disabilities, whereas Johnson and Myklebust (1967) indicated that these students frequently manifest problems in distinguishing between fact and fiction. A high degree of gullibility and confusion between fantasy and reality and between honesty and duplicity may result from failure to understand nonverbal clues as well as from the more obvious failure to comprehend the rationality and reasonableness of the words spoken. Children with learning disabilities have been described in a large body of professional literature as being deficient in social perception (Bryan and Bryan, 1978; Lerner, 1981; Minskoff, 1980a, 1980b, 1982; Siegel and Gold, 1982; Wiig and Harris, 1974; Wiig and Semel, 1976). Social perception deficits manifest themselves in problems interpreting kinetic, vocalic (paralanguage), proxemic, and artifactual clues, and they result in misunderstanding of the attitudes, feelings, and intentions of others. Social imperceptions lead to difficulties in making appropriate social judgments. Wallbrown, Fremont, Nelson, Wilson, and Fischer (1979) pointed out ample evidence that many children who have been diagnosed as being behaviorally disordered are in fact children with social imperceptions. Minskoff (1982) stipulated that social perception difficulties are the most serious of all types of learning disabilities, and she developed programs of instruction for teaching children how to discriminate, understand, and meaningfully use facial expressions and other kinetic clues (1980a). Minskoff also designed programs for developing competency in proxemic, vocalic, and artifactual clues (1980b). Siegel, Siegel, and Siegel (1978) emphasized the importance of educational programming in the area of nonverbal communication. They suggested a variety of teaching techniques such as using filmstrips, silent movies, and pantomimes to improve body-language understanding and expression. They also placed emphasis on the importance of programming for the improvement of the nonverbal aspects of conversational speech. Johnson and Myklebust (1967) suggested that children with learning disabilities initially require practice in observing and interpreting the facial expressions of a single individual. In the latter stages of the program, they advocated the use of situational pictures in which body-language clues are interpreted as part of the overall situational context. Valletutti and Bender (1985) identified three general educational objectives in the nonverbal sphere that might serve as annual goals in a student's IEP:

1. The student will respond to and use natural or commonly accepted gestures in a manner that allows him to function optimally.
2. The student will respond to and use vocal tone patterns in a manner that allows him to function optimally.
3. The student will respond to and use facial expressions in a manner that allows him to function optimally. (p. 28)

CONCLUSION

Teachers must be creative risk takers and insightful enough to design educational experiences in the largely ignored area of nonverbal communication. Although more and more programs are being designed to assist students who experience deficits or deficiencies in the nonverbal domain, much of this newly awakened attention has been devoted to the interpretation and expression of facial expressions as they correlate with emotional expression. Greater attention has to be directed to all identified aspects of nonverbal communication and how they affect social and emotional growth, how they affect cognitive progress and academic achievement, and how they affect day-to-day communication of all people, especially those individuals with discrepancies in both behavior and learning. Significant attention must be given to the nonverbal area, especially for young children with handicaps who, because of the severity of their disability, will have to rely on gestural language supplemented by augmentative communication devices as their means of communication.

REFERENCES

Bryan, T. H., and Bryan, J. H. (1978). *Understanding learning disabilities* (2nd ed.). Sherman Oaks, CA: Alfred.

Devito, J. A. (1978). *Communicology: An introduction to the study of communication.* New York: Harper & Row.

Egolf, D., and Chester, S. (1973). Nonverbal communication and the disorders of speech and language. *ASHA, 15,* 511–518.

Ekman, P., and Friesen, M. V. (1969). The repertoire of nonverbal behavior: Categories, origins, usage, and coding. *Semiotica, 1,* 31–39.

Johnson, D. J., and Myklebust, H. R. (1967). *Learning disabilities: Educational principles and practices.* New York: Grune & Stratton.

Krauss, R. M., Apple, W., Morency, N., Wenzel, C., and Winton, W. (1981). Verbal, vocal, and visible factors in judgments of another's affect. *Journal of Personality and Social Psychology, 40,* 312–320.

Lerner, J. W. (1981). *Learning disabilities* (3rd ed.). Boston: Houghton Mifflin.

Minskoff, E. H. (1980a). Teaching approach for developing nonverbal communication skills in students with social perception deficits, Part I. *Journal of Learning Disabilities, 13,* 118–124.

Minskoff, E. H. (1980b). Teaching approach for developing nonverbal communication skills in students with social perception deficits, Part 2: Proxemic, vocalic, and artifactual clues. *Journal of Learning Disabilities, 13,* 203–208.

Minskoff, E. H. (1982). Training LD students to cope with the everyday world. *Academic Therapy, 17,* 311–316.

Siegel, E., and Gold, R. (1982). *Educating the learning disabled.* New York: Macmillan.

Siegel, E., Siegel, R., and Siegel, P. (1978). *Help for the lonely child.* New York: Dutton.

Spignesi, A., and Shor, R. E. (1981). The judgment of facial expressions, contexts, and their combination. *Journal of General Psychology, 104,* 41–58.

Valletutti, P. (1987). Social and emotional problems of children with learning disabilities. In K. Kavale, S. Forness, and M. Bender (Eds.), *Handbook of learning disabilities* (Vol. 1), (pp. 211–226). Boston: College-Hill.

Valletutti, P. J., and Bender, M. (1985). *Teaching the moderately and severely handicapped: Curriculum objectives, strategies, and activities* (Vol. II, 2nd ed.). Austin, TX: PRO-ED.

Wallbrown, F. H., Fremont, T. S., Nelson, E., Wilson, J., and Fischer, J. (1979). Emotional disturbance or social misperception? An important classroom management question. *Journal of Learning Disabilities, 12,* 645–648.

Weiss, C. E., and Lillywhite, H. S. (1981). *Communicative disorders: Prevention and early identification* (2nd ed.). St. Louis: Mosby.

Wiig, E. H., and Harris, S. P. (1974). Perception and interpretation of nonverbally expressed emotions by adolescents with learning disabilities. *Perceptual and Motor Skills, 38,* 239–245.

Wiig, E. H., and Semel, E. M. (1976). *Language disabilities in children and adolescents.* Columbus, OH: Merrill.

CHAPTER 6

The Role of Assessment in the Educational Evaluation of Young Children with Handicaps

PETER J. VALLETUTTI
MICHAEL BENDER

Assessment for educational purposes is a multifaceted and multi-dimensional process, which involves collecting data, charting strengths and weaknesses, and making appropriate decisions. From this general and specific information, students can be screened and referred for program planning. Relevant decisions about students fall into five general types, namely, those involving referral, screening, classification, instructional planning, and evaluation of student progress. These types of educational and related service decisions are influenced and shaped by the nature of the tasks of education because assessments should be conducted in terms of goals. Educational goals or desired learning outcomes may be separated into three distinct areas: academic, social/emotional, and physical. Educational assessments relevant to these goals must then concentrate on behaviors subsumed under these behavioral domains.

INFORMAL AND FORMAL ASSESSMENT

Although there are a variety of methods or techniques for obtaining assessment data, assessment strategies may be viewed as being of two distinct types: formal or informal. Any assessment that involves anything other than a norm-referenced, standardized test is generally considered to be **informal assessment.** **Formal**, norm-referenced measures provide information concerning how a student has performed on a standardized test instrument as compared to the performance of his or her grade- or age-level peers. The standardized achievement test is an example of a common norm-referenced test. Often norm-referenced instruments, including standardized tests of intelligence, have little direct application to programming, unless educators look beneath and beyond scores obtained and conduct an in-depth analysis of test items and an appraisal of the student's processes during the test procedure in an attempt to identify pertinent school-related skills demonstrated by the student both on the test and while taking the test.

As educators have become more sophisticated and insightful, they have discovered that the value of most norm-referenced tests is restricted primarily to screening, referral, and classification. Not only are referral, screening, and classification essential administrative imperatives, they are also required by both federal and state laws. Appropriate and early identification and logically deduced classification systems are needed so that individuals with handicaps may be discovered and provided with a free and appropriate public educational placement and related services in the least restrictive educational environment.

The practice of classifying or labeling, however, implies a homogeneity of condition and a uniformity of instructional needs that is not warranted. The assignment of a legally mandated diagnostic label without a comprehensive analysis of the student's actual performance ignores the need to teach the whole child and is, at the same time, antithetical to the individualization of instruction, which is at the heart of the special education process.

Recognizing that the application of a label and the organization of a special program do not automatically translate into programming decisions, educators are increasingly willing to risk reliance on informal assessment techniques that more clearly illuminate the teaching/learning process. Educators are now less likely to depend on norm-referenced tests, which have earned greater acceptance by other practitioners who fail to see that a diagnostic procedure that does not lead to meaningful and successful intervention is a largely sterile and myopic exercise. Educators have come to realize that norm-referenced tests, especially those that measure intelligence, have limited applicability to the act and art of teaching.

As educators have come to realize that effective assessment requires their active and constant input, they have discovered that learners provide diagnostic data on a continuous basis as they interact with their environment and as they attempt to meet the requirements of assigned or expected educational tasks. Because behaviors that occur naturally and in direct response to educational activities are the best indicators of actual knowledge and skills, educators have become more involved in curriculum-based assessment (CBA).

Curriculum-based assessment uses the material to be learned as the basis for assessing the degree to which the information has been learned (Tucker, 1985). The title *CBA* may be confusing because emphasis is placed on instruction as well as on assessment. In this respect, teachers using CBA need to know how to collect and interpret data, as well as how to use it for improving instruction. (See Figure 6-1.) CBA focuses on the student's performance relative to instructional objectives and content. Strategies for observing students and methods for recording performance are therefore necessary for a systematic evaluation process. A framework is also needed to provide a structure for directed observations, and a listing of identified curriculum objectives provides such a framework.

Because many professionals appear uncomfortable with the idea of informal assessment strategies, equating them with unscientific approaches, the nature and types of informal assessment need to be described in sufficient detail to explicate not only their variety but also their applicability to education. Historical sources of diagnostic information include *observations* of previous teachers and anecdotal records, both informal and objective procedures, as well as the perusal of medical records; the results of *tests* designed by school curriculum committees and individual classroom teachers as recorded in the student's cumulative record; the *judgments* made by previous educational, therapeutic, and medical specialists and by previous teachers; and the parent's memory of developmental milestones and significant physical, social, and emotional incidents.

Current sources also involve observations, tests, and judgments. Sources that are current certainly have greater diagnostic relevance than historical sources; however, teachers must be cognizant of the fact that even current information must be viewed carefully because children are dynamic human beings who are ever-changing and, it is hoped, growing and progressing. This point is particularly valid in evaluating diagnostic information obtained from and about young children with handicaps who often grow in unexpected and unanticipated spurts. When one examines the various current sources, it is obvious that most of these sources also involve informal approaches and include observations of both the student's work products and the processes employed by the student in carrying out a specific task; the results of criterion-referenced, teacher-made

Student's name _____   Special physical restrictions (if any) _____

Curriculum area: _____

                                            Evaluator(s) _____

Unit objective: _____

Specific instructional objective	Response*	Number of observations and by whom	Dates	Observations and their programming implications
1.				
2.				

* Response legend: NA — not applicable; NR — no response; NATT — not attempted; PP — partial performance; CAR — completed, assistance required; P — physical guidance; G — gestural prompts; V — verbal cues; IF — independent functioning; DFS — demonstrated in functional situation; T — teacher; P, SP — parent, surrogate parent; OTM — other team member (specify).

Figure 6-1. Sample format for a CBA checklist. (Adapted from Bender, M, and Valletutti, P. J. *Teaching the moderately and severely handicapped: A functional curriculum for self-care, motor skills, and household management* (Vol. 1, 2nd ed.). Austin, TX: PRO-ED. Copyright 1985 by PRO-ED, Inc. By permission.)

tests; and judgments made by parents as well as teachers and other professionals as they appear in anecdotal records, progress reports, and responses to more structured rating scales.

CRITERION-REFERENCED TESTS

Perhaps, the most productive informal procedure is the use of criterion-referenced tests that measure a student's performance of curriculum-oriented skills in terms of previously identified mastery levels. Criterion-referenced measures provide teachers with information concerning those skills students either have or do not have in their behavioral repertoire. Because skills are typically based on a continuum of subskills, teachers can then program to correct deficit areas from the appropriate perspective of existing skills. In addition to providing teachers with information that leads to productive educational prescriptions, criterion-referenced measures provide a post-intervention instrument to evaluate the effectiveness of instruction while offering immediate feedback to students regarding their performance on specific learning tasks. The use of checklists based on generally accepted instructional objectives is currently receiving significant attention as a teacher-made, teacher-administered, informal, criterion-referenced procedure (Bender and Bender, 1979).

Checklists offer a straightforward and effective way of obtaining information about a student. Checklists are currently being used (Battelle Developmental Inventory, 1984; Developmental Activities Screening Inventory, 1984; Learning Accomplishment Profile, 1977) as a means of rating children entering preschool programs in order to assess whether or not the child has performed each of the listed behaviors at some time in the past or as part of his or her everyday activities. The usefulness of some checklists and rating scales (as of any instrument that relies on informant knowledge) depends highly on the reliability of the sources being consulted. Unhappily, many checklists are completed by individuals who are unaware of a child's actual abilities, especially with respect to those abilities exhibited during nonschool hours in pragmatic situations. The two major purposes for using behavior checklists appear to be description and prescription. If diagnosis is the major purpose, any checklist that comprehensively and accurately measures the behaviors in question is appropriate. A prescriptive checklist additionally enumerates suggestions or strategies for remediating or treating identified discrepancies in performance.

LOCATING, IDENTIFYING, AND EVALUATING CHILDREN WITH HANDICAPS

As a consequence of Public Law 94-142 (1975), and more recently Public Law 99-457 (1986), the various public school systems are engaged in intensive efforts to locate, identify, and evaluate all children with handicaps regardless of type or degree of disability. The federally mandated process of Public Law 94-142 has required school systems to conduct child-find programs designed to locate all children with handicaps in their community. Various approaches to locating these children have been documented, including public awareness campaigns, parental notices and questionnaires, house-to-house and telephone surveys, agency and physician contacts, and informal teacher-parent interactions (Payne and Patton, 1981). Some states have established high-risk registers for identifying infants who may be handicapped at birth. Criteria for placement on such registers vary but generally include hereditary history of abnormality, low birth weight, intrauterine infections, high bilirubin levels, and obvious physical abnormalities. In addition, hospitals throughout the United States have established high-risk nurseries for neonates who fall below criteria for healthy development.

In addition to the referral approach exemplified in the procedures just identified, some local education agencies engage in a screening campaign, at which time various segments of the population are periodically screened. Regardless of the approach used to locate children with handicaps, screening procedures are necessary to distinguish those who require more intensive scrutiny from those who may not require further study.

In the latter part of 1986, landmark legislation was passed concerning early intervention programs. Public Law 99-457, titled The Education of the Handicapped Amendments of 1986, specifically addressed:

(1) reauthorizing the discretionary programs of the Education of the Handicapped Act, (2) providing incentives to States to serve an estimated additional 70,000 handicapped children 3 through 5 who currently were not being served, (260,000 children were currently being provided services) and (3) creating a new discretionary program to address the special needs of handicapped infants and toddlers (birth through age two) and their families. (NASDE, 1987)

The act authorized a total of $125 million for fiscal years 1987 and 1988 for the new birth–2 program, and after four years, each state — if it wanted to continue receiving federal financial assistance under the birth–2 and 3–5 programs — must have in place, among other things, a policy to provide appropriate early intervention services to all infants and toddlers with handicaps in the state.

Legally, the classification of a child as handicapped, and thus in need of special education services, requires interdisciplinary action. This element in the assessment process, which is the antecedent of any placement decisions, must involve a comprehensive educational assessment. This multidimensional evaluation can include (in addition to the standard individual test of general intellectual functioning) teacher recommendations, a sociological background study, an investigation of adaptive behavior, and standard school-related measures, including achievement test scores. Moreover, evaluations relevant to specifically identified areas of concern are pursued, for example, a speech-language-hearing evaluation, a medical evaluation, and an occupational or physical therapy assessment.

EVALUATION FOR PROGRAMMING PURPOSES

Subsequent to the assessment process that decides whether a student should or should not be designated as a handicapped student and provided with an appropriate program placement, an individualized education plan (IEP) must be developed by appropriate school personnel and the student's parents or legal guardians. As part of this educational prescription, assessment information must be provided that indicates the student's present performance level. It is in this diagnostic process that the results of *all* assessment procedures should come together in a vivid portrait of the child as he or she performs the myriad tasks required of him or her in the dynamic, functional interaction with the school, the home, and the general community.

PROBLEMS IN INTERPRETING THE RESULTS OF STANDARDIZED TESTS

Before using specific tests of achievement, intelligence, and adaptive behavior, it seems important to review some of the caveats in the tests themselves and in the test procedures that should be considered in the administration of tests and in the interpretation of test results.

Caution must be taken when interpreting the results of standardized tests because it cannot be assumed that the testing situation was an optimal one. For example, the evaluator may have been unable to establish a comfortable and productive rapport, for a variety of reasons, including a mismatch in his or her temperament with that of the student. In other cases, the evaluator may have varied the presentation of test stimuli or scored the test incorrectly. At other times, contamination of test results may arise from the child him or herself.

Perhaps the greatest concern relevant to the interpretation of the results of standardized tests has been the application of norms that are irrelevant to those students whose life experiences are markedly different from those of the population on whom the test was standardized. Differences in the acculturation process may be a function of ethnic origin, socioeconomic class, and even geography. Given the fact that there are so many regional dialects and variations in climate and natural environment in the United States, these differences in experiences can account for some variations in test performance. Children whose experiences differ from those on which the test was standardized are thus at a distinct disadvantage, and their incorrect or inadequate performance may not be a function of intellectual restriction but of experiential circumstance. The cultural bias of most standardized tests is probably best illustrated by exploring those tests specifically designed for minority populations, that is, *The Black Intelligence Test of Cultural Homogeneity,* based on urban black culture, and the *Hana-Butta Test* based on Hawaiian culture (Payne and Patton, 1981).

In an effort to correct for variations in experiential background, a number of culture-free, or culture-fair, intelligence tests have been created. The culture-fair concept is predicated on the assumption that test items are selected either because all children of a given age have had the opportunity to familiarize themselves with the test material or that the test material is novel to all, and further, that all students are equally motivated. Obviously, culture-free tests have been less than successful because the United States is a culturally diverse society. The following are examples of frequently or historically used culture-free tests:

The Draw-A-Man Test (Harris, 1963)
The Culture Fair Intelligence Tests (Cattell, 1973)
The Progressive Matrices (Raven, 1960)
The Coloured Progressive Matrices (Raven, 1947)

Many psychologists believe in the need for culture-free tests because children from ethnic minorities, from economically disadvantaged families, and from rural areas do poorly on intelligence tests that are commonly used. This poorer performance is viewed by these psychologists as validation of tests being biased against such populations. Other interpret such poor performance as supporting the fact that these groups are less intelligent. However, it is important to understand that many ethnic minority groups who do poorly on intelligence tests also have difficulty succeeding at school and at work.

Another facet of evaluation, which unfortunately receives little attention, relates to the internal and external environments that may influence a child during the evaluation process. In terms of the child, for example, had the child been sick immediately prior to or during the test? Was the child on any medication? Did the child appear to be highly anxious? If any of these conditions existed, more time should have been devoted to developing a rapport, or the decision should have been made as to whether or not the child was in a satisfactory state for testing. In some cases, for example, when a child appears to be highly medicated, rescheduling the evaluation should be considered.

Basic biological needs may also affect the evaluation process. Children, especially infants, who are hungry or thirsty, may not perform at optimal levels unless these needs are satisfied. For example, many young children need to be reminded to go to the bathroom before the evaluation begins, otherwise they may interrupt the evaluation session at a critical time or be uncomfortable during testing.

The time of day of an evaluation may also have an effect on the results. It has been hypothesized that it is better to evaluate children early in the morning because they are most alert and less tired at that time. However, this may not be so if the child has not had a good night's sleep, is hungry, or is not fully awake when he or she arrives for the evaluation.

There are also some situational factors that should be considered, for example, the type of distractions within the testing room, the type of furniture (size) the child may have to sit on, and the quality of the lighting in the test environment. Also, the testing of infants often requires a free, flat surface so that postural or other gross motor capacities can be demonstrated. Therefore, the testing rooms should be a comfortable size (not too confining or too vast) with a place to lie down. Part of the room should have a rug or mat for floor activities. The temperature in the room should be comfortable, and the room should be well lit and, if possible, soundproofed or away from distracting noises. It is equally important that the room not look too much like a physician's office. It is also advisable that the evaluator be dressed in pleasant everyday attire, avoiding white coats and references to his or her degree status. Referring to the evaluator as *Dr.* Smith may terrify a child who might then expect a needle rather than a test.

Also to be considered is the length of the trip to the evaluation site and the type of transportation used. Even weather conditions may be a contributing factor. It is also important to remember that the rapport established between the child and evaluator may not depend solely on verbal communication. Bender and Valletutti (1976) cautioned that nonverbal communication plays an important role in communication and may at times be of greater importance to the communication act than the verbal content. Nonverbal elements include body language, gestures, and vocal inflections and tones.

Moreover, evaluation is a highly personal process, and instruments are often selected because the evaluator is most familiar with them. It is hoped that such instruments are still appropriate, but too often instrument selection is determined on the basis of the following:

- The instrument's availability at the facility
- The instrument with which the evaluator has been trained
- The instrument the evaluator was told to use
- The lack of knowledge about alternative instruments
- The ease of scoring and interpretation

When standardized, norm-referenced tests that were developed for use with nonhandicapped children are used with children having handicaps, evaluators frequently modify the method of presentation, the mode of response, or both. These modifications are made in an effort to nullify or minimize the impact of the handicap on test results while accommodating the child's sensory and motoric restrictions. Unhappily, any change in the administration of a standardized test makes it no longer standardized because the norms are no longer applicable. Therefore, when modifications are made to accommodate a child with handicaps, interpretation of results must be tempered by the knowledge the comparison to the norms is no longer possible.

Teachers should be aware that, in testing situations, a student's performance varies on different types of tests, all purporting to measure the same knowledge and skills. Identifying how a student tests best is as important as identifying how a student learns best. Designing appropriate testing experiences that accommodate individual student temperament (Thomas and Chess, 1977; Thomas, Chess, and Birch, 1968) and cognitive style (Valletutti and Salpino,

1979) is as much a part of individualizing programs as is designing learning experiences.

INTELLECTUAL ASSESSMENT OF YOUNG CHILDREN: BIRTH TO 3 YEARS

Unquestionably, early identification of children who are suspected of being at high risk for developmental disabilities is potentially the single most powerful means at hand for reducing the impact of that exceptionality. Deficit areas that are identified can be treated, whereas serious problems that go unrecognized may only grow worse. American children still do not receive regular systematic health care and developmental evaluations before school age. In addition, the greatest burden of developmental anomalies occurs among those people who have the least contact with the health-related professions. The identification of developmental disabilities based on accurate and early observation is vital to the success of therapeutic and educational interventions. In most instances, detection and diagnosis of a biological or psychological abnormality can lead to remediation programs or intervention procedures that may ultimately result in a child who is less handicapped. Early diagnosis is especially important for children born or raised in poverty areas because programs of early stimulation or enrichment for this population are most likely to make a developmental difference.

Carefully and precisely administered and interpreted educational and psychological tests often define a type or degree of handicap that might not be evident on clinical examination. When a question of differential diagnosis arises, tests of an educational or psychological nature may often provide clues from which a definitive diagnosis may be reached, and thus, an appropriate intervention strategy may be formulated.

Perhaps the principal value of utilizing educational and psychological tests in the early years of a child's life is to provide baselines from which future growth may be measured. In essence, these baselines provide the means to measure the success of intervention programs in an objective way rather than on subjective impressions of program success.

There is no single measure of a child's first years more widely discussed than those measures associated with intelligence. Unfortunately, there is a tendency to assess infants and young children solely in terms of an intelligence quotient. Numerical scores, whether they are IQs, grade-level scores, or percentiles, must be viewed cautiously; they cannot and do not capture the essence of any child in all that child's myriad dimensions. The ultimate success of children in school and society does not always reflect earlier prognoses arrived at from psychological or educational tests. This phenomenon is especially pertinent when considering the results of tests given at early ages.

It is important to remember that many psychologists and educators who work with children who are handicapped are traditionally oriented toward the medical model, which searches out deficiencies, abnormalities, and etiologically significant factors. What is more important than the identification of discrepancies is a clear and precise appraisal of the child's current status in terms of knowledge, skills, and concepts already possessed.

Historically, the study of intellectual functioning has focused on older children, with little attention paid to infants. It has long been assumed that infants are preoccupied with systems that simply react motorically to sensory stimuli without attention or thought to the relationships existing among the stimulus, the cognitive process, and the response events. Because infants are unable to verbalize about what and how they are thinking, little applied research has been conducted in this area until recently. In large part, the paucity of research on this issue is probably because of those developmental theories that have long postulated that the early developmental stages are exclusively sensorimotor with no cognitive functioning worthy of investigation occurring until the achievement of sufficient language skills. The controversy continues as to whether infants can think without the necessary language to represent events and phenomena; and evidence has now been gathered that contradicts earlier assumptions about what does and does not occur in early infancy.

Some early articles that reviewed various intervention efforts throughout the United States, such as those by Starr (1971), Caldwell (1975), and Meier (1975), all indicated that it is important to assess not only the individual infant but also the context within which the infant is growing and developing if one is to arrive at a valid prediction of whether or not the child will eventually be a handicapped learner. Starr has emphasized that

Historically, developmental psychology has dramatically turned in the last ten years from the maturational viewpoint of development espoused by Gesell and others toward a view which has varied between strict environmentalism and moderate interactionism. In general, psychologists have been most interested in environmental effects given the genetic status of a particular individual with whom they are dealing. Within this context they must assess the effects of the environment and, if possible, eliminate deleterious environmental effects while providing appropriate experience. (Starr, 1971, p. 153)

ASSESSMENT INSTRUMENTS

Before using specific instruments that may be appropriate for infant assessment, there are some general factors that must be considered when evaluating this population.

1. Generally, the first five years of life are broken down into the infancy period, which extends from birth to 18 months, and the preschool period, which extends from 18 months to 5 years.

2. A number of tests for infants address sensorimotor development, and most developmental scales require that examiners observe the child as he or she responds to objects and ask the parents or guardians for additional information.

3. It is important to remember that performance tests generally involve the manipulation of objects. Nonlanguage tests require no language from either the

evaluator or the student, and instructions can be given in gesture, in panto-mime, or by demonstration.

4. Tests administered during the first year of life have poor predictive validity, whereas tests given after 18 months have moderate predictive validity (McCall, Hogarty, and Hurlburt, 1972).

5. Because most intelligence tests result in an IQ figure that is supposedly a person's general intellectual level, it is presumed that tasks on such tests cover a broad range of cognitive dimensions. In reality, however, most IQ tests are overloaded with some tasks (i.e., in the verbal area), whereas other cognitive areas are underrepresented or not covered at all.

6. It is presumed that infants who have low IQs during the first years of life will have low IQs later. However, studies have shown that some infants who were considered "slow" are not slow at later ages (Wilson and Harspring, 1972). Therefore, children should be retested at later ages at periodic intervals.

7. Some of the differences observed in the cognitive development of infants can be attributed to heredity, to environment, and to the interaction of the two (Clarke-Stewart, 1977). For example, Hanson (1975) conducted a longitudinal study across three periods (birth to 3 years, 4 to 6 years, and 7 to 10 years). He found that certain environmental variables were related to scores obtained on the Stanford-Binet. Variables such as the freedom to engage in verbal expres-sion, parental involvement with the child, emphasis on independent perform-ance, and the freedom to explore one's environment were all significantly related to intelligence at each age level.

CONCLUSION

Past research with nonhandicapped infants has generally shown that tests given to children under the age of 2 have poor ability to predict preschool, school, or adult intelligence. Therefore, one must be extremely cautious when using infant tests, except to assess current developmental status, and avoid pre-dictions about future ability level or about time lines for skill acquisition. Before considering the use of any instrument, it should be reviewed both for validity and reliability, and the population for which the instrument was developed and normed should be verified.

Without question there are numerous problems in the screening and assess-ment of infants. Perhaps the most notable are the following:

1. Some motivational techniques and incentives may be required to get wide-scale screening under way
2. The significance of a delay can be determined only in relation to the expected performance of the individual child
3. Professionals still fail to identify many infants with severe handicaps, although they are the most clearly identifiable
4. Severe handicapping conditions are not concentrated in any particular social level

5. Unless early screening and programming efforts are legally mandated with consequences for noncompliance, there is little hope that service delivery gaps can be closed rapidly

Moreover, there needs to be continued research and development of screening and assessment instruments. Once a delay has been identified, it is important that there exists identifiable screening devices that are more discriminating than gross screening. There is also a tremendous need for follow-up procedures to be included as part of the overall assessment scheme. It is imperative that those who evaluate children know what to look for, know how to stimulate the expression of a disability if it does not appear, and when and how to intervene during the evaluation process. The following are characteristics of a good assessment instrument:

It can be administered by qualified personnel
It measures small increments in an evolving sequence of development
It leads directly to intervention efforts

Careful and accurate measurement can only be justified if it leads to action, specifically the development of appropriate intervention programs. Knowing that a child may be handicapped or at high risk for developmental disabilities is valuable only if the next and critical step of programming is taken.

The individual evaluator must not only be well trained in test administration but must also have a comprehensive understanding of human growth and development. Even though instruments developed by individuals such as Bayley (1969), Uzgiris and Hunt (1975), Kaufman and Kaufman (1983), and others have done much to provide the diagnostician with needed tools that have been sorely lacking over the years, they must be viewed carefully in terms of whether or not they are appropriate for the children being discussed. It is also imperative that a young child be evaluated over time under various conditions. It is only *then* that a more accurate assessment can be obtained, one that will reveal the important information necessary for intervention to begin in a well-conceived plan with evaluation strategies specified. It is also clear that infant and neonate educational and psychological evaluation is still in its own infancy, and it is hoped that the next several years will provide the practitioner with information that will lead to more effective and efficient remediation and intervention techniques in educational and therapeutic programming.

Any discussion of early cognitive development testing, especially in terms of infants, requires an additional cautionary note. The state of the infant at the time of testing (i.e., arousal level and the degree of wakefulness and alertness) must be considered in all screening and assessment efforts.

The child's so-called biological clock (i.e., sleeping, waking for feeding, needing to urinate) all influence the outcome of evaluations. Sleep patterns, as well as travel time to the evaluation site and the time of day the evaluation is conducted, also affect assessment outcomes.

A final and critical area to consider in the evaluation of young children with handicaps is adaptive behavior. As defined by the American Association on Mental Retardation, *adaptive behavior* refers to the "effectiveness or degree with which individuals meet the standards of personal independence and social responsibility expected of their age and cultural group" (Grossman, 1983, p. 157). It also includes the ability of individuals to function independently, to maintain themselves, and to assume the demands placed on them by society. In essence, adaptive behavior is a very broad area, and no one instrument can accurately measure all domains.

The adaptive area has often been neglected in the assessment of children with handicaps, especially in terms of adaptation to the natural and social demands of their environment. This is a most critical assessment area because how well this type of child adapts in early years may very well indicate how he or she will function in future years. With this in mind, instruments such as *The Vineland Adaptive Behavior Scales* (Sparrow, Balla, and Cicchetti, 1984), *The Balthazar* (Balthazar, 1973), and the *Adaptive Behavior Scale* (Nihira, Foster, Shellhaas, and Leland, 1974) are being used to assess this most critical area, an area especially pertinent to teachers who hope to prepare children to assume adult roles upon their exit from school.

Whereas individuals such as Piaget recorded the behavior of normal infants and young children, few professionals in the past were trained to evaluate children with handicaps. It has been only recently that evaluators and those charged with the responsibility of assessing these special children have recognized the need for specialized instruments, special training in presenting test information, and knowledge of all the behavioral aspects and components that make up an appropriate and fair evaluation system.

REFERENCES

Balthazar, E. E. (1973). *Balthazar Scales of Adaptive Behavior.* Palo Alto, CA: Consulting Psychologists Press.

Battelle Developmental Inventory. (1984). Allen, TX: Teaching Resources.

Bayley, N. (1969). *Bayley Scales of Infant Development.* New York: Psychological Corporation.

Bender, M., and Bender, R. (1979). *Disadvantaged preschool children: A source book for teachers.* Baltimore: Brookes.

Bender, M., and Valletutti, P. J. (1976). *Teaching the moderately and severely handicapped. Vol II: Communication, socialization, safety, and leisure time skills.* Baltimore: University Park Press.

Caldwell, B. E. (1975). Early stimulation of the mentally retarded. In J. Wortis (Ed.), *Mental retardation and developmental disabilities* (Vol. 3). New York: Brunner/Mazel.

Cattell, R. B. (1973). *Culture Fair Intelligence Test.* Champaign, IL: Institute for Personality and Ability Testing.

Clarke-Stewart, K. W. (1977). *Child care in the family.* New York: Academic Press.

Developmental Activities Screening Inventory (DASI-II). (1984). Austin, TX: PRO-ED.

Grossman, H. J. (1983). *Manual on terminology and classification in mental retardation, 1973 Revision.* American Association on Mental Deficiency. Baltimore: Gramond/Pridemark Press.

Hanson, R. A. (1975). Consistency and stability of home environmental measures related to IQ. *Child Development, 46,* 470–480.

Harris, D. (1963). *Children's drawing as measures of intellectual maturity.* Orlando, FL: Harcourt

Brace Jovanovich.

Kaufman, A. S., and Kaufman, N. L. (1983). *Kaufman Assessment Battery for Children: Administration and scoring manual.* Circle Pines, MN: American Guidance Service.

Learning Accomplishment Profile (Diagnostic Edition, Revised) (1977). Chapel Hill, NC: Chapel Hill Training Outreach Project.

McCall, R. B., Hogarty, P. S., and Hurlburt, N. (1972). Transitions in infant sensorimotor development and the prediction of childhood IQ. *American Psychologist, 27,* 728–748.

NASDE. (1987). *1987 Liaison Bulletin, 12*(12). Washington, DC: National Association of State Directors of Education.

Nihira, K., Foster, R., Shellhaas, M., and Leland, H. (1974). *Adaptive Behavior Scale.* Washington, DC: American Association on Mental Deficiency.

Payne, J. S., and Patton, J. R. (1981). *Mental retardation.* Columbus, OH: Merrill.

Public Law 94-142. Education of All Handicapped Children Act of 1975. Washington, DC: Office of Education.

Public Law 99-457, The Education of All Handicapped Amendments of 1986. Washington, DC: Office of Education.

Raven, J. C. (1947). *Coloured Progressive Matrices.* London: Lewis.

Raven, J. C. (1960). *Guide to using the Standard Progressive Matrices.* London: Lewis.

Sparrow, S. S., Balla, D. A., and Cicchetti, D. U. (1984). *Vineland Adaptive Behavior Scales.* Circle Pines, MN: American Guidance Service.

Starr, R. H., Jr. (1971). Cognitive development in infancy: Assessment, acceleration, and actualization. *Merrill-Palmer Quarterly of Behavior and Development, 17,* 153–185.

Thomas, A., and Chess, S. (1977). *Temperament and development.* New York: Brunner/Mazel.

Thomas, A., Chess, S., and Birch, H. (1968). *Temperament and behavior disorders in children.* New York: New York University Press.

Tucker, J. A. (1985). Curriculum-based assessment: an introduction. *Exceptional Children, 52*(3), 199–204.

Uzgiris, I. C., and Hunt, J. McV. (1975). *Assessment in infancy. Ordinal Scales of Psychological Development.* Urbana, IL: University of Illinois Press.

Valletutti, P. J., and Salpino, A. O. (1979). *Individualizing educational objectives and programs: A modular approach.* Baltimore: University Park Press.

Wilson, R. S., and Harspring, E. B. (1972). Mental and motor development in infant twins. *Developmental Psychology, 7,* 277–287.

CHAPTER 7

Teacher Assessment of Speech and Language Development of Infants and Other Young Children

PETER J. VALLETUTTI

The key diagnostic skill required of teachers, regardless of the students served, is the ability to observe student behavior selectively and insightfully. On a daily basis, as teachers interact with students and as students interact with them and perform classroom tasks, teachers have an unparalleled opportunity to process an abundance of auditory and visual data, some of which are irrelevant to the instructional process and some of which are highly relevant. In the case of the instructional process, **relevant behaviors** can be defined as those behaviors of students that provide teachers with instructional insights. **Instructional insight** refers to the essential first step in the professional decision-making process through which a teacher arrives at judgments about what and how to teach an identified student or group of students.

THE NATURE OF INFORMAL ASSESSMENT

Teacher observation of student behavior may be viewed as the quintessential informal diagnostic procedure, whether it is the fleeting observation of here-and-now behavior or the analysis of student products. For example, the analysis of a student's spelling skills on a writing exercise involves the observation of the written work produced by that student. When the behavior is concretized in some way, either in a student product or recorded on audio or videotape, the processes involved in observation are more easily accomplished. The capriciousness of memory and the interference of the abundant stimuli from all the students in a class make the process of data on oral communication skills a most challenging task. When student performance is not captured either in recordings or in tangible products, observations and decisions on their instructional relevancy must be made rapidly by teachers who must ever be alert to those behaviors that have instructional relevancy.

When a teacher is responsible for facilitating the oral and nonverbal communication skills of infants and other young children, it is clear that insightful observations are not easily made. Teachers must see most of what is occurring; must hear most of the sounds produced; and must have a mind set that allows for the rapid processing of diverse auditory and visual stimuli, for the formulation of diagnostic-prescriptive hypotheses, and for the development of program plans to be retained and then recorded at a convenient time each school day.

A successful teacher must observe both process and product, even when the product is a fleeting one, as in the production of sound. Concentrating solely on product and ignoring process may either create problems in the present or have the potential for causing problems in the future. Evaluating a finished product and commenting on its flaws is neither effective nor efficient teaching; competent teachers stop a faulty process to drive home a point while it is occurring, just as they would stop an unsafe behavior while it is occurring and not wait for injury or disaster. A case in point is the young child who, in attempting to make the /m/ phoneme, presses her or his lips together with thumb and forefinger. While an acoustically acceptable /m/ may be produced in this way, the process error or difficulty will be disturbing to the listeners or viewers and will interfere at a later time with rapid speech production when and if the child progresses to the point at which he or she is able to communicate in word combinations, phrases, and sentences. A child who produces the /f/ and /v/ phonemes with lower incisors against the upper lip may be able to approximate those sounds sufficiently but will have a cosmetic defect that is likely to be so disconcerting to listeners that they will focus on how the person looks when speaking rather than on what is being said. In early handwriting instruction, it is critical to work on process — that is, the alignment of the student's body; the relationship of the head, hands, and writing implement to the paper; and the position of the legs and feet relative to the desk and floor. It is not sufficient to describe the formation of a letter, provide a model to copy, and to examine the imitated product; the process observations must be made not only for the day's product but for the future when in adulthood writing is expected to be a rapid yet legible endeavor.

Diagnostic data obtained through observation may result from viewing the student's performance as it is expressed naturally and spontaneously in the ebb and flow of his or her life, or it may be obtained through teacher-organized experiences and tasks that are both evaluative and instructional in intent. Although naturally occurring behaviors are more likely to be a part of the student's behavioral repertoire, teachers cannot always afford to wait for a behavior to occur naturally. Structured experiences must be provided in an attempt to elicit responses considered essential to an understanding of that student's performance or performance potential pertinent to a circumscribed curricular area.

STRUCTURED OBSERVATIONS

With respect to the development of communication skills, teachers observing very young children are primarily concerned with demonstrated skills in the areas of nonverbal and oral communication. Structured experiences are designed then to elicit responses that are more likely to lead to insightful diagnosis and relevant instruction. How may teachers prepare themselves for insightful and systematic observation? Teachers must engage in a cognitive exercise in which their knowledge of the subject to be taught suggests a series of pertinent diagnostic questions that will logically lead to meaningful instructional goals and objectives as well as to instructional priorities. It should be noted that the pivotal diagnostic question underlying all others is one that focuses on *demonstrated skills* rather than on errors, problems, or lack of skill: What skills, knowledge, and concepts does the student already possess (through demonstration) that will serve as the basis for future teaching and learning?

NONVERBAL COMMUNICATION

In the case of nonverbal communication, the following questions provide a conceptual framework for subsequent observations. The particular questions posed depend, of course, on preliminary, get-acquainted interactions from which a decision is made about where to begin to explore the student's performance.

1. What commonly used gestures does the student respond to appropriately? How consistent are these responses? Do these responses occur naturally? Do they occur only in structured interactions focused on this aspect of behavior?

2. What commonly used gestures does the student use appropriately, either as the sole communicative act or to reinforce a simultaneous speech act? How consistent is the use of these gestures? Does the student use them automatically and naturally? Do they occur only in structured interactions focused on this aspect of behavior?

3. Does the student respond to the vocal message of a speaker by responding appropriately to its emotional content, with or without understanding the words themselves? How consistent are these responses? Do these responses occur naturally? Do they occur only in structured interactions focused on this aspect of behavior?

4. Does the student's production of voice, with or without speech, communicate his or her feelings and emotional state appropriate to the circumstances and situation? With what consistency does the student's voice communicate his or her feelings? Does this behavior occur automatically and naturally? Does it occur only in structured interactons focused on this aspect of behavior?

5. Does the student respond to the emotional content of a speaker's message, with or without understanding the words, by responding appropriately to the speaker's facial expression and other body-language clues? How consistent is the student's response? Do these responses occur naturally? Do they occur only in structured interactions focused on this aspect of behavior?

6. Does the student indicate his or her feelings or emotional state through appropriate facial expressions and other body-language clues? With what consistency does the student's body language accurately communicate his or her feelings? Does this behavior occur automatically and naturally? Does it occur only in structured interactions focused on this aspect of behavior?

ORAL COMMUNICATION

In the case of oral communication, the questions to be answered are more numerous and complex. Again the central diagnostic question is the same, and the particular questions considered depend on the hypothesized level of functioning, that is, a presumed level based on case history data and any information gleaned from preliminary get-acquainted interactions with the student.

Auditory Processes and Comprehension

1. Has the student's hearing been tested? If not, what behaviors seem to indicate that the student is hearing? What is the nature of any auditory stimuli to which the student responds? If a hearing loss has been diagnosed, what implications are there for your teaching practices and objectives?

2. Does the student respond to sound; that is, is the student aware of the presence of sound? What sounds does the student respond to and in what ways does he or she demonstrate awareness of sound; that is, is it just attending behavior or is there an appropriate response, for example, dancing or moving to the sound of music? Do these responses occur naturally? Do they occur only in structured interactions focused on this aspect of behavior?

3. Does the student localize sounds heard; that is, does the student turn in the direction of the sound-producing object or person? Does he or she do so with consistency? Do these responses occur naturally? Do they occur only in structured interactions focused on this aspect of behavior?

4. Does the student respond differentially to various environmental sounds? If so, which ones? Is the differential response appropriate? How consistent are these responses? Do these responses occur naturally? Do they occur only in structured interactions focused on this aspect of behavior?

5. Does the student respond to the speech of others? If so, to what persons does he or she respond? How consistent are these responses? Do these responses occur naturally? Do they occur only in structured interactions focused on this aspect of behavior?

6. Does the student appear to comprehend words? If so, what words does he or she appear to understand with sufficient consistency? What is the nature of these words, that is, nouns or verbs? To what environmental aspects of the student's life do they refer? Under what circumstances and in what situations does the student demonstrate comprehension of the individual words identified? Do these responses occur naturally? Do they occur only in structured interactions focused on this aspect of behavior?

7. Does the student appear to comprehend word combinations and phrases? Does he or she appear to understand with sufficient consistency? What is the nature of these word combinations and phrases. Under what circumstances and in what situations does the student demonstrate comprehension of the words and phrases identified? Do these responses occur naturally? Do they occur only in structured interactions focused on this aspect of behavior?

Speech Behaviors

1. Does the student's speech mechanism appear to be structurally normal?

2. Does the student's speech mechanism appear to be functioning normally during eating and drinking activities?

3. What movements of the articulators does the student make during eating and drinking activities?

4. Does the student engage in vocal play? If so, what sounds and sound patterns does he or she make during vocal play?

5. Does the student imitate sounds and sound patterns? If so what sounds and sound patterns does he or she imitate? Whom does the student imitate and under what circumstances?

6. Is the student using individual sounds to communicate his or her needs and wants? If so, what sounds are used and for what referents? How consistent

is the student's use of these sounds? Under what circumstances and in what situations does he or she use sounds expressively? With whom does the student initiate this type of communication?

7. Does the student use individual words to communicate his or her needs and wants? If so, what words does the student say with consistency? What types of words are used? How may these words be classified or grouped? Under what circumstances and in what situations does the student use individual words? With whom is the student likely to speak? How intelligible are these utterances? What sounds and sound patterns does the student say with acceptable articulation? If the articulation of the words is not acceptable, what sound patterns within the words are articulated acceptably and which ones are close to being articulated satisfactorily? What interests and concerns are demonstrated by the words the student uses; that is, what words (and thus their referents) appear to have significant emotional content or intensity? Are there indications that the words spoken are used because of their meaning or because of their sound patterns? If they are used because of their sound pattenrs, what are these patterns?

8. Does the student use word combinations and phrases to communicate his or her needs and wants? If so, what word combinations or phrases does the student say consistently? What is the nature of these combinations; that is, are they noun-verb, verb-noun, or adjective-noun combinations? Are they grammatically or syntactically correct? What grammatical and syntactical patterns are used. How intelligible are these utterances? What sounds and sound patterns does the student say with acceptable articulation? If the articulation is not acceptable, what sounds and sound patterns are articulated acceptably, and which ones are close to being articulated acceptably? What interests and concerns are demonstrated by the word combinations and phrases spoken; that is, what objects and persons in the student's environment appear to possess significant emotional content? Under what circumstances and in what situations does the student use word combinations and phrases? With whom is the student likely to communicate?

RECORDING ASSESSMENT DATA

Effective and efficient diagnostic teachers must not only be insightful observers but must have a system for recording these observations. The system involves not only the creation and use of an appropriate form but also the time for recording observational data while they are still current. This practice is valuable for identifying instructional goals and objectives and also provides a format and structure for charting student progress toward these objectives and goals.

The daily diary, or log, of these observations provides instructional insight, and the observations may be recorded in narrative form or in a checklist format. A brief narrative that describes relevant student behaviors might be written in diary form or as an appendix to the lesson plan. This lesson plan approach is a logical one because the recorded results of a lesson ought to be the necessary denouement to that lesson. Any plan of action, including a lesson plan, implies a hypothesized result. The practice of recording results at the end of a lesson plan not only provides a record of student behavior and progress but also furnishes teachers with information by which they can measure the appropriateness of their planning and the efficacy of their teaching. Ideally, each lesson should improve or expand on the student's knowledge, skills, and concepts. Whenever a student fails to accomplish teacher-specified objectives, it may not always be the student's fault; it may be a function of the teacher's inaccurate perception of the student's current level of performance or the teacher's inappropriate or faulty methodology.

Teachers may wish to avoid narrative reports because of their time-consuming nature and choose instead to use a diagnostic checklist. A diagnostic checklist may be used by itself, or it may be supplemented with some brief exposition. Those key behaviors deemed necessary for effective functioning in the area of nonverbal and oral communication serve not only to suggest the scope and sequence of the curriculum but also to suggest the framework and content of a curriculum-based diagnostic checklist. A diagnostic checklist serves as a preintervention and postintervention evaluative device and as a complementary document that both mirrors and drives the curriculum.

To clarify its nature and function, a sample checklist is presented in Figure 7-1. A response legend is necessary to clarify the exact nature of the observed behavior and, when pertinent, the assistance provided to obtain the desired result.

TEACHER-MADE INVENTORIES

As part of the diagnostic process and in response to the central diagnostic question (What skills, knowledge, and concepts does the student already possess [through demonstration] that will serve as the base for future teaching?), teachers may wish to develop a teacher-made inventory that will provide in-depth information on a student's performance in a specific curriculum area. In designing any inventory, one considers not only the nature of the behavior to be observed but also the nature of the stimulus required to obtain the desired response. In addition, consideration must be given to the range of possible behaviors if the proposed in-depth exploration is to thoroughly and truly gauge the student's performance.

In the area of oral communication skills, once the key observational questions have been posed and answered, teachers may wish to engage in a detailed diagnostic study of the scope of the student's performance in a given area, for example, when it has been determined that the student already comprehends some individual words. The *nature of the stimulus* may be the use of real objects (or toy miniatures), photographs, and pictures in the analysis of noun comprehension. In the case of verbs, the stimulus might be one-word teacher-tendered

Student's name: **Ray Gunn**

Behavioral curriculum area: **Nonverbal Communication Skills**

Special learning conditions/physical restrictions: **NA**

Form completed by: **Mary McKnight Carpenter** (Teacher)

Parent: **Nancy B. Gunn**

Team member: **Joseph Esperanza** (Speech pathologist)

Key behaviors	Student performance as observed by	Observational notes
1. The student responds appropriately to commonly used gestures.	DFC By: Parent	On 9/23, Ray responded to his mother's goodbye wave by crying. On 9/25, Ray responded to my Come-here gesture when signalled on playground.
2. The student uses commonly used gestures to express his needs and wants.	CP/AR(PG) By: TM and T	On 10/10, Ray waved goodby to Mr. Esperanza when leaving therapy. On 10/14, Ray pointed to his mouth to indicate he wanted a cookie. On both occasions, he needed physical guidance to make the gesture clear to an observer.

(continued)

Figure 7-1 *(continued)*

Key behaviors	Student performance as observed by	Observational notes
3. The student responds appropriately to the vocal message of speakers.	DSLA By: T	On 10/14, Ray responded by comforting a puppet who was expressing sadness in a story. On 10/16, during a role pay, Ray stopped an activity when the puppett voiced anger.
4. The student's voice communicates his feelings to others.	DFC By: PA and T	On 11/16, Ray vocalized sadness when a peer denied him a toy. On 11/18, Ray indicated his pleasure at being caressed by his mother.
5. The student responds appropriately to the facial expressions and body language of others.	PP/AR(VC) By: T	On 12/12, Ray did not at first respond to my facial expression of sadness during a story until he was told to look at my face and see how sad I was.
6. The student communicates his feelings with appropriate facial expressions and other body language.	DFC By: T and TM	On 1/7, Ray smiled repeatedly when Mr. Esperanza read him a happy tale. On 1/9, Ray showed fear when a visitor to the class, dressed as a clown, frightened him.

Figure 7-1. Sample diagnostic checklist. *Student performance:* DFC = demonstrated in functional context; DSLA = demonstrated in structured learning activity; CP/AR = completed performance/assistance required; PP = partial performance; PP/AR = partial performance but assistance required. *Type of assistance:* PG = physical guidance; G = gestural prompt; VC = verbal cue. *Observers:* T = teacher; PA = parent (or other adult in the home); TM = team member. Sample annotated CBA checklist. (Adapted from Valletutti, P. J., and Bender, M. *Teaching the moderately and severely handicapped: A functional curriculum for communication and socialization* (Vol. 2, 2nd ed.). Austin, TX: PRO-ED. Copyright 1985 by PRO-ED, Inc. By permission.)

commands or photographs and pictures that depict people performing various gross and fine motor acts. The stimulus for testing understanding of polar adjectives might be the use of objects and pictures that demonstrate or depict opposite qualities.

The *nature of the response* for ascertaining noun comprehension might be pointing to the named item (because speech may be minimally present or absent in a student to whom this particular inventory might be given). The nature of the response for determining verb comprehension might be encouraging the student to perform the action named or to point to pictures showing a same-age child demonstrating the action named. In the case of adjectival comprehension, the student response might involve pointing to the named member of a pair of contrasting objects or pictures.

The next step in constructing an inventory is to design individual subtests and their subsumed test items. A sample teacher-designed inventory that ascertains the student's oral comprehension follows.

INVENTORY: ORAL COMPREHENSION OF COMMONLY USED NOUNS, ACTION VERBS, AND ADJECTIVES

SECTION A. COMPREHENSION OF COMMONLY USED NOUNS

Subtest 1. Noun Comprehension: Object Pairs

Teacher directions: For each of the real objects or their miniatures (e.g., toy cars, a doll house, and doll house furniture) shown to the student, ask the child to point to the object named. Test comprehension for each item three times in three separate pairings of objects. Place a check mark on the line immediately preceding each noun if it has been identified correctly on three occasions.

HOME

Appliances		**Clothing**	
____ Sink	____ Vacuum	____ Shoe	____ Coat
____ Stove	____ Fan	____ Sock	____ Mitten
____ Refrigerator		____ Underwear	____ Glove
____ Iron	____ Ironing board	____ Hat	____ Dress
____ Clock	____ Telephone	____ Pants	____ Shirt
____ Dishwasher		____ Blouse	____ Tie
____ Washer	____ Dryer	____ Snowsuit	____ Sweater
____ Toaster		____ Jacket	

Food and Beverages

Dairy	**Fruit**		**Fruit Juices**
____ Milk	____ Apple	____ Pineapple	____ Apple juice
____ Cheese	____ Orange	____ Peach	____ Orange juice
____ Butter	____ Grapes	____ Pear	____ Grape juice
____ Margarine	____ Watermelon	____ Lemon	
____ Eggs			

Meat

____ Hot dog
____ Hamburger
____ Chicken
____ Fish
____ Turkey

Starches

____ Rice
____ Spaghetti
____ Pizza
____ Bread

Condiments

____ Salt
____ Pepper
____ Ketchup
____ Mustard
____ Mayonnaise

Vegetables

____ Corn
____ Peas
____ Carrot
____ Lettuce
____ Tomato
____ Celery
____ Potato
____ Onions

Sweets

____ Cookie
____ Candy
____ Ice cream
____ Cake
____ Pie
____ Cracker
____ Jelly
____ Pudding

Structural Items

____ Floor
____ Wall
____ Ceiling
____ Window
____ Door
____ Closet
____ Rug

Grooming Items/Devices

____ Comb
____ Hairbrush
____ Toothbrush
____ Toothpaste
____ Soap
____ Water
____ Ring
____ Towel
____ Watch
____ Ribbon
____ Eyeglasses

Furniture and Accessories

____ Table
____ Chair
____ Sofa
____ Lamp
____ Bookcase
____ Television (TV)
____ Radio
____ Stereo
____ Plant
____ Dresser
____ Bureau
____ Crib
____ Playpen
____ Bathtub
____ Toilet
____ Mirror
____ Pictures
____ Curtains
____ Blinds
____ Drapes
____ Bed
____ Bedspread
____ Mattress
____ Blanket
____ Pillow
____ Sheet
____ Vase
____ Light
____ Shower

Tools and Cleaning Equipment

____ Hammer
____ Screwdriver
____ Broom
____ Mop
____ Sponge
____ Paper towels

Utensils and Kitchenware

____ Spoon
____ Fork
____ Knife
____ Cup
____ Bottle
____ Glass
____ Saucer
____ Dish
____ Pot
____ Pan

Toys

____ Ball
____ Doll
____ Balloon
____ Car
____ Truck
____ Block
____ Clay
____ Train
____ Puzzle
____ Game
____ Pail
____ Shovel

Outside the House

____ Mailbox
____ Fence
____ Gate
____ Garden
____ Hose
____ Lawn mower
____ Garage
____ Swing
____ Seesaw

SCHOOL

____ Desk
____ Chair
____ Chalkboard
____ Chalk
____ Eraser
____ Book
____ Picture
____ Plant
____ Record
____ Phonograph
____ Pen
____ Pencil
____ Crayon
____ Stars
____ Scissors
____ Paste

COMMUNITY

People

____ Baby
____ Boy
____ Girl
____ Man
____ Woman

Vehicles

____ Bicycle
____ Baby carriage
____ Wagon
____ Bus
____ Train
____ Car
____ Truck

Animals/Pets

____ Dog
____ Cat
____ Horse
____ Rabbit
____ Bird
____ Fish

Natural Objects

____ Tree
____ Flower

Man-made Objects

____ Building
____ Store
____ Bridge

Insects

____ Fly
____ Bee
____ Ant
____ Spider

Zoo Animals

____ Lion
____ Tiger
____ Elephant
____ Bear
____ Giraffe
____ Monkey
____ Snake

Farm Animals

____ Cow
____ Chicken
____ Pig
____ Duck
____ Sheep
____ Goat

BODY PARTS

____ Hair
____ Eyes
____ Nose
____ Ears
____ Mouth
____ Teeth

____ Tongue
____ Lips
____ Head
____ Face
____ Hands
____ Fingers

____ Arms
____ Legs
____ Feet
____ Toes

Subtest 2. Noun Comprehension: Object Trios

Teacher Directions: Follow the same directions as in Subtest 1. This time, however, place three objects in front of the student for identification.

Subtest 3. Noun Comprehension: Photograph Pairs

Teacher Directions: Follow the same directions as in Subtest 1. This time, however, use photographs of the items.

Subtest 4. Noun Comprehension: Photograph Trios

Teacher Directions: Follow the same directions as in Subtest 2. This time, however, use photographs of the items.

Subtest 5. Noun Comprehension: Picture Pairs

Teacher Directions: Follow the same directions as in Subtest 1. This time, however, use pictures of the items.

Subtest 6: Noun Comprehension: Picture Trios

Teacher Directions: Follow the same directions as in Subtest 2. This time, however, use pictures of the items.

SECTION B: COMPREHENSION OF COMMONLY USED ACTION VERBS

Subtest 7. Action Verb Comprehension: One Word Commands

Teacher Directions: Model the imitation of the action to be tested in order to make certain that the student understands what is expected and is able to perform the desired behavior. Then say each command and observe the student's performance.

Gross Motor	Upper Extremities	Hand	Face
____ Walk	____ Throw	____ Touch	____ Open (eyes)
____ Jump	____ Catch	____ Reach	____ Shut (eyes)
____ Hop	____ Eat	____ Hold	____ Kiss
____ Run	____ Drink	____ Point	____ Chew
____ Skip	____ Reach	____ Pass	____ Smile
____ Sit		____ Wave	
		____ Clap	
		____ Open	
		____ Shut	

Subtest 8. Action Verb Comprehension: Photograph or Picture Pairs

Teacher Directions: Show the student photographs or pictures of two distinct actions. Ask the student to point to the picture or photograph of a same-age child performing the action named. Test comprehension for each item three times in three separate pairings.

Subtest 9. Action Verb Comprehension: Photograph or Picture Trios

Teacher Directions: Follow the same directions as in Subtest 8. This time, however, place three photographs or pictures in front of the student.

SECTION C. COMPREHENSION OF COMMONLY USED POLAR ADJECTIVES

Subtest 10. Comprehension of Polar Adjectives: Object Pairs

Teacher Directions: Show the student paired objects that demonstrate contrasting qualities. Each presentation involves showing two opposites that are the same in all aspects except for the contrasting quality being tested. Test the comprehension for both adjectival elements in each contrasting pair by using three separate physical representations of each quality examined.

Visual

____ Long-short (pencils)
____ Tall-short (adult figures)
____ Fat-thin (toy clowns)
____ Big-small (toy cars)

Auditory

____ Loud-soft (bells)

Proprioceptive

____ Light-heavy (books)

Tactile

____ Smooth-rough (sandpaper and tissue paper)

Olfactory

____ Nice-bad (flower/bottle of perfume and rotten egg)

Gustatory

____ Sweet-sour (candy and lemon)

TRANSLATING OBSERVATIONAL DATA INTO A STATEMENT OF THE CURRENT LEVEL OF PERFORMANCE

Once sufficient data has been collected to illuminate the nature of the student relevant to his or her performance in the pertinent behavioral domain (in this case nonverbal and oral communication skills), a narrative portrait of that student can be sketched. This student profile then serves as the foundation from which specific instructional outcomes may be projected. It should be clear to all educators that the educational needs of a student arise from the dynamic life and nature of the student as viewed from the professional perspective of educators who are preparing children and youth for the demands that will be made of them in adulthood. Thus, instructional objectives are designed on an individual basis in order to achieve the long-term goals that are honored for all persons in a society, whether thay have handicaps or not.

For example, consider the responses to the following observational questions:

Does the student respond to various environmental sounds?

Yes.

If so, which ones does the student respond to?

The doorbell, the telephone, the vacuum cleaner, the radio, the barking of a dog, the opening of the refrigerator door, and the scratching of the cat against the door.

Is the differential response appropriate?

Yes, the student runs to the door, picks up the telephone, avoids the vacuum, dances to the music played on the radio, gives the dog a biscuit, indicates hunger, and opens the door to let the cat in.

Given these responses, the current level of performance statement can be simply phrased: *Student A responds appropriately to the following sounds: doorbell, vacuum cleaner, radio, barking of a dog, opening of a refrigerator, and scratching of a cat.* A test or grade/age-equivalent score can never provide this needed detail. The numerical neatness of a score on a standardized test appears to be a highly efficient description of a student, but in reality, it has little programming effectiveness because it cannot possibly provide the specifics needed to individualize an educational program that is both the letter and intent of state and federal laws dealing with the education of young children who are handicapped.

A portrait that deals with relevant student behavior is not easily captured, nor is it long-lived. Therefore, instructional goals and objectives can never, in reality, remain currently meaningful or realistic. A statement of the current level of performance is out-dated by the time it is formulated because the student progresses, at times even regresses, and because the child's environment and external stimuli change. That is why the student's profile must be modified as new details are added and as previously recorded informaton becomes history. Goals and instructional objectives must be changed as the student changes, calling for flexibility in planning and teaching that is seldom rewarded and seldom appreciated by those educators whose expectations of teachers and students are driven by curricula and age or grade expectancies. Being a flexible professional is a high-risk behavior, not only because it may be threatening to persons higher up in the school's hierarchy but also because it calls for heightened responsiveness and rapid responses to newly demonstrated and newly emerging behaviors. Although flexibility in planning and teaching is subject to greater error than responding to more fully supported observational data from the past, it can be highly facilitative of learning when it is shaped by fresh insights and triggered by newly evolving behavior.

ESTABLISHING EDUCATIONAL GOALS AND OBJECTIVES

Once consistent data has been collected and a descriptive narrative of the student has been written, educational goals and objectives are identifiable. In addition, a priority ordering of these goals and objectives must be made. A priority ordering depends on a variety of factors, including the likelihood of the student's rapid success based on partial mastery, the utility of a skill or knowledge to the student, the parental needs and concerns, the school system's emphases, the therapeutic imperatives, and the teacher's appraisal of the student's needs.

For example, in the process of selecting instructional objectives for Student B, it has been observed that, during the past several weeks, she frequently articulates the /s/ as she moves about the classroom and as she explores and investigates the school playground's equipment. Interestingly, she has made no other consonant sound in the hearing of others; the only other sounds she makes when engaging either in vocal play or in reflexive vocalization are vowel sounds. She particularly enjoys playing with a well-used rag doll, grown more ragged with this student's aggressive attention. She manipulates the doll for minutes at a time (uncharacteristically long for this student) while sitting in the classroom rocking chair. The instructional objective suggested by this observation might be: *Student B will get her rag doll and play with it in response to an adult saying, "Cissie."* (the doll's newly acquired and specially selected name). A further objective might logically be *Student B will make the /s/ sound when she wants to obtain her rag doll that is placed out of her reach or out of her sight.* A third objective might be a behavioral one in which the amount of time her attention is directed toward "Cissie" is increased. Thus, a distinct individualized objective has been fashioned directly from observational data and not from a school-generated or computerized list of possible objectives for special students based on the type and degree of handicap and on the age of the individual.

Another example is Student C who responds to simple one-step commands involving the preposition *on* but fails to respond appropriately to any other preposition that denotes position. This attribute has been substantiated during several recent class sessions, at which time he successfully placed a variety of familiar objects on various surfaces and pieces of furniture. Specifically, he responded to the following commands: *Put the spoon on the table, Put the book on the desk, Put the car on the floor,* and *Set the doll down on the chair.* However, when he was asked to put various toys and objects *in* the drawer, boxes, and containers, he failed to do so. In most cases, he started to place the toy on the recipient container, hesitated, looked puzzled, turned to seek help, and stopped. Thus the instructional objective that reasonably emerges from this teacher-organized and structured evaluative experience might be *Student C will place various familiar objects in drawers and other receptacles in response to one-step commands. Sample commands include, "Put the spoon in the drawer," "Put the book in the box," "Put the car in the garage,"* and *"Put the doll in the crib."*

SELECTING TEACHING STRATEGIES AND TECHNIQUES

So far this chapter has addressed the role of the teacher in determining *what* should be taught to a particular student. Also important is *how* to teach that student. Insights on how to teach may also result from skillful observation of the student as he or she interacts with the people and things in the environment. These observations help determine what the student's interests are, for it is often the student's interests that should shape the teaching/learning act and the materials used. For example, the first words spoken by a child are invariably the names of people and things that have emotional intensity for that child. They are not always phonetically simple words, as may be noted in the speech of a young child who says *Dee-Dee* for his beloved sister, Delores. In the absense of articulating maturity, the intensity of the word will win out all the time, and the word will become part of the child's vocabulary, imperfect as it may be. If this is the case, then the words to be learned should be chosen from the persons and things that are emotionally tied to the child's life. *How* to reinforce a child may also be determined through careful observation. A favored toy, a favorite activity, a favored record, and a favorite snack may all serve as reinforcers for one child but may be distasteful and boring to others.

Observational data on *how* to teach and reinforce a student should be supplemented by information obtained from parents and other caregivers. Although relying on information obtained from others may not be as comfortable to teachers as their own observations, it can be an excellent source of diagnostic data, not only for *how* but also for *what* to teach. Such information may provide data on activities that are essential to the child's functioning in the home setting, data that are not readily available, except as may emerge from classroom simulations. In addition, observations from others may supply information resulting from the many one-to-one parent-child interactions that are not as easily available to teachers in classroom settings. Such observations may also furnish data concerning behaviors that have occurred in familiar surroundings but which are absent in the less familiar and perhaps more threatening classroom environment.

A favored toy such as a teddy bear may be just the thing to help the child develop comprehension for various action verbs: *Look, Teddy is dancing! Now, Teddy is walking! Be quiet now; Teddy is sleeping. Now you make Teddy walk! Make Teddy dance! Now Teddy is tired; put Teddy to sleep.* Make a game out of what otherwise might be a boring, didactic lesson. It may be all that is needed for the student to pay attention and learn. Questions relevant to selecting stimulating and motivating materials and approaches include the following:

What toys and games excite the student's interests?
What foods does the student prefer?
What types of activities capture and hold the student's attention?
What stories, books, records, rhymes, and songs appear to interest the student?

For more details on *how* to teach communication skills to the young child with handicaps see Chapters 8, 9, and 10.

SELECTING ASSESSMENT STRATEGIES

The selection of appropriate strategies for assessing learning outcomes is not an esoteric task. It is simply a preintervention and postintervention phenomenon. The techniques employed for assessing preintervention procedures must merely be replicated on a postintervention basis. For example, if a teacher asked *What commonly used gestures does the student respond to appropriately?* as part of the initial diagnostic process, then he or she must make only a slight alteration after treatment by asking *What additional commonly used gestures does the student now respond to appropriately?* The assessment strategy then becomes clear, that is, *teacher observation.* The teacher must observe the student functioning in natural settings or in specially constructed interactions to determine whether he or she is responding appropriately to any new commonly used (or uncommonly used) gestures as well as retaining those previously acquired. Teacher observation of student growth includes evaluation of both process and product, either as the behaviors occur naturally or in response to oral or written tests.

Therefore, a teacher-made test is a legitimate informal assessment strategy if the test duplicates the initial test stimuli and format with appropriate changes in content to reflect the essential hope that there are newly acquired skills, knowledge, and concepts.

CONCLUSION

Even though teachers must learn to be insightful observers of student behavior, they must not ignore key diagnostic information available from the child's parents who interact in real-life situations with their child in the home and in the community. Moreover, teachers must be responsive to the wealth of diagnostic information available from speech and language pathologists, not only for their specialized assessments but also for their suggestions of productive and creative language stimulation and development activities. The team members (the teacher, the parents, and the speech and language pathologist) must consult together regularly and must coordinate their efforts so that communication skills are facilitated and so that young children who are handicapped may communicate with others as successfully and with as much pleasure as possible, regardless of the type or severity of the handicap.

SUGGESTED READINGS

Bagnato, S. J., and Neisworth, J. T. (1981). *Linking developmental assessment and curricula: Prescriptions for early intervention.* Rockville, MD: Aspen Systems.

Ballard, K. D. (1983). A model for behavioral assessment of developmentally handicapped children. *Exceptional Children, 30,* 175–184.

Bennett, R. E. (1981). Assessment of exceptional children: Guidelines for practice. *Diagnostique, 7,* 5–13.

Blankenship, C. S. (1985). Using curriculum-based data to make instructional decisions. *Exceptional Children, 52,* 233–238.

Bliss, L. S. (1985). A symptom approach to the intervention of childhood language disorders. *Journal of Communication Disorders, 18,* 91–108.

Boucher, C. R. (1982). Formative testing to teach children with learning problems. *Teaching Exceptional Children, 14,* 177–181.

Bricker, D. D. (Ed.). (1982). *Intervention with at-risk and handicapped infants: From research to application.* Baltimore: University Park Press.

Bromley, K. D., and Jalongo, M. R. (1984). Song picture books and the language disordered child. *Teaching Exceptional Children, 16,* 115–119.

Calhoun, M. L., and Newson, E. (1984). Parents as experts: An assessment approach for hard-to-test children. *Diagnostique, 9,* 239–244.

Casby, M. W., and Cumpata, J. F. (1986). A protocol for the assessment of prelinguistic intentional communication. *Journal of Communication Disorders, 19,* 251–260.

Connell, P. J. (1986). Teaching subjecthood to language-disordered children. *Journal of Speech and Hearing Research, 29,* 481–492.

Coggins, T. E., Olswang, L. B., and Guthrie, J. (1987). Assessing communicative intents in young children: Low structured observation or elicitation tasks? *Journal of Speech and Hearing Disorders, 52,* 44–49.

Culatta, B. (1983). Story retelling as a communicative performance screening tool. _Language, Speech, and Hearing Services in Schools, 14_, 66–74.

Curtis, W. S., and Donlon, E. T. (1985). _Observational evaluation of severely multihandicapped children._ Lewiston, NY: C. H. Hogrefe.

Deno, S. L. (1985). Curriculum-based measurement: The emerging alternative. _Exceptional Children, 52_, 219–232.

Dollaghan, C. (1985). Child meets word: "Fast mapping" in preschool children. _Journal of Speech and Hearing Research, 28_, 449–454.

Evans, S. S., and Evans, W. H. (1986). A perspective on assessment for instruction. Section I: Perspectives on instructional assessment. _Pointer, 30_, 9–12.

Fallen, N. H., and Umansky, W. (1985). _Young children with special needs_ (2nd ed.). Columbus, OH: Merrill.

Foster, S. (1985). The development of discourse topic skills by infants and young children. _Topics in Language Disorders, 5_, 31–45.

Frank, A. R., and Ehly, S. W. (1983). Strategies for parental involvement in planning and implementing IEPs. _Journal for Special Educators, 19_, 45–50.

Fuchs, L. S., and Fuchs, D. (1986). Effects of systematic formative evaluation: A meta-analysis. _Exceptional Children, 53_, 199–208.

Fujiki, M., and Willbrand, M. L. (1982). A comparison of four informal methods of language evaluation. _Language, Speech, and Hearing Services in Schools, 13_, 42–52.

Gickling, E. E., and Thompson, V. P. (1985). A personal view of curriculum-based assessment. _Exceptional Children, 52_, 205–218.

Gulliford, R. (1983). The school's role in assessment. Special education. _Forward Trends, 10_, 6–9.

Handen, B. L., Feldman, R. S., and Honigman, A. (1987). Comparison of parent and teacher assessments of developmentally delayed children's behavior. _Exceptional Children, 54_, 137–144.

Hansen, L., and Weaver, J. (1983). _Strategies to develop communication, mobility, and object manipulative skills within the curriculum domains for elementary age severely handicapped students._ Madison, WI: Madison Public Schools.

Hargis, C. H. (1987). _Curriculum based assessment: A primer._ Springfield, IL: Thomas.

Hartshorne, T. S., and Johnston, D. W. (1982). The use of behavioral assessment. _Diagnostique, 7_, 212–220.

Heidinger, V. A. (1984). _Analysing syntax and semantics: A self-instructional approach for teachers and clinicians._ Washington, DC: Gallaudet College Press.

Heron, T. E., and Heward, W. L. (1982). Ecological assessment: Implications for teachers of learning disabled students. _Learning Disability Quarterly, 5_, 117–125.

Holdgrafer, G., and Dunst, C. J. (1986). Communicative competence: From research to practice. _Topics in Early Childhood Special Education, 6_, 1–22.

Humphries, T. W., and Wilson, A. K. (1986). An instructional-based model for assessing learning disabilities. _Canadian Journal of Special Education, 2_, 55–66.

Illerbrun, D., and Greenough, P. (1983). Classroom/clinical diagnosis of young language learning disabled children: An integrated approach. _Special Education in Canada, 57_, 23–27.

Johnson, A. R., Johnston, E. B., and Weinrich, B. D. (1984). Assessing pragmatic skills in children. _Language, Speech, and Hearing Services in Schools, 15_, 2–9.

Kendall, P. C., and Braswell, L. (1982). Assessment for cognitive-behavioral interventions in the schools. _School Psychology Review, 11_, 21–31.

Lederer, J. B. (1983). _Measuring pupil progress in special education._ Paramus, NJ: Bergen County Special Services School District.

McConkey, R. (1985). _Working with parents: A practical guide for teachers and therapists._ Cambridge, MA: Brookline Books.

McLoughlin, J. A., and Lewis, R. B. (1981). _Assessing special students: Strategies and procedures._ Columbus, OH: Merrill.

Mecham, M. J., and Willbrand, M. L. (1985). _Treatment approaches to learning disabilities in children._ Springfield, IL: Thomas.

Meyers, J., and Lytle, S. (1986). Assessment of the learning process. _Exceptional Children, 53_, 138–144.

Nation, J. E., and Aram, D. M. (1984). *Diagnosis of speech and language disorders* (2nd ed.). Boston: College-Hill.

Nelson, N. W. (1986). Individual processing in classroom settings. *Topics in Language Disorders, 6*, 13–27.

Paget, K. D. (1984). Assessment in early childhood education. *Diagnostique, 10*, 76–87.

Reed, J. (Ed.). (1981). The earliest years. *Children Today, 10*, 2–45.

Roffman, A. J. (1983). *The classroom teacher's guide to mainstreaming.* Springfield, IL: Thomas.

Sapir, S. G., and Cort, R. H. (Eds.). (1982). *Children with special needs: Case studies in the clinical teaching process.* New York: Brunner/Mazel.

Schiefelbusch, R. L. (Ed.). (1986). *Language competence: Assessment and intervention.* Boston: College-Hill.

Schlieper, A. E. (1982). A note on frames of reference in the assessment of learning disabilities. *Journal of Learning Disabilities, 15*, 84–85.

Shirmer, B. R. (1984). Dynamic model of oral and/or signed language diagnosis. *Language, Speech, and Hearing Services in Schools, 15*, 76–82.

Shore, K. (1986). *The special education handbook: A comprehensive guide for parents and educators.* New York: Teachers College Press.

Simon, C. S. (1984). Functional-pragmatic evaluation of communication skills in school-age children. *Language, Speech, and Hearing Services in Schools, 15*, 83–97.

Stephens, T. M. (1982). *Teaching children basic skills: A curriculum handbook* (2nd ed.). Columbus, OH: Merrill.

Sugai, G. (1985). Case study: Designing instruction from IEPs. *Teaching Exceptional Children, 17*, 232–239.

Taylor, R. L. (1984). *Assessment of exceptional students: Educational and psychological procedures.* Englewood Cliffs, NJ: Prentice-Hall.

Thurlow, M. L., and Ysseldyke, J. E. (1982). Instructional planning: Information collected by school psychologists vs information considered useful by teachers. *Journal of School Psychology, 20*, 3–10.

Tucker, J. A. (1985). Curriculum-based assessment: An introduction. *Exceptional Children, 52*, 199–204.

Turnbull, K. K., and Hughes, D. L. (1987). A pragmatic analysis of speech and language IEP conferences. *Language, Speech, and Hearing Services in Schools, 18*, 275–286.

Wiig, E. H. (1984). Assessment of communicative disorders. *Diagnostique, 10*, 67–75.

Wood, J. W., and Aldridge, J. T. (1985). Adapting tests for mainstreamed students. *Academic Therapy, 20*, 419–426.

Wren, C. T. (1985). Collecting language samples from children with syntax problems. *Language, Speech, and Hearing Services in Schools, 16*, 83–102.

Ysseldyke, J. E., and Algozzine, B. (1984). *Introduction to special education.* Boston: Houghton Mifflin.

CHAPTER 8

Organizing the
Instructional Experience

PETER J. VALLETUTTI

The teaching/learning experience, in terms of its instructional content, should ideally flow from a thorough assessment of the student with primary emphasis on the skills, knowledge, and concepts that have already been demonstrated. This exercise requires a richly detailed, descriptive narrative that articulates the student's behaviors relevant to specific areas of educational emphasis or concern. Because the purview of this book is language development in the young child, designing the instructional sequence and structuring the learning environment requires initial attention to the precise reporting of the student's abilities in both nonverbal and verbal communication competencies, including oral language comprehension; oral language expression; and to a lesser degree, written language comprehension and expression. The typical practice of simply indicating the scores obtained by a student on a battery of formal tests is not sufficient to illustrate and vivify the student's performance or to suggest what the student should be taught. The teacher must be a keen observer and recorder of significant behavioral events so that lessons emerge based on the reality of the student and not on facile labels, available materials, or instructional biases.

CURRENT LEVEL OF PERFORMANCE NARRATIVE

Basic to the design of individualized instructional experiences is a thorough analysis of the individual student's current performance level. The importance of this critical assessment process is recognized in the provisions of PL 94-142, The Education for All Handicapped Children Act (Federal Register, 1977), and in parallel state laws. Specifically, the requirements of the mandated IEP include a report on the student's current level of performance (Federal Register, 1977). Unfortunately, most school systems attend to the letter of the law, ignoring its deeper intent, namely, the need to describe the individual student in sufficient detail so that the designed program plan arises from the comprehensive evaluation of that student's present performance and thus addresses that student's special education and related service needs.

An example of an appropriate current level of performance narrative follows. Although evaluation reports usually begin with a background section, a current level of performance statement need not do so because the intent is not to recount history but to describe current status.

MARVIN ROLLO'S LANGUAGE DEVELOPMENT

I. NONVERBAL COMMUNICATION SKILLS

A. Gestures: Comprehension

Marvin stops an activity when someone shakes his or her finger or shakes his or her head. He also looks at objects or people pointed to. He usually waves good-bye in response to the good-bye wave of a departing person and responds to the "hello" gesture by gesturing "hello" in return. However, he does not respond when someone makes the "give me" gesture, nor does he respond when someone greets him with an extended hand for the hand-shaking ritual. (N.B., a current level of performance statment may include behaviors that are absent or incomplete only after the behaviors that are present are fully explicated. These unacquired behaviors should only be included in the narrative when they suggest a progamming possibility.)

B. Gestures: Expression

Marvin points to desired objects and gains a person's attention by waving his hands in front of that person's face. He also indicates "give me" when he wishes to play with a toy he cannot reach. As yet, however, he does not use any need differentiating gestures that indicate he is hungry, thirsty, tired, or ill.

C. Paralanguage (the ability to interpret and to express appropriately the non-word communication elements of the vocalization process)

Marvin responds to the vocal expression of happiness or pleasure by con-tinuing an activity in which he is engaged. Similarly, he discontinues an activ-ity in which he is engaged when someone vocalizes anger or displeasure.

D. Facial Expressions

Marvin responds to a smile by smiling in turn and will continue an activity when someone shows approval by smiling. He shows that he is sad by curl-ing his lower lip and pulling his eyebrows in toward the bridge of his nose.

II. VERBAL COMMUNICATION SKILLS

A. Precursor Oral Language Skills

Marvin babbles duplicated syllables (ba-ba, me-me) and initiates vocal play with toys. Also, he vocalizes displeasure when a needed or favored object is withdrawn, and similarly, he vocalizes pleasure or satisfaction when given a favored or desired object. He vocalizes to music and, at times, initiates vocal play with familiar people in his environment (mother, a neighbor, grand-mother). He does echo individual sounds and consonant-vowel combina-tions but, as yet, has not echoed individual words or phrases in songs or rhymes or as spoken by others.

B. Oral Language Comprehension

Marvin looks at a familiar object (light, car, and baby) or significant person (mommy and daddy) named. In addition, he terminates a behavior when warned, "No!" He responds by pointing the the appropriate object when directed to *Show me the (object)!* or when asked *Where is the object?* He also re-sponds appropriately to the commands *Give me the (object)* and *Get the (object)* when the object involved is a familiar one. When asked, he does point to simple pictures (such as cow and cat) found in children's picture books. As yet, he has not pointed to parts of his face on request, although he occasion-ally points to another person's nose when asked.

C. Oral Language Expression

Most of the time Marvin says "dada" when seeking the attention of father; however, he also says "dada" when attempting to gain the attention of his mother or grandmother. *Car* does appear to be his first word; he says this upon seeing a car or a picture of one.

A narrative based on observations that provide insight into the instructional process must supplement (and cannot be supplanted by) scores obtained on formal diagnostic tests.

ESTABLISHING ANNUAL GOALS AND SHORT-TERM INSTRUCTIONAL OBJECTIVES

Once the present performance level has been determined, long-range or annual goals can then be formulated. Every handicapped student must have an IEP (Federal Register, 1977), and one of the requirements of this legal prescription is the identification of annual special education and related service goals. An instructional experience or lesson plan cannot be organized and logically envisioned unless appropriate annual or long-range goals are specified and serve as the organizing element for individualized lesson plans. For example, an appropriate long-range goal for Marvin might be *Marvin will express his needs by saying two words in noun/verb combinations*. Given the fact that Marvin appears to be using several individual words with meaningful reference in his communicative speech, a reasonable annual goal might be the acquisition of connected speech involving two-word combinations, namely noun/verb ones. A goal is typically broader in scope than an objective and is envisioned as attainable in the distant future.

After annual goals have been stipulated in the IEP contract between the school system and the student's parents or guardians, short-term instructional objectives that will contribute to the realization of these goals must then be formulated. These short-term instructional objectives become the specific objectives that behaviorally shape each instructional experience (Valletutti and Bender, 1982) and are therefore written in behavioral (measurable) terms. Specific short-term instructional objectives that will contribute to the acquisition of the annual goal stated for Marvin include the following:

Marvin will say the names of common objects.
Marvin will answer the question *What is this?*
Marvin will indicate his wants by saying nouns.
Marvin will name the actions of people by using verbs.
Marvin will name the action capabilities of common objects by using verbs.

Each of these short-term intructional objectives are prerequisite to the realization of the annual goal and, therefore, act as the focus for the daily instructional experience. Annual goals and their short-term instructional objectives are set by the IEP committee based on the identified needs of the child.

THE NATURE OF THE TEACHER-STUDENT INTERACTION: METHODS AND MATERIALS

Although the informal assessment narrative leads to the identification of long-range and short-term objectives, these objectives merely specify *what* the teacher/programmer expects the learning outcomes to be. *How* the teacher-student interaction should proceed becomes the next organizational task. This aspect of the overall instructional task involves the selection of appropriate materials, the identification of reinforcement preferences, the establishment of a suitable reinforcement schedule, and the specifications of the subject matter that will most likely capture the interest and thus motivate the performance of the student.

The selection of materials is based in part on the appropriateness of the material to the subject to be taught (e.g., real objects are to be used to develop noun comprehension and usage) and in part on the interests of the student. Materials and equipment appropriate to stimulating and developing language in young children with handicaps need not be esoteric; they are included in Table 8-1.

Although the use of a child's picture book may be seen as a suitable means of facilitating the noun vocabulary of a young child, the selection of a specific book depends greatly on the pictures found therein. The teacher needs to ask *Does this book contain clear illustrations that will interest this particular student.* For example, Marvin has begun to vocalize "buh-buh-buh" upon seeing pictures of dolls and babies; therefore, the word baby is a logical one to develop, and a picture book that contains at least one picture of a baby should be used in the instructional experience. Another example involves playing a children's record to stimulate Marvin's vocalization. Because Marvin has been observed interrupting his free, largely undirected play whenever the song "This Old Man" is played, this record should be used to facilitate Marvin's language development, even if it merely stimulates his vocalization.

Further, the identificaton of reinforcement preferences and a suitable reinforcement schedule should be explored. It may be necessary at this point to conduct a number of informal interviews with the student's parents or caregivers. Asking parents what toys their child enjoys, what his or her favorite foods are, what nursery rhymes or commercial jingles capture his or her interest, and what book he or she thumbs through — all may provide answers to what might be used as reinforcers as well as instructional materials. Additionally, there is a need to establish a reinforcement schedule, recognizing that various students have various response rates, that the programming must modify the types of reinforcers toward more socially mature ones, and that the schedule of reinforcement must be modified toward a more natural one.

The specification of the subject matter that will most likely capture the interest and motivate the performance of the child is the final element in response to the question of *how* to teach the student, and it requires that the teacher be a subject matter specialist who determines which subcategory or aspect of the subject matter is most likely to interest the pupil and thus prove more successful. Vocalization may be stimulated by playing records, by vocalizing during

Table 8-1. MATERIALS AND EQUIPMENT USED IN STIMULATING LANGUAGE IN YOUNG CHILDREN WITH HANDICAPS

Materials	Equipment
Alphabet blocks	Cassette or tape recorder
Audio tapes	Chalkboards
Balls and bean bags	Child-size kitchen equipment
Books	Doll carriage
Building blocks (assorted sizes)	Doll house and furniture
Catalogs	Earphones
Clay	File cabinets (for pictures)
Clocks	Film strip projector
Colored chalk, crayons, magic markers, paintbrushes, pastels, and pencils for drawing and painting	Flannel board
Coloring books	Musical instruments (non rhythm, e.g., autoharps and harmonicas)
Construction paper	Pillows and floor cushions
Dolls and doll clothing	Record player
Dress-up clothes	Rhythm instruments
Film strips	Rocking chair
Flannel board cutouts (labels, pictures, and characters)	Sand box or sand table
Games (commerical and teacher-made)	Small table and chairs
Magazines	Storage (open) for books, records, tapes
Modeling clay	Telephones (real and toy)
Models	Television and video cassette records
Objects (for sensory stimulation)	Trunk (for dress-up clothes)
Objects (for vocabulary development)	Typewriter
Paints	Viewmaster and slides
Paste and glue	Water play table
Records	
Pictures and photographs	
Play money	
Puzzles	
Song books	
Stuffed animals	
Tea sets, pots and pans, toy cooking utensils, and toy silverware	
Toys	
Video tapes	
Word boxes	
Writing paper	

free play; by engaging in chanting, singing, and other rhythmic games; by talking about pictures, photographs, or books; and by listening to simple rhymes, chants, or jingles. Because Marvin vocalizes more when he hears selected television commercials, those video recordings of commercials that have stimulated him to vocalize should be emphasized over the use of children's records that have proven to be minimally stimulating.

THE NATURE OF THE TEACHER-STUDENT INTERACTION: TEACHER PERSONALITY AND TEMPERAMENT

Teachers should appreciate the effects of the classroom's social climate on student learning and on behavior as well as on establishing an effective interpersonal milieu. First, teachers must understand that peers significantly influence and reinforce the attitudes and behavior of group members (Bronfenbrenner, 1970). Therefore, in establishing an instructional group, teachers and administrators must match students not only in terms of their knowledge and skill profiles but also in terms of their personal interactions. Certainly, placing a student who possesses superior skill in an instructional group with a student who is functioning at a lower level can facilitate the development of both. Because of the significant effects of peer modeling on learning as well as on behavior, teachers must discover the forces at work in the classroom and utilize those students who are most likely to be modeled. Realizing that peers exert a major influence on the learning of classmates, teachers must not ignore the effects of their own personality, temperament, and behavior. To maximize their effect on students, teachers must behave in ways that communicate their caring interest, their own excitement in the teaching/learning interaction, and their confidence that there will be a successful outcome.

More than a knowledge of subject matter is necessary. Creativity in providing stimulating experiences, vitality, a sense of humor, and a genuine respect for the student's value as a human being are equally essential. Teachers should always remember that feelings and attitudes may be communicated both verbally and nonverbally. In recognition of the effect of teacher communication on student confidence, interest, and progress, various formal procedures have been developed for analyzing the nature of these interactions. Formal techniques force teachers to consider what they are communicating besides knowledge and skills. Videotaping and audiotaping lessons and then analyzing them to determine whether a responsive and stimulating environment has been fostered are endeavors critical to diagnosing verbal and nonverbal interactions. Videotaping is superior to audiotaping because it allows for the analysis of nonverbal communication elements. Nonverbal communication is usually more powerful than verbal communication whenever gestures and other body language, facial expressions, or vocal tone and inflections contradict the verbal message (Valletutti, 1983).

The design of the instructional experience requires that attention be paid to the student's learning style, to the teacher's learning style and temperament, and to the interaction between the temperament of the teacher and students. It is the interaction between the temperaments of teacher and student that determines learning outcomes more heavily than does the temperament of either teacher or student in isolation. Because learning styles reflect basic personality patterns, consideration should be given to the student's attention span, distractibility, activity level, approach and withdrawal, adaptability, intensity of reaction, impulsivity and reflection, and field dependence and independence (Thomas and Chess, 1977; Thomas, Chess, and Birch, 1968). Once these analyses are complete, teachers must then examine the effects of their own temperament, personality, and perceptions of the teaching task on the behavior and learning of the students. For example, a low-intensity student may be frightened and overwhelmed by a high-intensity teacher.

MOTIVATING THE STUDENT: THE ART OF TEACHING

Once the teacher has visualized the sequence of instructional steps that are likely to achieve the desired learning outcome, he or she must imagine a motivating action or activity that will secure the attention, fire the imagination, and stimulate the interest of the student. Often, the wise choice of materials and approaches will be sufficiently motivating, as might the application of the appropriate reinforcers and reinforcement schedules. At other times, teachers must use an approach or some material that involves surprise, suspense, and novelty. For example, a new toy or book, a hidden treasure, or an unexpected event may be just the spark needed to stimulate learning. It is the motivating activity that epitomizes the art of teaching. A challenging opening to an emerging lesson often spells the difference between the success or failure of a well-designed instructional sequence. The importance of the motivating event is especially pertinent when teaching infants and other young children, particularly those youngsters who have experienced delays or restrictions in learning and development and those children with severe impairments.

ORGANIZING THE INSTRUCTIONAL SEQUENCE: THE SCIENCE OF TEACHING

The instructional procedures that define and describe the sequence of instruction arise out of the specific, short-term, instructional objectives being taught. Instructional procedures are teacher-oriented and describe the actions to be taken to facilitate the student's continuous progress toward the desired outcome. Each step must proceed logically from motivation through demonstrated acquisition, and any accomplishment must be measured by appropriate teacher-identified assessment procedures. Each instructional step should clearly state the proposed teaching behavior (e.g., demonstrating, explaining, assisting, or challenging) as well as imply the anticipated student response to the teaching act. Throughout, however, there must be a logical sequence of interactions based on the student's particular constellation of abilities and discrepancies, the nature of the educational task, and an awareness of developmental sequences. For example, when attempting to help a student use noun plurals correctly, it is appropriate to begin the instructional segment by providing the child hands-on experience involving the singularity versus the plurality of concrete objects; then continue the segment by describing that objective reality orally (e.g., car, cars; book, books; and spoon, spoons). Of course, all of the initial concrete objects should have maximum emotional content for the student, and all of the plurals should end either with the /s/ or /z/ phoneme. Based on the student's responses, each instructional step should then proceed to higher levels of performance if possible (e.g., perhaps dealing with words of less emotional intensity or proceeding to nouns that do not form their plural by the addition of the phonemes /s/ or /z/).

THE PHYSICAL ENVIRONMENT AND ITS IMPACT ON LEARNING

It is clear that the quality of the classroom's interpersonal interactions have the greatest impact on a student's learning and behavior, but teachers must not overlook the effects of the physical environment in their design of instructional experiences. Failure to recognize the effect of the physical surroundings on student behavior may result in a spurious interpretation of that behavior and, consequently, inappropriate programming (Smith, Neisworth, and Green, 1978).

Perhaps the most important factor in the student environment is the size of the classroom, which must ideally be considered on a square-foot-per-student basis in relationship to the size and amount of furniture and equipment housed therein. The absence of clear boundaries between activity areas and crowded conditions may lead to student distractibility, restlessness, and interference with classmates. On the other hand, large classrooms with too much empty space are likely to have a deleterious effect on hyperactive and behaviorally disordered children. Students who function better when there are limited boundaries are apt to become anxious and frightened when classroom space is overwhelming.

The selection of classroom furniture is another dimension to be considered in the engineering of the classroom environment. The selection of furniture that is both safe and comfortable must be supplemented by classroom floor plans that include alternative seating arrangements, learning stations, space for physical activities and movements, and space for display areas (Abeson and Blacklow, 1971).

Seating arrangements are yet another factor to be considered in organizing the instructional experience. The participation of students with hearing impairments may be affected by their positions in the classroom. Indeed, the child with language impairment is likely to withdraw further from active communication if he or she is seated at too great a distance from the teacher or from peers who are language and speech models. Perhaps, the best approach to the arrangement of seats is to modify the seating patterns based on the nature of the learning activity. A circular seating pattern is conducive to group discussion; clusters of chairs and desks are appropriate to small group activities; whereas the traditional separation of teacher from students is ideal for teacher explanation or demonstration.

In addition to considering class size, furniture type and size, and seating arrangements, teachers must consider the effects of external factors on the teaching/learning interaction. External factors that contribute to the classroom milieu include noise level; type and adequacy of ventilation; sufficiency of lighting; number and types of windows (and the view from them); the presence of carpeting; and the nature, type, and amount of wall colors, textures, and classroom decorations (Valletutti and Salpino, 1979).

Besides the physical environment of the classroom, teachers must examine the environment of the school as a whole. For example, students with physical handicaps may require handrails throughout the building and special toilet cubicles that accommodate wheelchairs. They may also require rebuses, arrows, and other easily read signs to assist them in finding their way around the school, including visits to the speech-language pathologist.

ORGANIZING THE INSTRUCTIONAL EXPERIENCE: FOLLOW-UP AND FOLLOW-THROUGH

Prior to the execution of the lesson plan, the teacher should identify a projected follow-up activity. This professional endeavor is meant to ensure that the instructional sequence is respected. A follow-up activity is specified because the behavioral objective for that day's lesson is a realistic one that is achievable within the lesson's time constraints. If the objective was not attainable, it should not have been expressed and may be a function either of inadequate diagnosis of the students strengths, of inadequate programming, or of some unanticipated or unexpected intrapersonal or interpersonal occurrence that could not be forseen.

Whatever the reason, if the student fails to attain the specified objective, then a new instructional plan must be written on an ad hoc basis to address the specific problems that arose during that learning experience. These ad hoc plans are remedial, not developmental, in nature and are, therefore, different in content and format. Otherwise, the follow-up activity is pursued, devoted to reinforcing the previously acquired behavior or to reinforcing a new one that logically arises from the preceding skill acquisition.

Attention should especially be directed to the follow-through process. Although follow-through deals in part with posttesting, it is primarily directed toward the carry-over process. This process involves all those significant caregivers in the student's life, including the child's parents or guardians. It is particularly critical to the all-important carry-over process in which skills acquired in the classroom or learning area are reinforced, practiced, and applied in pragmatic situations or settings. Therefore, part of the responsibility of the teacher working with young children who have language delay or impairment is to train other caregivers in providing their own instructional experiences. Parents, especially, must be shown how they can help their child practice skills as they interact with their child in the home and in the community. Parents must be helped to understand the nature of realistic goals, effective methods, and appropriate and motivating materials. They must understand the essence of behavior modification techniques, including the identification of reinforcers, the establishment of a reinforcement schedule, and the need for consistency. Parents must also be assisted in defining appropriate times and places to have their language lessons, understanding that pressure to perform can be as destructive as indifference.

CONCLUSION

Organizing the instructional experience initially involves a comprehensive evaluation of the student's current level of performance relevant to language acquisition, including the creation of a narrative portrait of the child that primarily describes the child's abilities: skills, knowledge, and concepts. Whenever discrepancies in performance are chronicled, they should ideally be written from the perspective of an ability (e.g., Although Marvin does not vocalize either the /t/ or the /n/ sound, he does place his tongue against the gum ridge [alveolar ridge] when he vocalizes the /d/ sound).

Subsequent to the evaluation process, annual goals and short-term instructional objectives are established to define *what* is to be taught. Then the teacher must decide *how* the student is to be taught, namely what materials to employ for instruction and reinforcement, what schedule of reinforcement to follow, and what subject matter to pursue. Next, the nature of the teacher-student interaction must be examined with particular attention to student and teacher personality and temperament variables. The creation of interesting, stimulating, and motivating lessons epitomizes the art of teaching, and the logical sequencing of teaching/learning events designed to assist the student in achieving the instructional objective at a previously determined mastery level exemplifies the science of teaching. The physical environment's impact on teaching/learning must always be considered because it is a key element in facilitating or inhibiting learning outcomes. Finally, follow-up and follow-through procedures must be established, with special consideration given to the role of parents in posttesting activities and in facilitating the carry-over of emerging language skills as the child functions in the home and in the life of the community.

REFERENCES

Abeson, A., and Blacklow, J. (Eds.). (1971). *Environmental design: New relevance for special education.* Arlington, VA: Council for Exceptional Children.

Bronfenbrenner, U. (1970). *Two worlds of childhood: U.S. and U.S.S.R.* New York: Russell Sage Foundation.

Federal Register. (1977). Education of handicapped children. Washington, DC: *Federal Register* (42) 42474–42518.

Smith, R. M., Neisworth, J. T., and Green, J. G. (1978). *Evaluating educational environments.* Columbus, OH: Merrill.

Thomas, A., and Chess, S. (1977). *Temperament and development.* New York: Brunner/Mazel.

Thomas, A., Chess, S., and Birch, H. (1968). *Temperament and behavior disorders in children.* New York: New York University Press.

Valletutti, P. (1983). The social and emotional problems of children with learning disabilities. *Learning Disabilities, 2,* 17–29.

Valletutti, P. J., and Bender, M. (1982). *Teaching interpersonal and community living skills.* Baltimore: University Park Press.

Valletutti, P. J., and Salpino, A. O. (1979). *Individualizing educational objectives and programs: A modular approach.* Baltimore: University Park Press.

CHAPTER 9

Stimulating Speech and Language Development of Infants and Other Young Children

MARY McKNIGHT-TAYLOR

The goals of language instruction for exceptional children parallel those for children who are developing at the expected rate of general skill acquisition. Special education instruction is designed to enable young children to interact purposefully and appropriately in various group situations as well as in one-to-one settings. All individuals, particularly young children, need to be able to acquire, store, and retrieve information; develop ideas; and identify thoughts and emotions. Further, they must be able to communicate information, ideas, and emotions in various ways. Children who have acquired this skill are able to demonstrate a wide range of options for communication, as well as being able to recognize what is appropriate and understandable to others and being able to select language that is appropriate to the situation and intelligible to others.

Speech is the result of a human need to connect with others or to respond to the persons or events in one's environment. Freeman (1977) described the importance of language and communication skills, In the discussion of the normal pattern of language acquisition, the following timetable was outlined.

Children learn to understand and speak the language of their culture; in fact by 3 years of age most children are able to engage in fairly sophisticated conversation. They appropriately produce a sufficient number of the sounds of their native language to be understood. They comprehend the sentences of other people and put words together in meaningful sentences. Considering the complexities involved in mastering these skills, it is amazing that most children accomplish the task at all, let alone in so brief a time. (p. 9)

ACQUISITION OF COMMUNICATION SKILLS BY CHILDREN WITH SPECIAL NEEDS

Children with special needs acquire and use language at a rate and level of proficiency much different from children without handicapping conditions. Children and handicapping conditions may be classified in many ways. One general dimension is development, in which group membership (the labels assigned) is based on the presence and level of intactness of the various systems existing in human beings. There may exist developmental delays, developmental disorders, or developmental disabilities. Each of these classifications includes adaptive behavior and the ability to communicate at least basic needs (Ehlers, Prothero, and Langone, 1982). A measure of the need for intensive intervention would be the type and severity of the handicapping condition or conditions that have been identified in the infants and young children assigned special services. The development of speech and communications skills is contingent on a mental and emotional level of competence that enables the individual to sequence thoughts and produce signals that are understood by an audience. Parts of this process may be crippled if it is impossible to receive information, store it, and analyze it. If experiential possibilities are limited from birth, or if they make no sense to the individual, neither receptive nor expressive exchanges are possible. An additional problem may exist if several organs are impaired or if severe emotional problems exist, disrupting or preventing the establishment of the relationships necessary for communication.

Intragroup verbal and nonverbal comunications depend on particular codes, which may be culturally derived. The language, or linguistic code, used may be oral or written. **Speech** is described as the oral delivery of phonetic units produced by the inner directed movements of the articulators (tongue, teeth, palate, lips, and jaw) and the vocal tract. It is primarily referred to as a mechanical process, even though it is linked to cognitive and affective factors. There is a rationale for separating speech training from language and communication activities, and this separation helps clarify the roles and jurisdictions of the speech, language, and hearing pathologist (SLP) and of the classroom teacher. Speech disorders may require intensive and prolonged intervention by SLPs. Language and communication problems may also require the service of speech personnel, especially for the development of diagnostic and prescriptive profiles. If the profile is normal, the classroom teacher has primary responsibility for planning and implementation; if abnormalities exist or pathology is present, primary responsibility rests with the SLP. However, activities designed to facilitate language and communication skills are the domain of the classroom teacher. In addition to the guidance of SLPs, teachers may use one other consultative source, namely, early childhood curriculum guides, including those that are not specific to language but deal with other content areas in early childhood.

RATIONALE FOR LANGUAGE STIMULATION ACTIVITIES

School activities, even if they are not specifically designated as language training, provide skill development in areas that are incidental to identified, content-specific objectives. Language stimulation activities are designed to increase auditory comprehension and expression. Activities are also geared toward increasing the scope of content and the quality of meaningful productons. The flexibility of young children in assuming the roles of speaker and listener is increased using these activities. Developing intelligibility of speech in children is an important consideration for classroom teachers because children who cannot make themselves understood soon cease trying. Feelings of frustration and inadequacy may lead either to withdrawal or to aggressive behavior. Articulation disorders may persist in children with no specific maturational problems up to the age of 7 or 8 (Arlt and Goodban, 1976). Problems in articulation may be classified as omissions, substitutions, or distortions of vowel or consonant sounds. Children exhibiting all of these error patterns may either have maturational delays, speak English as a second language, or be truly in need of speech therapy. To increase language proficiency, teachers must provide both incentive and opportunity for speaking. Because early childhood communication is largely postural, gestural, or motoric, teachers can build in activities that use these modes for interactions between themselves and the children.

When processing, weighing, and judging something new — when responding to the opposing pulls of curiosity and fear — toddlers sometimes merely stare at the object or person. In a structured language and communicative session, the focus is on creating an environment in which speech is encouraged and in which all attempts are rewarded. However, most children with maturational delays will profit from indirect speech-improvement techniques used by classroom teachers:

- Immediate correct modeling of the child's vocalization with emphasis on the misarticulated portion
- Positive statements of approval when speech is clear
- Acceptance of articulation errors that are developmentally linked and correctable through growth and positive practice
- Stimulation of oral language with continuous reinforcement

SPECIAL CONCERNS FOR LANGUAGE STIMULATION IN VARIOUS DISABILITY GROUPS

The complexities of language acquisition and communication proficiency become more apparent as one examines those problems that are likely to interfere with the ability of young children to act on and react to persons and things in their environment. Children with special needs will have their language and communication capabilities distorted in ways that reflect the level and type of disability with which they must cope. The child who is physically disabled may have a severe limitation in the amount of sensory information that is obtained. Certainly those children who are visually or hearing impaired will receive incomplete information upon which to base their actions and responses. Children who are intellectually impaired may not be able to adequately interpret incoming stimuli and may not be able to communicate their impressions, feelings, or analyses of incoming information. McLean (1974) urged caution in the interpretation of data related to the language performance and intellectual assessment of children with mental retardation, and he described the dilemma that exists when one attempts to make connections between language retardation and mental functioning. The following quote illustrates his view.

Because it is relatively easy to establish the correlative relationship between "mental retardation" and language retardation, it is also easy to establish a cause-and-effect relationship between the two, i.e., mental retardation causes language retardation. The problem is that the correlation can be easily reversed, i.e., if a child is retarded in language he is most apt to be labeled mentally retarded. While it is totally rational to assume that some degree of intellectual integrity is necessary to acquire language, it is not rational to assume that any child who has not acquired language must be mentally retarded. (p. 473)

Language and communication stimulation for children who are disturbed has several important goals. Disturbed emotional states often result in disorders in thinking, in memory, in communication, and in interpersonal relationships. Withdrawn as well as aggressive states have a significant impact on the development, the quality, and the direction of language and communication efforts of young children. Language codes for children generally reflect the ways in which they perceive their world. If their attempts at communication are rewarded, they will continue to work at learning. However, if their efforts are met by unresponsiveness, misunderstanding, or rejection they may cease to try.

In communication efforts, articulation and intelligibility are important factors. Speech that is unintelligible might be the result of physical limitation (inadequate breath control), inappropriate pitch or loudness, or problems in actual speech production. Unintelligibility may also be defined as a disparity between the intent of the speaker and the interpretation of the audience for which the message is intended.

A classroom teacher must be concerned about at least three basic aspects of communication, and teaching/learning activities should be directed toward the following:

- Acquisition of coherent speech and age-appropriate language

- Provision of opportunities to use language

- Stimulation of thoughts and emotions that will provide samples of children's communication style and language content

SPEECH AND LANGUAGE STIMULATION TECHNIQUES

Initial programming for infants and other young children is directed toward assessment and stimulation of auditory receptive abilities using both visual and auditory modes, methods, and material. A musical mobile, for example, revolves and makes familiar music or presents familiar scenes or objects. Early stimulation activities are designed to develop in children an awareness of sound in its varied forms. This awareness progresses to an appreciation of sound as a vehicle for communication and enjoyment. (In the following sections, activities are presented that stimulate first general and then more specific involvement with sound.)

Creative classroom teachers use their classes as springboards for exploration and manipulation of the visual, auditory, and aesthetic dimensions that are readily available to the children. Although a large budget for material is desirable, the innovative use of standard classroom equipment and materials usually results in increased student involvement in some form of communication.

Essential to the skillful use of available materials is the teacher's personality, temperament, and skill. The teacher's sense of excitement about and pleasure in language will be transmitted to students if sessions are structured so that the student joins with the teacher in the joy of communication. This excitement can reinforce the idea that the youngster's thoughts, feelings, and vocalizations are important. Teachers should monitor their own interactions with children so that they encourage all efforts to communicate. The likelihood then becomes greater that students will adopt the mode of interaction that is modeled and rewarded. Oral communication develops on seven levels:

1. Basic or presymbolic behavior (sensation)
2. Awareness of the presence of sound
3. Localization of sound
4. Differential response to sounds
5. Memory for sound patterns
6. Receptive language (comprehension)
7. Expression (language)

LEVEL 1 — SENSATION

Activities at this level are designed to help infants and toddlers develop an appreciation for sound as a pleasurable, interesting, and novel sensory component in the environment. The teacher is essentially concerned with stimulating children's awareness of sound and of the power that is inherent in their ability to create sound through their own action. Activities involving common objects in the environment permit varied experiences for the creation of sound. Teachers may choose from environmental sounds that are common in the child's home or school life (Table 9-1).

The following activities will help the teacher evaluate the infant's response to sound. The goal is to have the child look toward sound sources, reach for objects, or by facial expression, indicate that they have heard the sound.

- Clap hands. Say, "Look at me." Take the child's face and turn it toward you. Encourage the child to respond to your hand clap in some way, perhaps by clapping also. Reward any response that indicates an awareness of sound such as smiling, cooing, or reaching towards your hands.

- Activate a mobile or a musical merry-go-round that combines motion with sound. The child may respond in a manner that indicates an awareness of the sound the merry-go-round is producing.

- Sing to the child. The child may indicate that he or she has identified the source of the sound by touching the singer's lips, by babbling, by rocking, or by making any other motion or sound that seems to indicate hearing.

LEVEL 2: AWARENESS OF THE PRESENCE OF SOUND

Activities at this level are designed to make the child aware of sound, and they focus on establishing that children hear and attend to the presence of sound.

**Table 9–1. ENVIRONMENTAL SOUNDS COMMON
IN HOME AND SCHOOL LIFE**

KITCHEN

Mixing eggs with egg beaters

Mixing a malted in a blender

Washing fruit then eating it

Toaster popping up and clicking as it
is put down

Stove timer-buzzer going off and
clicking as it is turned off

Tearing aluminum foil or plastic wrap

Cracking nuts

Taking ice out of trays

Pouring milk or cereal into a bowl

Opening/shutting refrigerator door

Popping popcorn

Opening a can

BATHROOM

Using electric toothbrush

Flushing the toilet

Using hair dryer

Filling tub

Using manual toothbrush

Closing the door for privacy

Running shower

Gargling with mouthwash

LIVING ROOM

Clock chiming

Playing radio

Watching television

Using electric broom

Using vacuum

Air conditioning/heating unit running

Playing records, tapes, disc player

Humidifier humming

Electric fan whirring

PLAY AREA

Percussion instruments (triangle,
piano, xylophone, drums, cymbals)

Wind instruments (recorder, horns,
whistles, flute)

Push toys with sirens or wheels that
turn

Musical blocks and balls designed for
children with low vision

Hanging musical mobiles

Sound toys, such as Sesame Street
Music Box

Musical workbench with pegs and
hammer

Cash register

Pull toys

Dolls that cry/speak when activated
by pulling a string

See and Say talking toys

Squeeze-and-squeak toys

Sound blocks

Pop-up/pop-out toys

String instruments (guitar,
auto-harp)

Clocks, timers

Telephone

Musical busy box

Children demonstrate that they do hear by some action or response. Initial activities are designed to gain the child's attention. While calling the child's name, the teacher may create distinctive sounds with any sound maker for a single session. The teacher should not, however, use more than one sound maker in any session; otherwise, the session becomes an auditory discrimination session rather than an awareness lesson. For each sound, a response should be established; for instance, upon hearing rattling keys, the child goes to the door. In building associations, it is important to have the expected response related to the sound maker (as in the example just given). Sounds may be produced in the following ways.

- Ring a bell
- Strike a note on a xylophone
- Clap your hands
- Blow a whistle
- Tap on a table
- Strum a guitar
- Jangle keys
- Clang cymbals
- Play a note or a sequence of chords on the piano

All of the sounds listed have definite, clear beginnings and durations. The session with the student moves from silence to sound. Those sounds produced by the teacher are the cue for the student to respond in some way; any action is acceptable. Establish an upbeat, spontaneous climate by smiling and reaching out to the student. Working on a mat allows for easy contact and, at early stages, facilitates turning the child's head toward the source of the sound. If the child can sit up unaided, teachers should stand or sit in front of the student with the sound-producing object in view.

LEVEL 3 — LOCALIZATION OF SOUND

After the child has begun to respond to the presence of sound or has begun to relate various objects to the sounds they create, activities at Level 3 should then be pursued. These activities are designed to help the child locate the source of sounds whenever and wherever they occur. In these activities sound makers must be hidden from view and then moved from location to location. In the beginning, the child should be shown the sound-producing item. Later the sound should be produced out of view. Be careful that sound is not diminished by too great a distance nor muffled by being buried under materials that are too heavily cushioned. Use screens, open desks, a piece of cardboard, or a jacket pocket. It may be necessary to utilize an aide, parent, or other volunteer to make the sound from various positions in the room while the teacher makes certain that the child is facing away from the person making the sounds. The sound-making equipment and materials used in the activities suggested in Levels 1 and 2 should be used in Level 3 activities.

- Use noisemakers such as a bell or a horn in a teaching session. The child learns to identify the sound that is made and demonstrates localization by looking at the person who is making the sound. The teaching assistant takes the object and walks around, making the sound periodically from various parts of the room. The child turns to the part of the room from which the sound comes.

- Encourage children to look for the source of the sound. Hide an object under a brown paper bag. Hiding behind a screen is probably a good idea because of the danger that children may imitate by "hiding" under a dangerous cover, something too heavy, something made of plastic, or something in which they might become trapped.

- Show children the object (whistle, triangle) that is going to make the sound. Make the sound and then ask the children to close their eyes. Give the object to an assistant and ask him or her to produce the sound from a different part of the room.

LEVEL 4 — DIFFERENTIAL RESPONSE TO SOUNDS

Activities at this level focus on differential student responses to sounds. Acquisition of auditory discrimination skills can now be monitored because sounds that are already recognized in isolation are paired with sound-specific requirements. Sounds presented alternately require the child to respond in various ways contingent on the stimulus provided; for example, at the rattle of keys, the child goes to a locked cabinet or door. At this level the child associates incoming sound with specified responses.

The child hears then discriminates or identifies the sound as the one that requires a specified action. The key to the assessment of mastery is the teacher's observation of student response in terms of accuracy and speed. The teacher notes consistency of responses. When it is fairly certain that the child is beginning to discriminate grossly different sounds, teachers may change the stimulus sounds so that they are similar in nature.

Stimulus	Response of Child
Run a vacuum cleaner	Cleans the floor
Tap on table	Gets a plate of cookies
Strum a guitar/clap hands	Child stands/comes for a hug
Clang of a cymbal during a noisy nonconstructive activity	Stops and waits for instruction
Play notes on a piano when child is on task at a table-top activity	Stops and waits for instruction
Blow whistle	Child puts on police hat and badge and role-plays directing traffic

The idea is to get an appropriate response from children, especially when the response flows naturally from the stimulus being given.

LEVEL 5 — MEMORY FOR SOUND PATTERNS

Activities at this level are created to encourage memory for sound patterns. The same sounds used in Levels 1–4 should be used at this level because the child is now familiar with them and has demonstrated differential responses. The Level-5 activities differ from those in Levels 1–2 in that the child must do more than discriminate various sounds. The child must now produce them in the pattern presented. A sequence of receptive and expressive productions should be pursued. The first activities should involve immediate imitation of sound patterns followed by a delay in imitation, and if appropriate, finally by a delay in imitation with distractors being presented, such as competing visual or auditory stimuli.

Activities that combine motor activity with vocalization help children to attend to and respond to sound. Teaching may begin by reinforcing name syllables by tapping on a drum, or clapping hands. Call out the names while clapping; for example, *Ma ry* (two strong drum beats, taps, or hand claps), or *Jim* (one strong drum beat, tap, or hand clap), or *Sa rah Jane* or *Ter ry Ann* (three beats, taps, or claps). The same practice is fun when directions are given (*Come here*, or *Look, John*). Similarly, children may clap their responses to roll call with *I am here* when their names are called. *Susan is absent* could be the group response if a child were absent.

Two sets of stimuli can be used to teach a child to attend to a sound. Use an inflated balloon. Let air out of the balloon so that it caresses the child's cheek. The child is introduced to the name *balloon* and may respond to the hissing sound of air escaping (s-s-s). The child also is exposed to the vocabulary associated with the activity: *blow up, air, full, all gone, empty, pop, flat*. This one activity with the balloon can be used for lessons ranging from simply describing the colors, sizes, and shapes of the balloons to developing science concepts. Use the plastic bubble wrap that comes in fragile packages and pop the bubbles. Encourage the child to squeeze and pop the bubbles; this helps develop the pincer grasp and provides the child with the opportunity to be a producer of sound.

- Give children birthday-party noisemakers and encourage them to "talk" to each other. Model short, simple patterns of sound in a non-directed, spontaneous way at first. Then direct the patterns of sound: the teacher blows; the child listens. Then the teacher and child blow at the same time, almost a battle of sound. Then the child blows, creating a special pattern of sound for the teacher and other children to duplicate.

- Use a wooden mallet or hammer to create sound patterns. In Maryland, there is a "crableg cracker" that can be used to tap on various unbreakable, mar-proof surfaces. Items to be tapped include hard surfaces such as metal, plastic, wood (solid and hollow), various sizes of drums, xylophones, and metal gongs. Also include materials that make no sound or very little sound, for example, cotton balls, corkboard, sand in a dish, or foam blocks.

- Use a buzzer board to create patterns of sound: long/short, soft/loud. Combine sound patterns with cards that have the same series of sounds represented by dots and dashes. Begin with short patterns. Present more complex patterns as the child demonstrates the ability to identify and produce the pattern presented. The child listens to sound, repeats the sound patterns, points to the card that represents the sound pattern, creates a sound pattern, and draws the pattern correctly (representing by shape and color the length or loudness of the pattern).

LEVEL 6 — RECEPTIVE LANGUAGE COMPREHENSION

The following activities are designed to facilitate the child's understanding of the words and phrases spoken by others:

- Practice activities in which children are asked to respond differentially to their names. They stand or wave while saying hello or giving an assigned word.

- Include activities in which children must indicate comprehension of the names of classmates. Group the children in a circle and play a "Good morning" game in which the children look at the child whose name is called. Have another child give that child a toy while verbalizing the child's name and naming the toy.

- Observe the child as he or she functions in the school setting and discuss with the parents to determine favored objects, toys, and foods. Select one item from your list of high-intensity objects and begin to work on developing comprehension for the oral symbol. For example, if a favored toy is ball, join the child in playing with the ball (bouncing it, rolling it, throwing it, and catching it). While playing with it, keep repeating the word "ball" in an attempt to stimulate auditory comprehension. At some point say, "ball" and gesture "give me." If this is successful, gradually add other words from your individualized list to the child's comprehension vocabulary.

- Play a game of mechanical doll or robot in which you issue commands and the child performs them.

- Conduct a treasure hunt in which you give the child oral clues to the location of items hidden in the classroom.

- Place various examples of the same object in front of the child. Ask him or her to identify an object by a distinguishing characteristic (e.g. "Give me the big truck," "Point to the round bead," and "Show me the red car.").

- Show the child photographs of selected family members, and ask him or her to identify the individuals by their relationship and/or name as appropriate (e.g., "Where is Daddy?" "Show me the picture of your Mommy," "Point to Aunt Mabel," "Where is your brother, Joey?").

- Ask the child to place various objects in different locations in the classroom: "Put the book on the shelf," "Hang your coat in the closet," "Put the plate under the flowerpot," "Put the boxes of crayons next to the boxes of scissors."

LEVEL 7 — EXPRESSION (LANGUAGE)

Expressive speech is stimulated by using stuffed animals or dolls for dramatic play. Have each doll's voice represented by a musical instrument. Nursery rhymes and familiar stories such as *The Three Bears* have strongly differentiated characters, and their storylines reinforce the difference in voice quality — from the gruff, deep, Papa Bear voice to the mild, Mama Bear and the tiny, Baby Bear voice. Other stories that lend themselves to this activity are *The Three Billy Goats Gruff, The Three Little Pigs, Little Red Riding Hood,* and *Cinderella.*

Because the repetition and practice of expressive language is the primary goal, the musical instruments are used as background music for each part or to introduce the character, whereas the child fills in the actual dialogue. Use stories that have strong repetitious elements, in both language and events, stories such as the *Old Woman and Her Pig:* An old woman coming from the market with a newly purchased pig encounters all sorts of problems. In each instance she wants the animals she meets to perform their usual acts, as indicated in her lament, which grows longer with each obstacle encountered and with each animal she meets as she tries to get home. Another such story is the *Little Red Hen.* The Little Red Hen finds a kernel of wheat and asks the barnyard animals one by one to help her plant the wheat. None will help. In each instance, the story continues with the Little Red Hen saying she will do it. When the story ends, all of the animals want to share in the bread that the Little Red Hen has made from the kernel of wheat, but the Little Red Hen eats it herself because she has done all the work. *The Gingerbread Boy* is another story that has a sequence of events repeated as the gingerbread boy goes about the countryside — having run away from the little old man and the little old woman who made him and bragging that he can run away from others as well.

The goal of the following activities is to develop skills in expressive communication. Children will use appropriate gestures, both voice and body movements, to express feelings.

- In the mirror game, have the child register a series of feelings and emotions before you and before a mirror. Demonstrate facial and posture appearance for various emotions. Show pictures of situations in which the resulting emotion is fairly clear, for example, a birthday party with the birthday child opening a present, a child on the ground with a skinned knee and a band aid, or a child holding an empty cone and looking down at a melting ball of ice cream.

- Have the child show the following emotions: sadness, happiness, surprise, anger, and fear.

- Have the child arrange to peel-and-paste features on faces in response to stimulus words such as the emotions just listed.

- Ask the child to listen and repeat the following words, which describe sounds associated with feelings and emotions: moan, sob, groan, cry, whisper, sing, whimper, shout, sigh, growl, howl, laugh, whine, roar, and chuckle.

- Use story pictures with strong cause-and-effect scenes such as might be found in a magazine picture, a drawing, or Plate 22 from the primary level Peabody Kit (Dunn and Smith, 1965). For example, in one scene children are playing stickball on a city street, and the ball is heading directly for a store window. The teacher could ask the following questions about the picture: What is going to happen to the ball? to the window? How will the store owner feel? the children? the batter? the people shopping in the store? What will they say? What sound will we hear? shouts from the store owner? cheering as the ball is hit? groans as they see where the ball is going? the crack of the ball on the bat? the clatter of the bat dropping to the ground?

MacDonald (1984) described a concept called *conversational engineering,* which is a pragmatic and important contribution to any study of methods for facilitating language in infants and young children. The need for social competence highlights the importance of early parent-child interactions and of establishing a model for classroom strategies to display the skills required in conversation to attain proficiency in language and communication skills.

An important concept in MacDonald's discussion is what he called *Balance Turns.* He suggested that this strategy of give and take helps the child develop a sense of competence and an appreciation for what the other person involved in the conversation has to say. Such skills include taking turns, listening and (what MacDonald described as a critical skill for social success) waiting and reflecting on what has been said.

Increase opportunities for dramatic play. After a comprehensive review has been gained of the child's family make-up and the names of some friends outside of school have been obtained, act out scenes that the child suggests or that you introduce. In this way, the children are encouraged to talk about activities and interaction patterns that are common in his or her relationships. In this way, a great deal of information can be obtained about supervision and child-rearing practices. Teachers can gain insight into the communication styles with which the child is accustomed, and should they be negative or harsh, the teacher can establish new rules for talking that encourage and value the child's verbalizations. In building conversation skills, good listening habits are important. Dramatic play activities give teachers a chance to model good speaking and good listening skills. Teachers may present a story, choosing among various characters and scenes. They may use the child's own name and suggestions after beginning sessions with the story. For example, (Daddy; Aunt Thelma, Uncle Cliff, or Aunt Michelle; or Gram) *and* (child's name) *were sitting on a bench outside of the supermarket. They were waiting for a taxi to take them and their eight bags of groceries home. It was Monday evening. They always went shopping for groceries on Monday. It was payday for* (child's name)*'s big brother and for Daddy.*

One might set a scene for a visit to a friend's house. Scenes would include a discussion of the way they traveled to get there, who went, what they were wearing, what they ate, what they wore, what special good things happened or what trouble they had along the way. The child acts out the scene (the shopping trip or the visit) and creates the dialogue, for example, "May I have these? I like them a lot," or "Do we have enough (milk, potatoes, cereal or bread)?"

Create stories whose content emphasizes environmental sounds, common speech sounds, or words related to activities at school, at home, and in the community. The following are suggested topics:

playground
games
transportation (ways to travel — local neighborhood, city, state, national, or international)
health and safety
hospital or clinic
park
toys
foods

When creating stories, work together so that each child is supplying details about the characters and the dialogue among the characters. Use the child's name for the main character of the story. In a poem, use the child's name as the basis for rhyming, if possible. If the words created are nonsense words, be certain to point out the difference between real words and nonsense words. When constructing picture stories, create assorted characters, animals, birds, and people representing various ages, sexes, races, and professions. Establish vocabulary lists from which to plan each session's dialogue.

Create stories that highlight information and vocabulary associated with the senses, particularly sight, sound, and smell. For example, tell a story about Tammy's day. *It was morning; Tammy's eyes popped open. The first thing that Tammy saw was ...*

a big, round ball.
a bright orange goldfish swimming around in a glass bowl.
two red and white balloons.
a sunshiny, yellow raincoat with apple-red buttons.
a thick, blue book of Mother Goose rhymes.
a large, white, lacy snowflake floating past the window.

Teachers may choose to provide multiple examples of items that Tammy might see upon awakening. Provide things that are colorful and within children's experiences. Be sure to alternate story lines. For example: *It was morning. Tammy lay quietly, listening to sounds outside the window* (or around the house). *Tammy heard ...* Or tell about Nancy or Kenneth's day:

Nancy's/Kenneth's apartement/house was quiet.
Nancy/Kenneth was curled up tight as a ball.
Nancy's/Kenneth's eyelashes were so long and dark that they seemed wet.
They rested on her/his round, brown cheeks as she/he slept.

The sky grew lighter, going from inky black to grey to pale blue.
Nancy/Kenneth lay quietly, eyes closed, listening to the sounds in the
     apartment/house.
Nancy/Kenneth heard . . .

Sounds to explore in the stories created could include sounds from urban, suburban, or rural scenes.

the roar of the subway
sirens (police or fire)
clanging of firetrucks, trolley cable cars, buses
sanitation trucks
street sweepers
horns honking
rain/hail falling, tapping on the windows or roof
wind blowing, whistling, howling
birds singing, chirping or specific bird sounds: the caw of a crow, the
     hoot of an owl
dog scratching/barking to go out/come in
cat scratching/mewing to go out/come in
sound of the shower
whistle of the kettle
bell on the oven
alarm clock buzzer
music on the radio
TV newscaster
Mother/father/aunt/uncle/big brother/big sister knocking on sister's/brother's
     or child's own door

Schedule conversation times during the school day. Vary the size and com-
position of the group so that the child has practice in initiating and responding
to communications from peers and adults. Pretend "tea parties" or "visits" may
be staged so that the child is alternately host and guest. Sessions may be initially
structured by teachers offering special topics such as, "Tell me about your new
(sister/brother/pet/cat/puppy/goldfish/bird)." Teachers might ask questions
to stimulate conversation:

- Ask questions that help the child develop a full descriptive vocabulary
  ("How tall, big, large is [object]?" "What color are [his/her/its] eyes?"
  "When/where did you get [object]?")

- Ask questions that will help the child develop a vocabulary that will
  facilitate expression of feelings; for example, "When you first saw your
  puppy, how did you feel?" (Don't ask "Were you happy?"; that question can be answered with a yes or no.)

- Ask questions that call on the child's memory and ability to order
  events; for example, "What did you see on your way to school?" (If

conversaton is slow, or if the child gives limited responses, a few props
will help). "How many of the things in this picture did you see? Point to
those things. Tell us about your trip."

- Ask the child to differentiate between reality or truth and make-
believe. Read Dr. Seuss' *To Think That I Saw It On Mulberry Street*. Using a
flannel board or a magnetic board, have students retell the story, order
events, and tell what was real and what was make-believe. Introduce
the words *imaginary* and *imagine*. If a discussion of truth and falsehood
develops, be certain to include the fact that one can *imagine* things that
are *true* or possible as well as things that are untrue or impossible.

Help parents set a scene that encourages oral fluency in children. Help them
create an environment conducive to an easy flow of conversation in small
groups and in a one-on-one setting.

- Establish confidence and a feeling of security in the child by accepting
his or her thoughts and feelings regardless of articulation or syntactical
conformity. Help the child frame thoughts into grammatically or socially
acceptable terms. Repeat what the child says, substituting the correct
version, rather than interrupting children as they speak.

- Set aside time for talks — a special corner, over a snack, as chores are
done. Let the child know that you are listening and require the child to
listen to you. Reinforce good listening with verbal praise and hugs and
by telling others what a good talker or listener the child has become.

- Encourage other expressive activities that result from involvement in
art, block building, dramatic play, story poems, action songs, finger
plays, and puppetry.

Conversation times are important to the development of social skills.
Children learn to share ideas and to listen to what others say. An additional
reason for scheduling conversation times is to provide children with a structured setting for talking with classmates, teachers, and other adults in the
classroom. The following activities and materials can be used to stimulate conversation, spark curiosity, and provide pleasure.

- Manipulative experiences increase children's perceptual-motor capabilities. They also provide hands-on experience with concrete examples of shape, texture, size, weight, color, thickness, and other attributes
of things in the home or school environment.

- Include artistic, musical, and dramatic experiences in each day's activity. Include beautiful, aesthetic, and ethnically relevant objects in the
teaching sessions. Establish guidelines for touching and handling
objects, and provide cushioned surfaces for exploration of the objects.
Provide additional assistance by cooperatively holding the object with
the child.

- Establish and use descriptive vocabularies that include synonyms for over-used or readiness-level words. For example, instead of *big,* use the word *huge;* instead of *little,* use the word *tiny;* or instead of *nice,* use the word *wonderful.*

- Combine unusual textures in instructional materials such as sand, bark, seed pods, shells, and woods of various types, both rough and finished. Include color pictures showing scenes in various seasons at various times of the day. The day sky and the night sky, for instance, will have differential appeal and impact.

- Sharpen observational skills. Build vocabularies that include descriptors of change. List change agents. Describe the changes that result from specific change agents, for example, time (aging, growth, or differences in the environment as time passes from morning to noon to night), temperature (cold, snow, freezing, ice thawing, heat, cooking, the sun, radiator, furnace), abrasion (sandpaper, rain, sleet), sharp instruments (cutting, scraping, peeling), pounding (wind or physical force, hammering), air (fan — hand or electric, air conditioner).

Read aloud to children. Choose action poems, stories with a strong repetitive theme, stories with easily detected cause-and-effect themes, nursery rhymes, classic stories, and stories with main characters who have identified disabilities. It is important to include stories with culturally representative heros and heroines, urban themes, suburban themes, and multiethnic themes.

In the *Sounds of Home* (Teacher's Edition), authors Martin and Brogan (1972) show how episodes repeat one another. They call that kind of structure in a story a repetitive sequence. They combine various print types either with the meaning of the words or with the images they create. The story "What is Big?" is taken from *Sounds of Numbers:* a boy named Tommy compares himself with a goat, a horse, an elephant, a whale, and a dinosaur. Each time he does so, he says "(the animal) is bigger than I am." When he gets to the dinosaur, which is the largest creature, the familiar sentence structure is abandoned, and the typeface is greatly enlarged to say, "A dinosaur IS THE BIGGEST THING I KNOW" (p. 26). Children's voices and dramatic portrayals could reflect the small, large, big, and bigger theme of the story. Other ideas for experiences with books are as follows:

- Select three-dimensional books with manipulative or textured pages, cloth books, and pop-up books to keep the child's interest. A reference book that is particularly helpful and inexpensive is the *Read-Aloud Handbook* (Trelease, 1982).

- Use various questioning techniques. Divergent production is preferred to convergent production. Guilford's Structure of the Intellect (SI) (1968) suggests that cognitive processes are enhanced if children are provided with opportunities to give a wide range of responses. Questions should be used that call for many varied responses, each of which may be correct. Most classrooms use questions that require one right answer (convergent production: 2 + 2 = 4). The Fitzgerald Key (1966) questioning strategies help children think logically and choose the appropriate vocabulary to interpret oral or written material. Listening to teachers, children choose from vocabulary related to times (when), things (what), places (where), methods (how), and causes (why).

- Show that the child's remarks are valued. Retell some points that were shared by the child. Say, "Jamie said . . ." or "Jamie, tell the class what you thought about . . ." But make certain the child is willing to share the item. Share a letter that you write to another teacher (in which the children are praised for something they said or made). Help children choose options after they have explored possibilities for communicating thoughts and ideas. Let children know that it is desirable to use various forms for communicating.

CONCLUSION

The activities presented and the resources suggested were collected to help teachers plan and implement sound educational activities for beginning learners. The following goals for language and communication skill training may serve as a framework for planning activities and monitoring pupil progress:

- Develop a receptivity in young children to interactive situations
- Develop a recognition of and a response to spoken language
- Give children the tools for expressing their wants, needs, and thoughts
- Provide practice in, and develop skill in, extracting meaning from oral and gestural communication
- Provide an opportunity for creative expression
- Develop speech skills that ensure safety and survival of young children
- Develop language skills for participation in school, home, and community

Maintaining the link between home and school is an important part of language and communication training. Skilled teachers use the school materials as vehicles for maintaining the gains made both in school and at home. The curriculum materials used in the classroom for infants and toddlers with special needs should be used to train parents for follow-up activities at home.

Early, innovative intervention is important if young children are to become effective communicators. Children with a wide range of handicapping conditions can be helped to communicate at least basic needs, given systematic and creative practice. An overriding principle in language stimulation should be that language is a vehicle for connecting with others. The reciprocal nature of communication demands that young children be able to understand others as well as to make themselves understood. Improved skill in communication permits more elaborate and creative exchanges. Language stimulation activities are empowering activities; if successfully implemented, children are able to communicate in a number of ways.

The isolation that may result because of handicapping conditions may be lessened if children are able to communicate their thoughts, needs, and feelings to others. The song created in the PACER project captures the theme for language and communication efforts (Goldberg, Goldberg, Richardson, Nelson, Edmunds, and Bergenthal, 1981). The essence of the refrain used by the puppets and the children can be paraphrased as follows:

We may not all look alike,
We may not all talk alike,
We may not all walk alike,
But count me in.

When educational interventions push back or remove barriers for children with handicapping conditions, both the child and society benefit. Language stimulation activities draw on a variety of sources for content and teaching strategies. These activities involve the visual and performing arts, print and audio materials, toys and games, and everyday objects.

Language stimulation activities should combine receptive and expressive tasks that are based on multisensory experiments. Luria's (1961) work combined motor demands and vocalizations. Work by Fernald (1943) and Fitzgerald (1966) showed that young children generally profit from various combinations of sensory experiences, structural questioning techniques, and guided practice in interpreting and sharing their experiences.

REFERENCES

Arlt, A. B., and Goodban, M. T. (1976). A comparative study of articulation acquisition based on a study of 240 normals, aged 3 to 6. *Language, Speech and Hearing Services in Schools, 1,* 173–180.

Dr. Seuss. (1937). *To think that I saw it on Mulberry Street.* New York: Vanguard Press.

Dunn, L., and Smith, J. (1965). *Peabody Kit, Level #1.* Circle Pines, MN: American Guidance Service.

Ehlers, W. H., Prothero, J. C., and Langone, J. (1982). *Mental retardation and other developmental disabilities* (3rd ed.). Columbus, OH: Merrill.

Fernald, G. (1943). *Remedial techniques in the basic school subjects.* New York: McGraw-Hill.

Fitzgerald, E. (1966). *Straight language for the deaf.* Washington, DC: The Volta Bureau.

Freeman, G. G. (1977). *Speech and language services and the classroom teacher.* Minneapolis, MN: Bureau for the Education of the Handicapped, U.S. Department of Health, Education and Welfare.

Garcia, R. (1982). *Teaching in a pluralistic society: concepts, models, strategies.* New York: Harper and Row.

Goldberg, P. F., Goldberg, G., Leaf, R., Richardson, J., Nelson, L., Edmunds, P., and Berganthal, M. (1981). *Evaluation report for 1980–81, PACER Center, Inc., and a summary of years 1978-81 for the Parents Helping Parents program and the Count Me In project.* Minneapolis, MN: University of Minnesota.

Guilford, J. P. (1968). *Intelligence, creativity and their educational implications.* San Diego, CA: Robert R. Knapp.

Luria, A. R. (1961). *The role of speech in the regulation of normal and abnormal behavior.* USSR/New York: Moscow Academy of Pedagogical Sciences/Liveright Publishing Corporation.

MacDonald, J. D. (1984). Conversation engineering: A pragmatic approach to early social competence. *Educational Seminars in Speech and Language, 5*(3), 171–183.

Martin, B., and Brogan, P. (1972). *Sounds of the home.* New York: Holt, Rinehart, and Winston.

McLean, J. (1974). Language development and communication disorders. In N. G. Haring (Ed.), *Behavior of exceptional children: An introduction to special education.* Columbus, OH: Charles E. Merrill.

Trelease, J. (1982). *The read-aloud handbook.* New York: Penguin Books.

CHAPTER 10

Speech and Language Problems and Their Remediation

AUDREY SMITH HOFFNUNG

The initial part of this chapter details problems encountered by children with language impairment and children with learning disabilities in various areas of language (as judged by the comparison of these two groups and by contrasting them with children exhibiting normal language and achievement). Various methods have recently been proposed to stimulate and facilitate language development; therefore, the latter part of the chapter stresses the procedures that are appropriate for a classroom situation or for parental use.

To respond verbally, a child must be able to produce the sounds of the language, but before the child has achieved a fully developed sound system, the child has already used some words, phrases, and sentences in meaningful situations. These productions utilize words, the lexicon of the language, and their semantic relations (which are learned) based on the experiences of the child in the real world.

Researchers have presented many theories of semantic development: Cognitive Theory of Semantics (Olson, 1970), Semantic Feature Hypothesis (Clark, 1973), Dynamic Function (Nelson, 1974), and Prototypical Complex Hypothesis (Bowerman, 1978). Basically, it is important that children possess the cognition necessary to develop the word, to understand the meaning of the word (reference), and to recognize and comprehend the objects or events to which the word refers (referent) (Olson, 1970). It is also important that children have multiple and interactive experiences because semantics is not learned in isolation. The Relational Semantics Theory (Stockman and Vaughn–Cooke, 1986) primarily stresses that a child must acquire an underlying knowledge concerning semantic categories such as action (ride, draw), possession (mine, John's hat), and location, (there, here) before these words can be encoded or expressed. Speakers of standard and nonstandard dialects acquire this underlying semantic knowledge; it is only the surface or spoken forms that are different (Stockman and Vaughn–Cooke, 1986).

SEMANTICS

LEXICON

Bates (1976) suggests that words must be meaningful to the child if they are to be learned. Children do not just learn the words but learn how to do things with the words they have learned, continually refining and narrowing or broadening their definitions. A child may learn a word for a particular set of circumstances that may or may not correspond to conventional usage. An example of this phenomenon occurs when a mother looks out of a window on a particularly stormy day and comments that it is *brutal* outside. If her young daughter replies that it is not *hot*, the mother might see this as a failure in comprehension. In recalling her own previous uses of the word, however, the mother might remember that she had used *brutal* frequently to describe the previous *hot* and *humid* summer. Obviously, the earlier and frequent use established the meaning of "uncomfortable heat" for the word *brutal* in the young child's mind. On this stormy day, the child's definition of *brutal* was extended to "cold, nasty, stormy" weather, but still was not broad enough to include "cruel" or "ruthless" (Webster's, 1969).

Children need experiences to understand the words of their environment. If they are not able to explore the environment, then the environment must be brought to them by giving them items and objects to hold and to touch, by helping them to functionally manipulate the items, by taking the children to various places (e.g., bakery, supermarket, department store, zoo, pool, beach, park, and for a walk [or a ride] down the street), and by talking, talking, talking. Initially, the speaker must use small sentences, must use simple sentences, and must speak slowly while paraphrasing or saying the same idea using various words and constructions.

In their study of normally developing children and children with language impairment, Leonard and colleagues (1982) found that both groups comprehended more objects (nouns) than action words (verbs) and spontaneously used a greater number of object words than action words. Also, they did not produce the words that they had failed on the comprehension probes. Leonard and colleagues suggested that the development of object words relies on perception information, whereas the development of action words is related to the child's understanding of semantic relations; that is, agents perform actions, and someone or something is the recipient of the action (Fillmore, 1968). Both groups of children used a greater number of **in-phonology words,** words composed of sounds that are within the child's sound repertoire; that is, the child is able to produce these particular sounds. Conversely, the children produced fewer words if the words were composed of sounds they were not able to produce. Therefore, if a child could use /m/ and /b/ but not /k/ or /l/, the child might say *moo* for *cow* and *baa* for *lamb*. Ingram (1976) stated that children avoid using words that are beyond their phonological capabilities if they have not yet acquired fifty words. Once the fifty words have been acquired, however, the children demonstrate an increased willingness to attempt words that are not within their phonological production ability.

What children learn about the world depends on their conceptual level; that is, when they learn about the actual word meaning, they have developed the lexical level (one aspect of semantics), and when they learn about the combination of words in a sentence, they have learned about semantic relations (another level of semantics) (Nelson, 1978).

COGNITION: CATEGORY DEVELOPMENT

One aspect of cognitive development is the ability to build categories. It is hypothesized that children must develop a concept of categories as a precursor to the development of linguistic categories. To examine semantic organizations in young children, Nelson (1978) tested 17 children between the ages of 3.6 years (Mean = 3.5 years) and 4.6 years (Mean = 4.7 years) using two conditions. In the first condition, the child was asked to *Tell me what* x *is* or *Tell me what* x *means*. The question type was varied in the second condition, in which the child was asked to *Tell me all you know about* x. The children were questioned about five objects and the relationship of the objects to the superordinate categories of the objects (either a space or a time probe relating to the objects or a property of the objects and their function). For instance, two objects in the study were a tiger and an apple. The superordinate categories were *animal* and *fruit*, respectively; the space-time concept was (space) *zoo* for the tiger and (time) *lunch* for the apple; the property was *striped* for the tiger and *red* for the apple; and the function was *run* and *eat*, respectively (p. 52).

The children's ability to categorize and to tell what they knew about an item increased with age. Age difference was not significant for answering the *Tell me what* x *is* question. The children in the younger group (below 4.2 years) and the older group (above 4.2 years) used function responses more frequently for both types of questions.

Both category (e.g., animal) and object (e.g., tiger) words were responded to by function (e.g., runs, growls) but, when the question was *Tell me what* x *is* (e.g., animal, tiger), more examples or properties (e.g., tiger skin, tiger stripes) or other information considered more peripheral and not in the central core (e.g., lives in the jungle) were used than when the question was *Tell me what you know about* x. Children, 3 to 5 years of age, were found to be consistent in their basic meaning of words and in the use of function as the core of the category and object concept. Nelson believes the child has developed an internal structure concerning the word meaning with functional information given the most importance. It is the functional information that provides information about relations.

Children also gave more responses when given function terms as the stimuli. When stimulated with the function word *run*, the child answered as if asked with what (sneakers), where it was negative (you walk on the rug), or for an evaluation (It's a naughty thing because you run too fast) (p. 64). When given *eat* the child answered as if asked with what (fork), what (meat), when (lunch), or a negative (Hay you don't eat) (p. 64). Nelson believes that children respond to a function term with a wide variety of information that includes person, place, thing, and information based on what they have experienced or have been taught.

Nelson believes the child has experiences and then acquires the concept of the word (see Chapter 3). Object terms are learned first because they fill a greater need (e.g., dog versus animal). Category is different from an object term, though both category and object are defined in terms of function. For object terms (e.g., dog), a child first learns function (e.g., move), then properties (e.g., fur), and then parts (e.g., tail). For categorical terms (e.g., animal), the child learns function (e.g., move), then examples of items in that category (e.g., lion, cat), and only later properties (e.g., fur) and parts (e.g., whiskers). Nelson quotes deVos (1975) who wrote that the ability to categorize linguistically may be preceded by the ability to categorize by function, which is a vital factor for language development.

Children may separate the roles of people in their environment by function. Alison (CA 1.4) spent a week at her grandparent's home. When her parents returned, they hugged her, tossed her up in the air, and played with her. During this period she started to look at them and whine. Alison finally went to her grandmother, raised her arms asking to be picked up, pointed to the kitchen, and when in the kitchen, pointed to the refrigerator. Alison was hungry. Her whining had not been interpreted correctly by her excited parents. For this period, she had separated the people in her environment by function: those who played with her and those who fed her.

For intervention, it is important to remember that children are able to identify functions and objects from categories but are unable to supply categories from functions or objects. A child given the category name (animal, clothes) can give the function (run, wear) or the object (tiger, coat) but may not be able to go from object or item (tiger, coat) to category (animal, clothes). It is hypothesized that object, category, and function are at different semantic levels. Once the linkage has been established between them in both directions, the child can respond to *tiger* as animal and to *animal* as tiger. The use of the category level achieves semantic economy because the function (e.g., run, wear) would not have to be stated by the child if the category was given (e.g., animal, clothes) (Nelson, 1978).

The environment, or naturalistic setting, provides a vast opportunity for the development of the names of objects and their use in a meaningful setting. Adults should provide the name, in context, and supply the function when using the object in a particular way, for example, (object) knife, (general function) cutting, (more specific function) slicing or dicing. The use of category (silverware or utensils) is used at a much later date. Some categories (clothes) are more common or more frequently used than others (vehicle).

Initially, it is necessary to work with the item and its many functions in real-world situations, then through play, and later through books or pictures. When having a snack, talk about all possible ingestible items (e.g., juice, milk cookies, and crackers) and all relevant items in the environment (chair, bench, table) and ask, "Do you want a cookie?" (yes/no question) "What do you want to drink?" "What do you want to eat?" or "Where do you want to sit?" Later add items such as container, box, plate, and napkin, and ask, "Do you want to hold the container?" "Do you want to pour the milk?" "Who's going to help me pour the milk?" "Who's going to drink the juice?" The questions and statements must be appropriate to the physical, mental, and linguistic level of the child. Stress the nouns or the names of the items, and stress verbs or the function or action (e.g., eat, drink, hold, and pour). Give the child choices if possible by asking, "Which cookies do you want, the vanilla or chocolate?" (properties, attributes, or adjectives). Later, syntactically and semantically vary your questions depending on the level of the child. For example, you could ask: "Which glass (specific noun to which the child can refer) do you want, the red one (color adjective + empty noun) or the blue one (color adjective + empty noun)?" or "The one with stripes (empty noun, with the descriptive adjective that has a more subtle visual attribute, following the noun) or the one with the stars (again, an empty noun followed by a visual attribute)?" It will be easier for the child to develop concepts about what he or she has seen, touched, or moved.

Pictures and their relationships to objects are on a higher cognitive level. Perhaps match the object (chair or ball) to the picture (chair or ball) to be sure the child understands the picture. Present the child with a number of different kinds of balls mixed in with various toys, and ask the child to give you all the balls. When the child has finished, proceed to roll them, bounce them, throw them, and catch them. An activity such as this can be supported by all the major theories. The movement is the function, whereas selecting the balls and touching them provides the child with visual (perceptual) and kinesthetic feedback as to the roundness (shape) of the ball. Include the ball that is most frequently seen or used in the child's environment in order to provide the child with the best examplar, or prototype, of a ball. The child must be an active participant to develop the concept.

Phonological difficulties may create lexical development difficulties. If a child uses the Strategy of Homonymy (Drachman, 1975), in which the same CV syllable is used for five distinct referents (e.g., /ba/ for boy, boat, bottle, bye, and ball), and if the child remains at this stage for a long time without rectifying the final consonant deletion process (boat) or the weak syllable deletion process (baby), bottle), will the child have five separate words, or will this strategy limit the ability to add new words to his or her vocabulary (e.g., ball, bed, bike, bite)? If the child has difficulty inducing the underlying linguistic rules (e.g., sounds *t* for *k* [tote for coat] or *p* for *f* [pour for four]) or morpheme inflections (-ed), it is suggested that he or she will have a problem in reading and in spelling (Rourke, 1983). If the child has difficulty in lexical development, it will be evident in the following:

- Poor symbolic representation (Kamhi, 1981; Kamhi, Catts, Koenig, and Lewis, 1984)

- Slow development of words and low vocabulary scores (Rourke, 1983)

- Word-finding problems (Leonard, Nippold, Kail, and Hale, 1983)

- Rapid naming or word fluency (Wiig, Semel, and Nystrom, 1982; Denckla and Rudel, 1976a, 1976b)

- Poor building of categories

- Use of circumlocution (German, 1982; Temple, 1988)

- Lack of descriptive information about pictures

- Delay in color naming

- Problems in the development of antonyms

- Problems in the development of synonyms

If phonological and lexical problems are combined with syntactical difficulties, the child may have difficulty with the following:

- encoding novel referents (Meline, 1988)

- recalling ideas

- asking for more information when needed for clarification of the message

- recognizing the inadequacy of provided verbal cues

- completing open-ended sentences (German, 1982) that require the use of specific referents or category words

- understanding jokes

- maintaining cohesion when telling a narrative (Liles, 1985)

- reading

- spelling

Focal lesions of the left hemisphere of the brain are related to language disorders and to the associated phonetically inaccurate (PI) spelling errors among children with learning disabilities (Horn, O'Donnell, and Leicht, 1988); auditory processing and phonemic segmenting problems are related to an underlying language disorder (Rourke, 1983); and auditory-verbal short-term memory deficits that can be analyzed by poor performance on short-term memory tests such as the Auditory Sequential Memory Test of the ITPA (Kirk, McCarthy, and Kirk, 1968) as well as dysgraphia are associated with deep or central acquired dyslexia (Temple, 1988). These children produce lexical errors that are basically semantic errors when using a synonym (e.g., couch for sofa, soda for pop) or words that share some of the same semantic features but are not synonyms (e.g., chair for sofa, girl for woman). The following are other error categories listed for dyslexic children (Temple, 1988):

- visual (e.g., bag becomes bat)

- derivational (e.g., activity becomes active)

- function-word substitution (e.g., at becomes in)

- circumlocution (e.g., pal — He's my friend.) (p. 16)

- influence of initial letter (e.g., plate to playing) (p. 20)

The errors produced by the children were commonly or frequently used nouns and were words that were easily imagined. Rourke (1983) concluded that children with learning disabilities are a heterogeneous group. In a study of children with learning disabilities from 9–14 years of age (Rourke, Young and Flewelling, 1971), a pattern of errors was found that was not apparent in a group of 5–8-year-olds with learning disabilities (Rourke, Dietrich, and Young, 1973). This younger group, when compared to a normal group of children, presented attentional deficits or long latency times when responding to auditory and visual stimuli, which suggests some processing difficulties. These process-ing difficulties in younger children may be masked because of their hyperactiv-ity, distractibility, and disruptiveness. One of the older groups with learning disabilities, which was labeled as the high performance–low verbal group (in contrast to the low performance–high verbal group) was found to be poorer in verbal ability, auditory perceptual ability, speech-sound perception, auditory discrimination, phonemic learning, phonemic segmentation, word recognition, spelling, and problem solving. Other problems of children with learning dis-abilities include poor sentence memory, auditory closure, digit span backward, phonetic synthesis, verbal fluency, and the presence of phonetically inaccurate spelling errors. The children are poor in logical-grammatic ability (Wiig, 1986; Wiig and Semel, 1974), for example, comparative relationships (bigger than, smaller than), passive relationships, possessive and familial relationships (Bill's father's hat), spatial relationships, temporal relationships, exceptions (except for), and conditional (if/then); and they demonstrate poor development of rules and strategies for processing information. Rourke believes that dyslexic children deal with processing print in a manner qualitatively different from that of the normal reader. Analysis of these differences and awareness of their pres-ence is of major importance, especially analysis of the verbal, auditory-percep-tual, visual-spatial, and visual-perception problems. Sound and sight are im-portant relationships in reading.

The three-phase theory of the development of reading (Frith, 1985) empha-sized the relationship between sound and reading. Initially, the child reads by sight (logographic phase) but must then decode the letters or graphemes into the sounds or phonemes of the language (alphabetic phase). In the third phase (orthographic) the child is able to analyze the graphemes as units or words. If a child has difficulty reading, he or she may be arrested at any phase. It has been observed that without intervention, there is little reduction of the problems list-ed as the child gets older, rather the increasing difficulty of the scholastic pro-gram occasions increasing problems in reading and spelling.

Suggestions

Stimulate the reception of words. Use a basic vocabulary for classroom and home exercises or projects and then vary, elaborate, and extend the vocabulary; for example, *Draw the line. Draw the line straight. Make a straight line. Don't make it crooked.* or *Draw a little line, a short line. Make it long, make it longer.* Use new books, or old books in a new way, to stimulate new vocabulary and to reinforce the for-merly learned words. See the Chapter Appendix for suggestions.

Stimulate verbal recognition, speech-sound perception, and auditory dis-crimination. Start with a gross differentiation of words before going to a fine differentiation of words. Use words that are dissimilar in vision, sound, and cat-egory (e.g., *baby, chair, hat, apple*). Present easily identifiable pictures. Next, pre-sent pictures that are close in sound, and have the children point to the one that you say. Use pictures that can be easily understood from the drawing. Teach the children those words that are not yet in their vocabulary. The following are examples of words that are close in sound:

hot (sun blazing)	hat (vowel difference [vd])
hot	hit (boy, bat, ball) (vd)
hat	pat (boy patting dog) (initial consonant difference [icd])
bat	pat (icd)
bat	boat (vd)
bat	beet (vegetable) (vd)
	beat (beat the drum) (vd)
bead (show real bead)	beat (final consonant difference [fcd])
bead	feed (mother feeding child) (icd)
feed	feet (irregular plural) (fcd)

If you can draw the pictures, have the child select words verbally presented and have him or her paste your drawn or copied pictures in a notebook or put them in a toy mailbox. When working for short-term memory stimulation, have the child select two pictures and later three pictures. If the child can select them in order, it will stimulate his or her sequencing ability. If the child cannot paste them, have the child indicate (look, touch) the picture desired. Be sure to change the items; it is confusing and boring when the same items are used time and time again.

Play sound games in school, in the car, at lunch, and when going for a walk; for example, *What starts with /b/?* (bat, ball, book), *What starts with /t/?* (tie, top, table), *What rhymes with fat?* (cat, hat, mat, sat), *What rhymes with bit?* (hit, kit, mitt, lit). Add morphemes; for example, *I have two books* (plural), *hats, cups, shoes, watches; I am* (activity verb + ing) *jumping, hiking, swimming, running, eating;* or *I* (activity verb + ed) *jumped, hiked, hugged, painted, hunted.* Play with phonetic synthesis (putting words together). Start with two sounds (b - oy, u - p, b - ye). If successful, use three sounds (c - a - t, p - e - n, p - i - g). If the child just repeats the sounds, ask him to blend them together to form a word. Finally, stimulate word fluency; for example, *Quickly name all the colors, all the people in this class, all the animals,* or *all the jobs that people have.*

COGNITION AND LANGUAGE

Researchers have been trying to determine the relationship between cognition and language, specifically in children with language impairment. However, they have generally realized differing results and have arrived at differing conclusions, possibly because of differences in methodology (such as, age-range differences and linguistic-age differences) or possibly because the children with language impairment are not a homogeneous group. Terrell, Schwartz, Prelock, and Messick (1984) and Roth and Clark (1987) worked with children whose linguistic ages were matched for the experimental and control groups but whose chronological ages varied. Nelson, Kamhi, and Apel (1987) matched the control and experimental groups for chronological and mental age but not for linguistic age.

Terrell and colleagues (1984) studied children with linguistic impairment, CA 2.8–4.1 years, and children with normal language, CA 1.1–1.10 years, who were matched for linguistic age (but not for chronological age). The children in both groups produced 25–75 words and were at the one-word stage of language development. Using the Symbolic Play Test (Lowe and Costello, 1976), Terrell and colleagues found that the children with linguistic impairment who were at least one year older, were on a higher level of symbolic play than were the children in their linguistically matched control group who were at least one year younger. Children with learning impairments also demonstrated nonverbal cognitive abilities that were not expressed by them verbally, such as sweeping the floor and pretending that a doll cooked the food. The authors concluded that the children's responses demonstrated a knowledge of agent, action, and object concepts. Roth and Clark (1987) suggested that the children with normal language in the study by Terrell and colleagues had not completed Piaget's sensorimotor Stage 6 (18–24 months) (Muma, 1978 classification) in which symbolic development is said to emerge (see Chapter 3).

Roth and Clark (1987) conducted a similar study. The children with language impairment had a mean CA of 6.7, and the children with normal language had a mean CA of 2.9. Again there was a vast difference in age, but the mean length of utterance differed only slightly at 3.31 and 3.37, respectively; thus they were matched for linguistic age. In this instance both groups were beyond the sensorimotor period when symbolic development is said to occur. Roth and Clark's findings were opposed to Terrell and colleagues'. The children with language impairment (who were tested with the same Symbolic Play Test) scored significantly lower than the much younger children with normal language in symbolic play (when a doll had to be put to bed or fed); in adaptation (when flexible use of toys to suit their play situation was required); in integration (when it was necessary to structure their play activities around a basic idea or core); in their play behavior; and on a social participation test. The poor performance of the children with language impairment was not just at the linguistic level. The authors commented that they did not believe that all of these children belonged to the same homogeneous group; rather the differences in their behaviors during the testing suggested that subgroups existed within language impaired groups (Roth and Clark, 1987).

Nelson and colleagues (1987) studied children with and without language impairment who were matched for CA (ranging from 5.2 to 6.8 years) and for MA. The Columbia Mental Maturity Scale was used, a performance test of mental ability that requires the child to know color, size, and shape at age-appropriate levels. The researchers were interested in learning about another cognitive ability, that is, the hypothesis testing ability of the child with language impairment. For example, the children in the study were asked to solve a problem in which the correct solution for all twenty card pairs presented was the size *large*, regardless of the shape (square or circle). The correct answer was based on the hypothesis formed from examples and from feedback provided by the experimenter. After reviewing their findings and the literature, Nelson and colleagues concluded that the children with language impairment had limited resources, not only in encoding but in memory, storage, and capacity for processing verbal material. These children had difficulty in both verbal and nonverbal areas.

Rice (1983) commented that children with language impairment have more general representation problems and that language development is just one manifestation of a more basic underlying problem. Children with language impairment do not always succeed at the level of their CA-matched control group, their MA-matched control group, or their MLU-matched control group. If they do poorly in a problem-solving task, is it because they lack the language needed to figure out the problem, the concepts, and the representation that would enable them to think about an object that is not visible? To acquire the words, or the lexicon, of the language, it is necessary for the child to understand the environment and to understand the relations among the elements of the environment.

SEMANTIC RELATIONS

Semantic functions indicate how words are related to each other in a sentence. Fillmore (1968) wrote extensively concerning the semantic roles for particular noun phrases. These semantic roles are called **cases**. For example, the noun phrase (NP) *the man* in the sentence *The man opens the door* is considered the *agent* of the sentence, whereas the NP *the man* is considered the *experiencer* in the sentence *The man saw the house*. By definition, an **agent** is the instigator of the action, whereas an **experiencer** experiences something. This type of case grammar analysis relates nouns to verbs. Different verbs require different cases. The verb *to open* requires an object but does not require an agent (e.g., *open it*). The agent may be deleted in an imperative structure. Semantic roles may be used to analyze the verbal and nonverbal behavior of children.

Olswang and Carpenter (1982a) studied the development of three children, aged 11–22 months, for a one-year period and suggested that the development of the concept of agent had its roots in a preverbal sensorimotor period, specifically the sensorimotor Stage V (12–18 months) (Piaget, 1954). In Stage V, Piaget noted that Jacqueline (CA 1.0) had gained the notion of causality when she was able to make toy chickens move by touching the ball that was attached to them. She understood the existence of the relationship when she made the ball move, which in turn made the chickens move. This is an example of a nonverbal action acting out the concept of *agent*. At age 1.3, Jacqueline placed a box in her mother's hand to have her mother open it. At this point she had recognized that another person could act as *agent;* that is, a person other than herself could perform the action. In their study, Olswang and Carpenter (1982a) found that children progress from a single recipient (a child in their study pushed the train), to nondirective multiple recipient acts (the child touched the train and then looked at her mother and fussed until her mother reactivated the battery-driven train), to directive multiple recipient acts (the child touched her mother, then touched the train to try to turn the switch; then touched her mother again, and then pointed to the switch), to new-adult recipient acts (the child gave the toy to an adult who had not been part of the play situation and pointed to the switch), and to unobserved adult recipient acts (when the train stopped, the child found no one in the room to turn the switch, picked up the toy, brought it to her mother in a different room, and pointed to the switch). Olswang and Carpenter hypothesized that this type of nonverbal behavior precedes the use of verbal utterances to express the concept of *agent*.

Following these children as they developed verbal utterances, Olswang and Carpenter (1982b) found that vocalizations (consonant-vowel formations) accompanied directive multiple acts to direct adults' attention to the desired object or action, and they found that single words, in this instance *mommy*, were also used to express the role of possessor and location. As the children reached the 12–18-month level, they started to use two-word utterances to express agent and action, for example, *Mommy open*. They suggested that the verbal expressions used by children at this age were expressing the underlying concepts that they had developed in the preverbal stage.

Connell (1986) studied six children with language impairment, ranging in age from 2.8 to 3.2 years, who were at the one-word stage of language development. Their language development corresponded to children who were at least one year younger. The comprehension level of these children, judged by the Preschool Language Scale (Zimmerman, Steiner, and Evatt, 1969), was delayed by 7 to 12 months relative to their CA. Connell's goal was to teach the semantic relations of agent, the instigator of the action, and patient, the recipient of the action; for example, *A cat* (agent) *kissed a worm* (patient) (p. 367). These roles or relations have been found in the early two-word utterances of children (Brown, 1973). The pictures used as stimuli presented unusual or atypical situations to assure the researcher that no predetermined bias existed — that the child had no previous experience with or knowledge of that particular event. It has been found that if a situation is typical or expected, the child will ignore the atypical semantic role and respond to what is known. The objects selected could be used for either agent or patient; that is, the semantic roles could be reversed (e.g., *The worm* [now agent] *kissed the cat* [now patient]). To be included in this study, the children had to learn all the object and action words used. When initially tested, the children did not produce or comprehend any of the three-word stimulus noun-verb-noun sentences (e.g., *bunny push boy*).

The six children who had received production training learned to produce the agent-action-patient sentence and to use it meaningfully. Comprehension training did not help the three recipients learn to comprehend the semantic roles. The question raised was how children could learn to produce but not to comprehend structures similar to the ones produced. This differs from many studies that have found children can learn to comprehend without production practice (Winitz, 1973; Leonard et al., 1982; Schwartz and Leonard, 1985). A number of explanations were provided by the author to explain why this occurred: (1) The child may know the production and comprehension aspects of the semantic role, but the testing procedure was not valid. Children may be responding to what they perceive, or to the situational cues, and may be ignoring what they know about semantic roles. (2) Strategies for learning production and comprehension are different, and children may learn comprehension through production (Clark and Hecht, 1984). (3) By using certain strategies, the children appear to use semantic roles but do not really comprehend them. It is possible that the processes available to production and to comprehension are not equal (Chapman and Kohn, 1978).

Therefore, when working with the child, an adult may model or use the desired semantic role in conversation to achieve comprehension and production but should never take the expression of the stimulated role as evidence that the child has fully acquired the role, for the child may be producing what he has heard a hundred times in the same situation, and this production may be memorized. The child must be able to produce novel utterances (i.e., utterances of his or her own creation), must generalize, and must respond appropriately to a statement or suggestion made by the speaker. In a natural situation, the adult may model by noting, "Look, Johnny's painting," "See, the fish is swimming," "The gerbil's eating," or "The dog is panting." The child's novel utterances "Me painting," "Daddy swim," "Mommy eat cookie," suggest an acquisition of the semantic role of agent. A grammatical error is still present in the use of the object pronoun (me) instead of the subject pronoun (I). Children with language impairment experience difficulty when attempting to correct grammatical errors (Liles, Schulman, and Bartlett, 1977) such as syntactical agreement, lexical violations, and word order.

Suggestions

As stated in Chapter 4, the use of questions can help develop the semantic roles of agent (Who is doing something), locative (Where), and object (What the agent is acting on). If these roles are not developed, the child will have difficulty in simple syntax and, of course, in more complex constructions when wishing to express more abstract ideas or when wishing to combine two ideas in one sentence. The passive and relative clause are complex constructions that are difficult for many children with language impairment or learning disability (Wiig and Semel, 1973; Byrne, 1981).

Passive Construction. *Susan washed the shirt* is a simple declarative sentence in the past tense. The reverse of this sentence, *The shirt washed Susan* is semantically anomalous, or a meaningless sentence. The first sentence indicates that Susan is the agent and can be stimulated by using toy figures so that "the boy" (toy figure) paints the house, "the daddy" hits the nail, and "the girl" throws the ball.

Using the "probable event strategy" (deVilliers and deVilliers, 1978), many children analyze sentences using the first noun phrase in the sentence as the agent. To teach passive construction, have the child fill in the second noun phrase when asked, "The house was painted by *whom*?" or "*Who* painted the house?" Have the child point to the boy figure, say *the boy*, and do the action. Do this for a number of actions (e.g., "The nail was hit by *whom*? Who hit the nail?" "The ball was thrown by *whom*? Who threw the ball?"). This type of passive construction is easier than the reversible type (e.g., *The girl was pushed by the boy*) in which either noun phrase (*the girl* or *the boy*) could realistically do the pushing. Therefore, be sure the child has the concept of agent and object in the declarative sentence and can use a nonreversible passive construction before stimulating a passive sentence that is reversible. To be able to verbalize a complete passive sentence, the child must be able to use two noun phrases, must be able to permute them, must add an auxiliary form of *to be* in the appropriate tense (present, past) before the verb, and add *by* after the verb.

Relative Clause Construction. The relative clause construction consists of two declarative sentences in the deep structure and therefore has two ideas that are combined into one sentence. For example, *The girl is walking* and *The girl is my sister* are combined with the use of a relative pronoun and transformational rules into *The girl who is walking is my sister.* In this sentence, the identical noun phrase (*the girl*) is deleted, and the relative pronoun (*who*) is added. There are times when two distinct subjects occur in the same sentence, for example *The girl is my sister* and *The dog is biting.* When the second sentence is embedded into the first sentence, a new sentence (*The girl the dog is biting is my sister*) is formed. The child then has to be questioned as to who is doing the biting and who is the sister. This is not as difficult as an embedded sentence for which the roles are not distinct, as in the sentence *The girl the baby is hitting is my sister.* Again, ask, "Who is your sister?" (the girl) and "Who is doing the hitting?" (the baby). This is more difficult than the previous sentence because both the girl and the baby are capable of hitting and of being someone's sister.

DISCOURSE

Knowledge is acquired and information is transmitted through discourse, which is the major language medium (Roth, 1986). Dyads, or conversation, and narratives are two forms of discourse. Having acquired some ability to use words and semantic relations, the child must learn to use them to converse, that is, to respond to replies or statements given to his or her requestives, assertives, or responsives or to the requestives, assertives, and responsives of others. The adult working with the child may wish to encourage the child to produce additional responses so that a dyad or conversation can be developed. This aspect of communication depends on the child's development and integration of cognitive, social, and linguistic systems. Conversation depends on a number of skills, for example, the communicative intention of the child, the context in which this communication takes place, the organization of the discourse, and the child's presupposition ability, or the ability to recognize the information needed by the listener to understand the conversation (Spekman and Roth, 1982; Roth and Spekman, 1984). Organization of discourse and presupposition are discussed in this section; information concerning communicative intentions and context were discussed in Chapters 3 and 4.

ORGANIZATION OF DISCOURSE

The analysis of conversation can be divided into a number of areas: turn-taking, topic initiation, maintenance, termination, breakdown, and repair (Spekman and Roth, 1982). Turn-taking occurs when the listener makes a contingent response, or answers the speaker's utterance; for example, Question: "Do you want to play ball?" Contingent Response: "Uh-huh, . . . bat." The response indicated agreement with the suggestion and provided additional information that the bat was in the other room. A mother's request *Please sit down and eat your lunch* could bring a response from the child, *Pizza?*, which is a request for additional information, that is, is pizza being served for lunch. Or the response could be *Pizza!* to indicate to the other person present that pizza is being served for lunch. The one word *Pizza* stated strongly provided the new information needed. A strong intonation pattern, or tonic prominence, is used to carry new or contrasting information (Halliday and Hasan, 1976). The word *Pizza* alone, out of context, would not have provided the information that the child was having pizza for lunch, but taken in context (lunchtime, lunch table, food, mother's request), the listener had sufficient information to understand more than what the one-word utterance conveys in isolation. The listener understood that the child was not just labeling the item on the plate but was indicating that this was his lunch and he was going to eat it. The words *for lunch* were not expressed for a number of reasons: (1) possibly because the child thought the listener understood the situation, (2) probably because the word *lunch* was not in the child's expressive lexicon, and (3) probably because the child was not able to use the new information *Pizza* plus the prepositional phrase *for lunch*. For an adult, the use of the single word *Pizza* would be an elliptical item because other relevant information had been supplied to the listener moments before, and it did not have to be restated.

The adult can ask questions of the child (e.g., who, where, what [object], what [verb], why, when, how, how come) to continue any dialogue. To continue the "Pizza" dialogue, the adult could question the child: Question: "Do you like pizza?" Response: "Yes." Question: "What else do you like?" Question: "Are you going to have broccoli too?" Question: "How about a glass of milk?" Question: "Is daddy coming home for lunch?" Response: "No." Question: "Why isn't daddy coming home for lunch?" Response: "Work." Question: "Where does daddy work?" or "What does daddy do?" Of course, the last two questions have been asked many times, and the answers have been taught. In real-life situations, the child can be encouraged to continue or maintain the conversation. At other times, the child can be stimulated to initiate conversation, to introduce new topics, and when the time comes, to terminate or end the conversation. Teaching the child to clarify or to repair breakdowns in conversation is more complex.

There are instances when there is a breakdown in the conversation or when the verbalization is not understood. Young children will repeat the same word over and over again, possibly because they do not have additional words in their vocabulary or because they are not able to recognize the fact that additional information (e.g., shape, size, color, location, person) is needed to clarify the comment or request. Upon realization of the child's intention, the adult could model the ways in which altering the utterance would aid the listener's understanding. For example, one day Evan (CA 2.3 years) was displeased with the way he was being pushed on the swing and said, "(unintelligible word) + *swing*" and then used a gesture. The gesture provided the meaning. He was questioned by the agent of the action: "Should I push you from the back? Do you want me to stand in back of you? OK, not in front (with a negative movement of the head). You don't want me in front?" It is hoped that Evan will be able to use the preposition *back* or the negative + *front* ("no front") the next time the situation occurs. These spatial terms could be used at other times and in other situations to foster the development of spatial concepts combined with their corresponding linguistic counterparts.

At that time Evan was not able to repair the breakdown in communication. On the other hand, Alison, his (CA 5.6-year-old) sister, was able to repair her communication. One example of a breakdown is a misunderstanding based on her excited outpouring of information. In this instance, the use of the personal reference (Halliday and Hasan, 1976) was not specifically named or designated, requiring the listener to ask for clarification. Alison: " . . . and she said I could come for lunch." Response: "Who said?" Alison: "Lindsay said." Alison could also repair incorrect information provided to her, for example, Question: "How was your dance class yesterday?" Response: "I didn't go yesterday, I went the day before."

Suggestions

Playing a game such as *Candy Land* may help the child learn to use rules; to turn-take; and to develop number concepts (1 and 2), color concepts (red, blue, green, yellow, purple, orange), and a sequence concept (accompanied by the following words: You're first, You're next, I'm last, You're before me, I'm after you). These terms and concepts should be provided just a few at a time, for it would be difficult to learn them all in one sitting.

CONVERSATIONAL ACTS (REQUESTS AND RESPONSES)

Brinton and Fujiki (1982) studied the use of choice questions, product questions, and requests for clarification in six dyads (conversations) of 12 children, six with normal language, and six with language impairment, ages 5.6 to 6.0. The children with language impairment produced and answered significantly fewer choice questions (e.g., Do you want the ball or the train?), did not request clarification of the choice questions if there was a breakdown in communication, produced significantly fewer product or *Wh* questions (who, what, where, when), asked for clarification of requests three times less frequently than the children with normal language, and used more "unrelated" categories or opened new topics in response to requests for clarification. The problem could be related to an inability to interact in discourse or to a linguistic problem in which the development of words, sounds, and syntax of the language is delayed. This pattern of poor conversational skills can also be found in children with learning disabilities. Bryan, Donahue, Pearl, and Sturm (1981) set up a mock TV show for which the children with and without learning disabilities took turns as TV show host and TV show guest. Although the children with learning disabilities used the same amount of turn-taking as the children with normal achievements, they were not able to sustain the dominant speaker role or to direct the questions to the listener, and they used fewer process questions, compared to choice or product questions. Process questions ask for explanation (e.g., What about your last job?) as compared to requests for direct information using *Wh* interrogatives in product questions (e.g., What work did you do?). The authors felt the problems of the children with learning disabilities may be due to their poor linguistic ability, their strategy deficits, or their lower social status. Children with learning disabilities have been found to have (1) a linguistic difficulty, for example, in the recall of words (Denckla and Rudel, 1976; Rudel, Denckla, and Broman, 1981) and in the comprehension and production of syntactic and morphological structures (Wiig, 1986); (2) a strategy deficit that is separate from a linguistic problem because the product question (Where do you watch TV?) and the process question (Why do you watch TV?) are syntactically similar, but the answers requested by the process questions are not as predictable as are the answers of the product questions; and (3) a problem in maintaining the role of the dominant speaker because of a low social image. The children in the study by Bryan and colleagues were in second and fourth grade. Ervin–Tripp and Gordon (1986) studied children ages 4 to 8 years and found that 70 percent of them were able to assume the role of dominant speaker and were able to direct their partner's attention to specific aspects of the conversation. In conversation, the dominant partner uses more directives, more imperatives, and more "Let's" suggestions, whereas the subordinate partner asks permission (Corsaro, 1979; Mitchell–Kernan and Kernan, 1977). The levels of authority are recognized as young as 2 years of age. Ervin–Tripp and Gordon found that children of this age use more politeness markers, (e.g., Juice, please.) to adults than to children their own age, unless they want something from the other child and think they may not get it. The development of auxiliaries (*can, may*) at approximately 3 years of age assists in the development of more linguistically polite utterances. It is important that these linguistic skills be developed, but their use in pragmatic situations must be taught.

PRESUPPOSITION

Communication requires that the participants in a dialogue interpret more than the literal meaning of the sentence. The speaker and listener share a certain amount of information. It is obvious to a stranger listening to the conversation of two friends that the friends are gleaning more from the conversation than is the eavesdropping stranger. In the sentence, *She did go!* the speaker recognizes the listener's understanding of *she* because the person (referent) had been discussed the previous day. This shared information is presupposed by the speakers (Rees and Shulman, 1978). In this instance, presupposition is a cohesive relation of identity by reference (Halliday and Hasan, 1976). A child may not be cognizant of what or who the speaker knows and therefore does not provide linguistic cohesion to his or her statement. To help a child in one or the other or both of these areas, it is necessary to determine the child's use of pronouns, specifically, whether the pronouns are preceded by noun referents and whether the choice of pronouns is grammatically accurate (*He went* vs the incorrect *Him went, They eat* vs the incorrect *Them eat*). Training can be combined to stimulate development in each of these areas. To teach pronominalization, Connell (1987) suggested that the therapist discuss with a child a person (the boy, the girl) in the environment or in the stimulus (picture) presented, naming the boy or the girl in the first sentence produced and then referring to that person using the appropriate pronoun (he or she) in the second sentence. This type of presentation provides a contrast between the two sentences that will aid the child in building the abstract rule needed for the use of pronouns. This type of procedure can also be used to stimulate the concept of presupposition and linguistic comprehension by having the therapist or the adult who is with the child ask, "Who's he?" thus causing the child to refer to the original noun referent.

Suggestions

Use a picture book such as *No Place to Play* (Newman and Lockhart, 1969), in which one of the boys asks his friend whether he wants to see his baseball cards, suggesting, "We can play with them " (p. 8, underlining mine). Ask, "What will the boys play with?" Or when the boys talk about making a box into a clubhouse and say, "Let's see how big it is inside" (p. 24, underlining mine), ask, "How big is it?" Or when the boys decide to ask brother Bill if he will make a door for them and say, "Maybe he will help us" (p. 27, underlining mine), ask, "Who is he?" This type of approach can be used with any picture in which the characters and objects are easily discernible.

NARRATIVES

Conversation is one of the forms of discourse; narrative is another. For both conversation and narrative, the speaker needs an ability (Roth, 1986) (1) to state a purpose or reason for the communication, (2) to select information that is pertinent to the message, (3) to maintain an easy-to-follow and easily understood exchange of information with the listener or conversation partner, (4) to repair any breakdown in communication, and (5) to understand the communication from the listener's perspective so as to include the necessary and appropriate items. In addition, narration requires that the speaker (1) introduce the narration, (2) organize the events in their proper sequence, (3) carry on a monologue, and (4) provide the content and sufficient information so that the listener will be able to understand the totality of the message. The speaker should be able to use syntactic complexity and varied lexicon as well as being able to provide a unified whole, or cohesive, text.

Comprehension

The gist recall paradigm has been used to evaluate children's comprehension of the narrative (Roth, 1986). The gist recall paradigm is based on constructive memory when children are to remember the content of the story that was told or read to them. The recall protocols are analyzed for the accuracy of the information recalled, the importance or saliency of the categories of the story recalled, and the accuracy of the temporal order of the story categories recalled. From her analysis of the literature concerning children with learning disabilities, Roth drew the conclusion that these children recall less information and draw fewer inferences from the stories told to them than do children with normal achievement.

Liles (1985) presented a film (visual and auditory stimuli) to 20 children with language impairment and to 20 children with normal language (age range 7.6 to 10.6 years), and she analyzed the comprehension and expressive abilities of these children relative to the film. She found no significant difference between the responses of the children with language impairment and those of the children with normal language when presented factual questions about the story (Can you tell me who some of the people were in the movie? Which of the boys were brothers?) (p. 131). But there were significant differences in responses to questions measuring story grammar knowledge. These questions were based on the story grammar categories of Stein and Glenn (1979). Rule 2 of Stein and Glenn stipulates that the story characters be introduced in the setting category of the story. Liles used two questions to tap the children's setting story grammar category knowledge, e.g., "Was Super Duper strong? How do you know?" (p. 131). The first part of the story grammar knowledge question is a yes/no question; the second part is a process question. There were many more process questions included in the story grammar knowledge questions than were included in the factual questions. Many of the process questions required that inferences be formed from the information presented in the film, for example, "Why did the boys decide not to tell their friends what happened that day?" (p. 131). Johnson (1982) found language comprehension difficulties that might have affected the story-telling ability of the 9.6-year-old girl (K) who had language impairment. Johnson stressed the importance of discovering which aspects of comprehension are poor, for example, attention, perception, or inference.

The question must be asked, do comprehension difficulties occur because the children's delayed or deviant language ability does not provide them with the necessary tools to hold information, contrast information, or think about information? Auditory memory may be poor, and language is fleeting, so underdeveloped symbolization may occur. Snyder (1984) suggested that the "visual perceptual deficits" alluded to by Strauss and Lehtinen (1974) could also be indicative of an underlying representational and perhaps sequential and analytic deficit. Other researchers found variable differences in the language impaired group. Some children could create a concept (Kamhi, 1981; Kamhi, Catts, Koenig, and Lewis, 1984), but others scored low in all areas of concept formation and still poorer on the Haptic Recognition Test, for which the children had to use touch to select items with similar curves. It is suggested that this task requires nonlinguistic symbolic skills and that "symbolic image plays a role in the development of spatial relations" (Kamhi, 1981). The children with language impairment offered unique responses or used response strategies different from those used by the normal MA-matched group. This suggests that, although the language impaired group was matched for mental age (on the Leiter Performance Scale, a nonlinguistic test [Arthur, 1952]) to a normal group, there were still delays in some specific areas of conceptual development; yet it is not believed that these differences are sufficient to explain linguistic deficiencies. The question remains as to whether linguistic deficiencies cause delays in cognitive development or whether it is cognitive ability that shapes linguistic ability (Ellis Weismer, 1985). How much does what we learn or what we are capable of abstracting depend on language? Cognition is necessary but may not be sufficient for linguistic development (Cromer, 1974).

Production

Johnson (1982) suggested that four perspectives be used in the analysis of the narrative: story grammar, script, text, and communication act. The **story grammar** perspective is based on Stein and Glenn's categorization. The **script** perspective concerns content or the speaker's or listener's real-life experience with a particular situation and the sequence of expected events that occur in that particular situation, for example, a dinnertime script in which the child would expect certain behaviors to take place. The **text** refers to the linguistic expression that must be used in narration to link sentences together to build cohesion. An example of this is anaphoric reference, or the use of a pronoun (it, she) to refer to a previously specified object or person (pen, girl). The telling of a narrative requires that a cohesive, meaningful unit be built. The last of the four perspectives, the **communication act,** refers to the need to provide the listener with the relevant information necessary to understand the story.

The 9.6-year-old child (K) (Johnson, 1982), with obvious and limited syntactic expressive ability, did not give the quantity of elaborative information usually provided by children of her age and, in addition, used two items of information that were out of temporal sequence. (K) gave a single episode and established no main character, no clear problem, no attempt, no result, and no reaction. The fifth graders of Stein and Glenn (1979) produced stories with one or more episodes and at times included episodes embedded in the main episodes. (K) did show evidence of the use of script. The story was about the hatching of an egg and (K) lives on a farm. But she used reduced linguistic expression to tie the story together, utilizing only the conjunction *and* before each sentence. (K) also seemed not to recognize the needs of her listeners. Again, the question must be asked whether what appeared to be her underestimation of the needs of the listener could be based in her linguistic expression and comprehension difficulties.

Is it linguistics or cognition that limits the children's use of inferences and that limits their ability to infer information beyond what is specifically stated in the message (Clark and Haviland, 1977)? Ellis Weismer (1985) found that second grade children with language impairment used fewer spatial and causal inferences than did their same-age group (matched for nonverbal ability) and their group matched for language equivalence (which was two years younger). The children were asked to answer yes/no questions regarding the verbal stories or picture stories presented to them. The tasks required the children to infer information that was not specifically stated in the verbal story or the picture story. Ellis Weismer suggested that the children were deficient in mental representation ability rather than verbal mediation ability and that their deficiency in mental representation hindered their ability to abstract and to integrate material.

In Liles' study (1985), a film was shown to children with and without language impairment. Under one condition, an adult did not share the movie with the children; under the second condition, an adult participated in the viewing of the film. It was found that both the children with and the children without language impairment provided more information, gave more personal references, and gave more cohesive ties to the adult listener who did not share the movie with them. The subjects in Liles' study had language impairment, but their problems were not as severe as (K)'s (Johnson, 1982). Liles screened out the children who could not produce grammatically adequate sentences and who would not be able to produce a sufficient number of sentences.

Roth and Spekman (1986) reported that children with learning disabilities have problems in narration in the absence of structural language problems. Their study focused on the narrative ability of 48 children with learning disabilities, ages 8–13.11, who exhibited normal structural language, and they were matched with 48 normally achieving children. The children with learning disabilities omitted more of the middle of the story, more of the planning actions, and more of the attitudes. They gave less linkage between episodes, used fewer minor settings, employed fewer complete episodes (children of 5 and 6 years are able to narrate a complete episode), provided less information, and used less inference, causing the listener to make inferences, sometimes erroneously, concerning the material presented. Roth and Spekman hypothesized that though the children with learning disabilities had an intact knowledge of the story structure, they had difficulty expressing this knowledge because they were not able to realize the perspective of the listener and had problems using cohesive techniques and complete syntax.

Suggestions

Children can be stimulated to make inferences. Using a popular storybook such as *The Three Little Pigs,* the children can be proffered questions so that they will have to infer, guess, or suggest what will happen next. For example,

The first pig meets a man and asks him for some straw to build a house.

Question: "Why did he want the straw?"

Answer: To build a house."

The pig builds his house, and the wolf comes by. He wants to be let in.

Question: "Who wants to be let in?"

Answer: "The wolf."

Question: "Why does he want to go in?"

Answer depends on inference based on previous experience with animals (books, zoo).

Question: "Would you let him in?"

Answer depends on reason, decision.

The wolf blew the house in.

Question: "What did the pig do?"

Answer: "Run away."

Question: "Why ?"

Answer depends on reason, inference.

METHODS

A variety of methods for intervention have been espoused in the literature, each supporting a slightly different approach in an attempt to realize the same goal: effective, lucid communication. Some methods stress trainer, teacher, or adult (significant other) dominance; others stress child initiation of the activity; and some stress teaching function in a naturalistic setting (indirect approach), whereas others include the more traditional (direct) structure. It is the responsibility of the significant others (SO) to choose the approach (or parts of a number of approaches, a more eclectic method) that they believe would most benefit the particular population under their guidance. It is possible that an indirect approach would be sufficient for some children, but for others, a more direct and structured procedure must accompany the naturalistic approach.

The reader should carefully analyze the research projects reported in the literature, not only for the results and the interpretation of the results, but for the choice of goals, stimuli, and methods used for intervention. There is still controversy in the literature concerning the value of various intervention procedures because of the variability of populations, stimuli, and the methods selected by the various researchers. Some researchers are interested in the generalization of the specific items that have been taught, whereas others are interested in the overall language improvement that is judged many times by comparisons of pretest and posttest scores on standardized tests. Tests do not always cue the researcher to subtle changes in behavior such as latency, speed of response, or reduction in the number of emotional outbursts.

Before intervention, the children must be tested to ascertain their level of functioning. A complete analysis should be undertaken so that development in all verbal areas and specific nonverbal areas will be noted. It is important that the speech-language pathologist who is familiar with and aware of children's hierarchical development, especially in the areas of cognition, speech, and language (content, structure, and function), be responsible for the program. Setting goals that are beyond the abilities of children with language impairment or with learning disabilities, or even setting goals beyond the abilities of a normally developing child at that period of development, leads to failure and frustration. The children with language impairment in Warren and Kaiser's study (1986a) had difficulty generalizing structures taught in a free-play situation. The researchers wisely raised questions concerning the functional use of the structures taught in a therapy room to a free-play situation; that is, though the children had been taught the use of subject noun in a sentence in a therapy room, it was not carried over to a play situation. Children in a play situation might delete the subject and verb of a sentence and request "Ball" (with or without a gesture), or delete the subject and demand, "Get train." The average person does the same thing saying, "Another fork please," when setting the table, or "Push the chair in," when straightening the room after dinner. Additional research into the use of particular structures by children with normal language in various settings and by people of various authority levels is needed to set the standards against which the children with language impairment or learning disabilities can be evaluated.

Suggestions

Have the child tell you a story with a number of different characters: a man, a dog, and a boy. If the characters are of the same category, the child must use finer skills to differentiate them. For instance, if the child is capable of differentiating four legged creatures, use a dog, a cat, and a horse. If the child knows colors and if you want to add differentiating adjectives, use a brown dog, a black dog, and a white dog as characters. Further differentiation might require the use of two adjectives, the big brown dog, and the little brown dog. If the child describes the picture by saying, "Ran," ask, "Who ran?"; all of the mentioned characters are capable of running, therefore the statement needs clarification. Accept *dog ran* if the child does not use three morphemes or does not use an article. Accept *He ran*, even though the pronoun *it* should be used to relate to an animal; most people use *he* or *she* when describing their pet's actions anyway.

NATURALISTIC METHOD

A new method of naturalistic teaching has been suggested as a procedure that can be used by parents, teachers, and members of the staff in institutional settings to teach functional language. The purpose is to increase language communication, verbal and nonverbal language skills, initiation of conversation, and participation in conversation interaction. This method has been used in a number of settings by a number of researchers, but substantiation of its long-term effects must still be documented by experimental studies. These studies are needed to substantiate the belief that this method provides strategies that help increase the use of forms (e.g., the sounds of the language, the morphemes or words, and the words plus inflections); the ability to use words of different categories, such as adjective, noun, or verb; and the application of correct sequences of words. In addition, generalization of these forms should occur with various words used in various combinations, and expansion of the use of form and content should extend to a variety of social situations and to a variety of people. The words should be used flexibly to express different functions: to inform (*It's raining,* or merely *Raining*), to negate (*Not here*), to affirm (*Tom's coat,* after someone stated that the coat belonged to Tom), or to question (*What's that*). Children usually improve language skills with age once a generalization of learned structures occurs. If one can foster accelerated generalization so that the child learns more rapidly than he has at previous stages, if utilization of language increases in frequency and spreads to broader areas, then one may be observing generalization because of strategies that have been learned by the child (Warren and Kaiser, 1986a). Warren and Kaiser (1986b) described one naturalistic teaching method, namely, incidental teaching, or incidental language teaching (ILT).

INCIDENTAL LANGUAGE TEACHING

Incidental language teaching was introduced as a viable method for stimulating initiation of language in a child (for the special education teacher, the parent, or the institutional staff members) because the stimulus decided upon can be presented a number of times a day in various naturalistic situations. The sessions are brief and require no rigid structure. When introduced, the stimulus can provide positive interaction between the child and caretaker because the caretaker will give the child the item desired. The child will have greater self-motivation to request the object, toy, or eatable desired if the child knows the object is directly within his grasp. It is necessary to ascertain which item(s) would be best suited to the child. With the help of the speech-language pathologist the teacher may decide what language target is sought and what language production or communicative action will be accepted. If it is determined that the child must request a toy before it is given to him, the toys are put on a shelf out of reach of the child, so that the child can look at the toy, point to the toy, or grunt for the toy. Prior to the lesson, the teacher and the SLP make a decision about the type of communication that will be accepted from the child before the toy is given to the child. Will pointing be sufficient? Must some vocalization or sound be produced? Will the child have to approximate the word with a CV formation, 'ba' for *ball* or 'ta' for *truck*. When the child produces the desired response, the child gets the toy, object, or other item desired. This item is now the contingent reinforcer, as it would be in a natural situation. The item is given contingent on the verbal or nonverbal request of the child. The child may respond to the teacher's question *What do you want?* which may be repeated many times, if necessary, to obtain the desired response *car*. In this case, the child would demonstrate comprehension of the auditory stimulus. The teacher may provide a questioning look if the child responds nonverbally and points, may repeat the question *What do you want?* again, and may model what the child is expected to say: *car, want car, red car, big car, want big red car.*

Various pragmatic acts require various competencies. Requesting is different from commanding, from questioning, and from holding a conversation. How should the skills necessary for each communicative intention be facilitated? In commenting, for instance, it is known that, when we perform a task or work on a project, we have a tendency to talk to ourselves or to talk to others about what we are doing. Encouraging a child to do this when performing an activity might help in vocabulary building, task analysis, and sequential ordering.

Suggestions

When a child is getting ready to paint, the child (1) might be asked what is needed for the activity; (2) would be encouraged to express the need for paint, a brush, water, paper, and a smock; (3) would be encouraged to state what is needed first (a smock), second (paint), third (a brush), and fourth (some paper); (4) would be asked what he or she is going to paint (a house, a tree, the sun [outside], a table, a chair, a window [inside], mommy, daddy, sister [family]); (5) would be provided with information about letting the picture dry; and (6) would be questioned about what he or she would like to do with the picture when it is finished. For example, multiple choices should be provided if no expressive language is forthcoming; the choices might be *Take it home, Give it to mommy, Hang it up, Leave it in school.* This type of task analysis helps the child sequence events (realize the order of events that occur when carrying out an activity and recognize a time differential; that is, this comes first in time, this is next, and this is last). The child will also realize that it takes time for something to dry. The child is learning cognitive strategies and how to verbalize them in concrete and meaningful ways. The adult continually monitors the adult-child interaction to discover the cause of the breakdown in communication. Do these breakdowns occur because the child lacks (1) an understanding of the event, (2) the vocabulary to encode his or her understanding of the event, (3) the syntactic structures necessary to combine words, (4) the desire to communicate, or (5) the intelligibility that enables the adult to interpret the child's message accurately? Recording the sesson on tape; taking notes on context, gesture, and body communication; and analyzing the recording will help determine the problem areas in need of attention. If the error response was not recognized during the initial session, the therapist and the teacher can plan activities in which the situation may occur again, thus providing a second opportunity to provide a stimulus, to model the correct response, and to determine the child's understanding of the situation events (scripts) so that the confusion can be corrected.

SENSEMAKING AND FINE TUNING

It is important that an adult judge the "sensemaking" (Duchan, 1986) of a child's communication. Children perceive an event in a certain manner and understand what makes up an event and what will happen. The adult must try to understand the child's perception of the event and the child's communication of the event; in other words, the adult must "fine tune" (Duchan, 1986) to the event. Duchan believes that when working to stimulate language, it is essential that the language be worked on in a context-oriented situation, one in which the event and its parts are understood and represented and in which the child's intentions are communicated. This is particularly suited for home, school, and institution intervention.

This type of context-oriented stimulation and intervention can be pragmatically interwoven with the everyday school activities of the child with language impairment or learning disabilities. For example, it can evolve around an eating experience that occurred at home by using dolls from the doll corner, and it can evolve from role-playing (mother, child, father, or sibling) by using as many or as few characters as deemed necessary or appropriate. A target goal should be set up so that there is some direction, even in a loosely structured session. The setting of goals (Connell, 1987; Craig, 1983; MacDonald and Blott, 1974) is an extremely important factor in language intervention and in focused language stimulation. The areas of functional use of language can be stimulated by the adult significant other in the child's environment. An adult-child dyad, or conversation, is encouraged when the child or the adult SO initiates the dialogue and when the adult SO models the new vocabulary words required for an eating event. These vocabulary words will vary depending on the level of the child and the needs or uses in the child's culture. Rice (1986) stresses the need for the person working with the child to recognize that a difference may exist between that person's culture and the child's culture so that the linguistic, the interpersonal, and the cultural aspects required for communicative competence are acknowledged. The vocabulary provided by the adult SO may at first consist of the names of items to be eaten (vegetables, meats, dairy products, or some specialties from the child's ethnic background), may then consist of vocabulary for needed actions (I want, Please pass the), and may proceed to a more advanced level at which a different event can be discussed while this event is taking place. In a natural dinner setting, parents might discuss the day's work, the child's activities of the day, or some local or world situation. In a school setting, activity such as this would be presented during the eating-dinner event. The child must learn to understand the event that is being enacted. An eating event at home with the family requires one set of acts, whereas an eating event in the cafeteria with other children from class requires another set of acts. Eating in a restaurant where a waitress is present and where the child is required to remain seated, to talk in a soft voice, and to wait longer before the food is served requires yet another understanding of the acts that make up the event. Duchan (1986) calls for an understanding of the acts (the structure) of the event by the child before any intervention can take place. The child must learn to understand what will happen in a natural situation, what act will follow what specific act in the event, and what the agenda is for that event. The child engages in activities on a daily basis (e.g., brushing teeth, getting dressed, eating various meals, going to school, taking a bath, and going to sleep) or frequently participates in activities (e.g., going visiting, going to the store, painting, and feeding the dog) that can be discussed and for which the needed verbalizations can be modeled. The adult helps the child make sense out of the situations, or aids in "sensemaking" (Duchan, 1986). The breadth of the event depends on the child's ability. The adult SO must be able to judge the child's level of comprehension and verbal production so that the modeling and conversation will be at the child's level or a little above the child's spontaneous production ability (Macnamara, 1972).

The modeling presented by the adult should provide the child with stimulation and should be at the appropriate level so that the child will be able to utilize part if not all of the model. The models presented by the adult should convey what the child would want to communicate; they might include *I want juice* (subject-verb-object), *I want more bread* (subject-verb-modifer-object), or *I want bread and jam* (subject-verb-object-conjunction-object). Using these utterances, the adult is providing the vocabulary and syntactic form that a child could use meaningfully. The last sentence is more complex than the two preceding ones; there are a greater number of words that must be retained in the child's memory in order to be produced, and there is a compound object (bread, jam) joined by a conjunction (and). The adult SO must be aware of exactly what stimuli are being presented to the child and must be "tuned" to the child, aware of the child's abilities in many areas and on many levels within those areas. The response from the child must also be analyzed.

The child can respond with a request to the product question *What do you want?* If the child answers, "Want ice cream," or "Ice cream," the adult SO can maintain the dyad by expanding the child's utterance: "Oh, you want ice cream. OK, here's your ice cream." The communication was understood and answered as it would have been in the world beyond the classroom or therapy room. The adult should try to understand and accept the verbalizations of the child whenever possible so that the child will gain intrinsic satisfaction by interacting in the dyad and by having his intentions understood and his needs fulfilled or at least acknowledged. If the child is able to use the *I want* construction or is able to respond to your question in a number of differing situations, then generalization will have occurred. It should be remembered that responding in this manner or at this level occurs at approximately 2 years of age in a normally developing child, whereas responding to a subordinate clause that utilizes *because* (e.g., I want to have lunch now because I'm hungry) requires the child to understand cause and effect, which is on a much higher level. In addition to this cognitive understanding of causation, children must learn to use language pragmatically; for instance, children must learn to request on varying levels. They must learn when it is socially acceptable to use a direct request (e.g., *I would like some lunch please*) in contrast to a more indirect request (e.g., *It's twelve o'clock; I had breakfast early this morning*) and when the indirect request (e.g., *That was a good cookie*) is preferred to a direct request (e.g., *I want another cookie*). Alexandra (CA 5.1) employed this indirect manner of requesting another pretzel when she was given just two, one for her and one for her brother who was playing outside. She said, "Thank you," and then added, "Miki has a friend over to visit." It is important to keep in mind that individual children have individual needs and abilities.

CHILD-CENTERED APPROACH

A naturalistic setting can be trainer-oriented, as previously noted, but some suggest that another approach , a child-centered approach, can be productive. In this approach (McDade and Varnedoe, 1987), the adult SO is taught to maintain the child's attention and to follow the child's lead. McDade and Varnedoe described a Parent Training Program in which the parents are taught to be skilled observers and to elicit the child's response by, for example, modifying the environment so that the child will need to communicate; by waiting for the child's verbalization in a natural setting, which has been found to be frustrating at times; or by providing feedback through praise or imitation of the child's utterance. The parent then uses the child's verbalization as a stimulus on which to base the language lesson, that is, the parent learns to prompt, expand, imitate, model, and to provide natural reinforcement as a technique to elicit good language. This approach assures that the adult SO will be speaking about topics that are of interest to the child. The use of words based on the topic that has the child's attention has been found to increase the development of language in the child (Cross, 1984). The use of stimuli that have been initiated by the child also increases the child's participation and reduces the number of refusals by the child to join in the activity; in addition, it insures that both the child and the adult are engaging in the same activity and are thus in need of and using the same vocabulary (McDade and Varnedoe, 1987). Of course, in a non-child-centered approach the adult SO can talk about the topic of interest to the child (without waiting for the child to verbalize) by noting the child's gaze, actions, and needs. In the early stages of language development, the use of semantically related or semantically contingent utterances by the adult SO to respond to the nonverbal actions of the child are believed to increase language productivity. Language development is said to be impeded by frequent changes in the topic that are not related to the items or actions that have the child's attention (Snow, Midkiff–Borunda, Small, and Proctor, 1984), yet it must be remembered that interaction in therapy is different from the interaction at home (Prutting, Bagshaw, Goldstein, Juskowitz, and Umen, 1978).

SOCIAL INTERACTION

Social interaction (Snow et al., 1984) is considered a natural way to facilitate a child's development of language; social skills can be taught to facilitate a child's acceptance by his peer group (Valletutti, 1987).

- Consider the child an active learner, and through social interaction recognize the child's learning strategies so that they may be used as a basis for intervention (Snow, 1977).

- Try to accept what the child is saying and do not correct. Give positive feedback. Accepting can be considered reinforcement by acknowledgement (Cross, 1984). For example,

"No go home now."   Response: "OK, we won't go home now."

"No eat."   Response: "Oh, you don't want to eat at home?"

"No eat."   Response: "Oh, you don't want to eat at home, you want to eat here." (A positive statement is added as an alternative to the negative statement.)

- Expansion can be used to clarify a breakdown in communication without rejecting the utterance. In many intervention programs modeling is provided only to aid the revision of syntactic structures. Expansion may help the co-conversants carry on a negotiation of meaning while maintaining the child's topic and focus of interest.

- Expansion can provide alternate means of expressing an idea. Snow and colleagues (1984) stress the use of social interaction in language therapy with conversation used as the language text, with bidirection and interaction in useful communication.

STRATEGIES

To develop grammar, a child must be able to understand the physical and social events of the world and relate this knowledge to the meanings and forms of language (Slobin, 1973). To do this, Slobin suggested that children develop principles or strategies that are based on their generating cognition. For example, children pay attention to the ends of words and learn to signal plural, having recognized that the plural requires a morphological inflection (hats). In English, plural morphemes added to nouns occur early in development (circa CA 3.0); but in Egyptian Arabic, because of the extreme syntactic complexity in the use of the plural (Slobin quoted Omar, 1970), children at the age of 15 still have difficulty using pluralization in their language. Linguistic development requires skills that are not identical with cognitive skills (Cromer, 1974). Slobin suggested the use of universal operating principles by speakers of any language of the world (he contrasted at least nine languages). The first universal operating principle presented states that a semantic notion, when presented grammatically as a suffix, will be learned earlier than the same notion expressed as a prefix; for example, (Slobin quoted Gheorgov, 1908) in Bulgarian, the article that is expressed as a noun suffix (a morpheme attached to the end of the noun) is learned earlier than the article in English and German, which precedes the noun (the boy, a house, Die Fledermaus); and in French, the *pas,* or the final member of the negative *ne . . . pas,* is learned before the initial member of the French negative ne (Slobin quoted Gregoire, 1937). This operating principle of attending to the ends of words (not necessarily a suffix) is violated by many children with language impairment who use the phonological process of final deletion (Hodson, 1980).

CONCLUSION

Intervention approaches suggested in this chapter have often been based on hypothetical and applicable formulations by members of the field, yet how does one explain all the problems encountered by the children with language impairment and learning disabilities? A short list of the problems faced by these children includes difficulties in memory, in storage, and in capacity for verbal processing (Nelson, Kamhi, and Apel, 1987); in producing and responding to questions and in clarifying their productions (Brinton and Fujiki, 1982); in directing questions and maintaining speaker dominance (Bryan et al., 1981); and in symbolic play, in flexible use of toys, and in social participation (Roth and Clark, 1987). These deficits are not equally apparent in each child. The language patterns seen today are similar to language patterns in evidence in the past.

Twenty-five years ago, it was noted by this author that some of the children at a center for the mentally retarded and emotionally disturbed omitted the final consonants of each word (e.g., boat, big). The children were grouped for their mental level of functioning, regrouped for known or suspected etiology, regrouped again for cultural background, and so on, but no explanatory variable was uncovered. Evaluations would now describe the children as using the phonological process of final deletion (Hodson, 1980) or an operating principle or strategy that excludes the final sounds of words (Slobin, 1973). The scientists in all fields are searching for the elusive cause. Is language the cause of the difficulty in problem solving, or is language one of the problems that cannot be solved by the child. If the children with language impairment cannot infer actions, can they induce rules? If they do not remember minor settings or quantities of information, can they remember enough information so that rules can be inferred? The problem areas in phonology, semantics, syntax, and pragmatics are now analyzed in great detail, and these analyses are leading to new intervention techniques. The field had made great strides, but we still have a long way to go.

CHAPTER APPENDIX

Suggested Books for Stimulation of Vocabulary and Concepts

The listing approximates a hierarchical level of complexity.

1. Burningham, J. (1974). *The snow.* New York: Thomas Y. Crowell.
   Very simple, small in size, one action to a page.

2. Kruger, S., and Britt, S. (1985). *Under my bed.* Mahwah, NJ: Troll Associates.
   Night script — going to bed, asking for a drink of water, fears of a child.

3. Rey, H. A. Curious George Series:
   Curious George, Curious George takes a job, Curious George rides a bike, Curious George gets a medal (younger books). *Curious George goes to the hospital* and *Curious George and the dump truck* (older books). Boston: Houghton Mifflin.
   The younger children (2–3 yrs.) will enjoy the pictures, the older children (4–6 yrs.) should be asked to consider the problems and the solutions.

4. Maris, R. (1985). *Is anyone home?* New York: Greenwillow Books.
   Good story to develop nonexistence. The door is closed and must be opened.

5. Maris, R. (1984). *Are you there bear?* New York: Greenwillow Books.
   Can be used to develop denial and spatial concepts. The child looks for a bear and sees a donkey ("That's not a bear") under the bed.

6. Hoban, T. (1973). *Over, under and through.* New York: Macmillan.
   Book of pictures of a child going over, under, and through objects.

7. Hoban, T. (1978). *Is it red? is it yellow? is it blue?* New York: Greenwillow Books.
   Interesting book about colors.

8. Zion, G., and Graham, M. (1956). *Harry the dirty dog.* (1958) *No roses for Harry.* New York: Harper & Row.
   Classic books. Good story line to follow and problems to be solved. Use for pictures for younger children.

9. Hautzig, D., and Mathieu, J. (1985). *A visit to the Seasame Street Hospital.* New York: Random House.
   This book can be used to discuss occupations, feelings, illnesses, activities, colors, procedures in a hospital, and more.

10. Tanaka, Hideyuki (1983). *The happy dog.* New York: Atheneum. (Originally published in Japan: Fukuinkan Shoeten)
    This is a wordless book. The dog's actions cause problems, and he reasons how to solve them. Teaches sequence and consequence.

11. Stone, R., and Frith, M. (1975). *Because a little bug went ka-choo.* New York: Random House.
    Each action leads to another action — cause and effect. The print rhymes. Use pictures for 2–6-year-olds and causality for older children.

12. Goor, R., and Goor, N. (1983). *Signs*. New York: Thomas Y. Crowell.
    This book contains the various signs seen on the street. Good for sight reading, recognition, and awareness.

13. Waber, B. (1962). *The house on East 88th Street*. (1969) *Lovable Lyle*. Boston: Houghton Mifflin.
    Use the books to expand vocabulary and provide ideas of the city. Many activities. About a crocodile.

14. Ruben, C. (1978). *True or false*. New York: J. B. Lippincott.
    Contains pictures and questions concerning the pictures. Asks, "True or False?"

15. Stevenson, J. (1982). *We can't sleep*. New York: Greenwillow Books.
    Many actions and reasons are given. Many pictures to a page. A 5–7-year-old would probably enjoy the book.

REFERENCES

Arthur, G. (1952). *The Arthur adaptation of the Leiter international performance scale.* Washington, DC: Psychological Service Center Press.

Bates, E. (1976). Pragmatics and sociolinguistics in child language. In D. Morehead and A. Morehead (Eds.), *Normal and deficient child language* (pp. 411–436). Baltimore, MD: University Park Press.

Bowerman, M. (1978). The acquisition of word meaning: An investigation of some current conflicts. In N. Waterson and C. Snow (Eds.), *The development of communicaiton* (pp. 263–287). New York: John Wiley.

Brinton, B. and Fujiki, M. (1982). A comparison of request-response sequences in the discourse of normal and language-disordered children. *Journal of Speech and Hearing Disorders, 47,* 57–62.

Brown, R. (1973). *A first language.* Campridge, MA: Harvard University Press.

Bryan, T., Donahue, M., Pearl, R., and Sturm, C. (1981). Learning disabled conversational skills: The "TV talk show." *Learning Disabled Quarterly, 4,* 250–259.

Byrne, B. (1981). Deficient syntactic control in poor readers: Is a weak phonetic memory code responsible? *Applied Psycholinguistics, 2,* 210–212.

Chapman, R., and Kohn, L. (1978). Comprehension strategies of two and three year olds: Animate agents or probable events? *Journal of Speech and Hearing Research, 21,* 746–761.

Clark, E. (1973). What's in a word? On the child's acquistion of semantics in his first language. In T. Moore (Ed.), *Cognitive development and the acquisition of language* (pp. 65–110). New York: Academic Press.

Clark, E., and Hecht, R. (1984). Comprehension and production in language acquisition. *Annual Review of Psychology, 34,* 325–332.

Clark, H., and Haviland, S. (1977). Comprehension and the given-new contract. In R. Freedle (Ed.), *Discourse: Production and comprehension,* Vol. 1. Norwood, NJ: Ablex.

Connell, P. (1986). Acquisition of semantic role by language-disordered children: Differences between production and comprehension. *Journal of Speech and Hearing Research, 29,* 336–374.

Connell, P. (1987). Teaching language rules as solutions to language problems: A baseball analogy. *Language, Speech and Hearing Services in Schools, 18,* 194–205.

Corsaro, W. (1979). Young children's conception of status and role. *Sociology of Education, 52,* 46–50.

Craig, H. (1983). Applications of pragmatic language models for intervention. In T. Gallagher and C. Prutting (Eds.), *Pragmatic assessment and language intervention issues in language* (pp. 101–127). Boston: College-Hill.

Cromer, R. (1974). The development of language and cognition. The cognition hypothesis. In B. Foss (Ed.), *New perspectives in child development* (pp. 184–252). Middlesex, England: Penguin Books.

Cross, T. (1984). Habilitating the language-impaired child: Ideas from studies of parent-child interaction. *Topics in Language Disorders, 4,* 1–14.

Denckla, M. B, and Rudel, R. G. (1976a). Naming the object-drawings by dyslexic and other learning-disabled children. *Brain and Language, 3,* 1–15.

Denckla, M., and Rudel, R. (1976b). Rapid "automized naming" (R. A. N.): Dyslexia differentiated from other learning disabilities. *Neuropsychologia, 14,* 471–479.

de Villiers, J., and de Villiers, P. (1978). *Language acquisition.* Cambridge, MA: Harvard.

de Vos, N. (1975). Unpublished paper. New Haven, CT: Yale University.

Drachman, G. (1975). Generative phonology and child language acquisition. *Working Papers in Linguistics* (Ohio State University), *15,* 146–149.

Duchan, J. (1986). Language intervention through sensemaking and finetuning. In R. Schiefelbusch (Ed.), *Language competence: Assessment and intervention* (pp. 187–212). Boston: College-Hill.

Ellis Weismer, S. (1985). Constructive comprehension abilities exhibited by language-disordered children. *Journal of Speech and Hearing Research, 28,* 175–184.

Ervin-Tripp, S., and Gordon, D. (1986). The development of requests. In R. Schiefelbusch (Ed.), *Language competence: Assessment and intervention* (pp. 61–95). Boston: College-Hill.

Fillmore, C. (1968). The case for case. In E. Bach and R. Harms (Eds.), *Universals in linguistic theory* (pp. 1–88). New York: Hold, Rinehart & Winston.

Frith, V. (1985). Beneath the surface of developmental dyslexia. In K. Patterson, J. Marshall, and M. Coltheart (Eds.), *Surface dyslexia: Neuropsychological and cognitive studies of phonological reading*. London: Erlbaum.

German, D. (1982). Word-finding substitutions in children with learning disabilities. *Language, Speech and Hearing Services in the Schools, 13,* 223–230.

Gheorgov, I. (1908). *Ein beitrag zur grammatischen entwicklung der kindersprache*. Leipzig, Germany: Engelmann.

Gregoire, A. (1937). *L'apprentissage due language: Vol. 1. Les deux premieres annees, Vol. 2. La troisieme annee et les annees suivantes*. Paris: Dorz. (Reprinted 1947, Paris/Liege: Dorz).

Halliday, M., and Hasan, R. (1976). *Cohesion in English*. New York: Longman.

Ingram, D. (1976). *Phonological disability in children*. London: Edward Arnold.

Hodson, B. W. (1980). *The assessment of phonological process*. Danville, IL: The Interstate Printers Publishers, Inc.

Horn, J., O'Donnell, J., and Leicht, D. (1988). Phonetically inaccurate spelling among learning-disabled, head-injured, and nondisabled young adults. *Brain and Language, 33,* 55–64.

Jansky, J. (1975). The marginally reading child. *Bulletin of Orton Society, 25,* 69–85.

Johnson, J. (1982). Narratives: A new look at communication problems in older language-disordered children. *Language, Speech and Hearing Services in the Schools, 13,* 144–155.

Kamhi, A. (1981). Nonlinguistic symbolic and conceptual abilities of language-impaired and normally developing children. *Journal of Speech and Hearing Research, 24,* 446–453.

Kamhi, A., Catts, H., Koenig, L., and Lewis, B. (1984). Hypothesis-testing and nonlinguistic symbolic abilities in language-impaired children. *Journal of Speech and Hearing Disorders, 49,* 169–176.

Kirk, S., McCarthy, J., and Kirk, W. (1968). *Illinois Test of Psycholinguistic Abilities* (Rev. ed.). Urbana, IL: University of Illinois Press.

Leonard, L., Nippold, M., Kail, R., and Hale, C. (1983). Picture naming in language-impaired children: Differentiation lexical storage from retrieval. *Journal of Speech and Hearing Disorders, 26,* 609–615.

Leonard, L., Schwartz, R., Chapman, K., Rowan, L., Prelock, P., Terrell, B., Weiss, A., and Messick, C. (1982). Early lexical acquisition in children with specific language impairment. *Journal of Speech and Hearing Research, 25,* 554–564.

Liles, B. (1985). Cohesion in the narratives of normal and language-disordered children. *Journal of Speech and Hearing Research, 28,* 123–133.

Liles, B., Schulman, M., and Bartlett, S. (1977). Judgments of grammaticality in normal and language-disordered children. *Journal of Speech and Hearing Disorders, 42,* 199–210.

Lowe, M., and Costello, A. (1976). *The Symbolic Play Test*. Windsor, Great Britian: NFER Publishing.

MacDonald, J., and Blott, J. (1974). Environmental language intervention. The rationale for a diagnostic and training strategy through rules, context, and generalization. *Journal of Speech and Hearing Disorders, 39,* 244–256.

Macnamara, J. (1972). Cognitive basis of language learning in infants. *Psychological Review, 79,* 1–13.

McDade, H., and Varnedoe, D. (1987). Training parents to be language facilitators. *Topics in Language Disorders, 7,* 19–30.

Meline, T. (1988). The encoding of novel referents by language-impaired children. *Language, Speech and Hearing Services in the Schools, 19,* 119–127.

Mitchell–Kernan, C., and Kernan, K. (1977). Pragmatics of directive choice among children. In S. Ervin–Tripp and C. Mitchell–Kernan (Eds.), *Child discourse* (pp. 189–208). New York: Academic Press.

Muma, J. (1978). *Language handbook — Concepts, assessment, intervention*. Englewood Cliffs, NJ: Prentice-Hall.

Nelson, K. (1974). Concept, word and sentence: Interrelations in acquisition and development. *Psychological Review, 81,* 267–285.

Nelson, K. (1978). Semantic development and the development of semantic memory. In K. E. Nelson (Ed.), *Child language* (Vol. 1, pp. 39–80). New York: Wiley.

Nelson, L., Kamhi, A., and Apel, K. (1987). Cognitive strengths and weaknesses in language-impaired children: One more look. *Journal of Speech and Hearing Disorders, 52,* 36–43.

Newman, P., and Lockhart, D. (1969). *No place to play.* New York: Grosset & Dunlap.

Olson, D. R. (1970). Language and thought: Aspects of a cognitive theory of semantics. *Psychological Review, 77,* 257–273.

Olswang, L., and Carpenter, R. (1982a). The ontogenesis of agent: Cognitive notion. *Journal of Speech and Hearing Research, 25,* 297–306.

Olswang, L., and Carpenter, R. (1982b). The ontogenesis of agent: Linguistic expression. *Journal of Speech and Hearing Research, 25,* 306–314.

Omar, M. (1970). *The acquisition of Egyptian Arabic as a native language.* Unpublished doctoral dissertation, Georgetown University.

Piaget, J. (1954). *The construction of reality in the child.* New York: Ballantine Books.

Prutting, C., Bagshaw, N., Goldstein, H., Juskowitz, S., and Umen, I. (1978). Clinician-child discourse: Some preliminary questions. *Journal of Speech and Hearing Disorders, 43,* 123–139.

Rees, N., and Shulman, M. (1978). I don't understand what you mean by comprehension. *Journal of Speech and Hearing Disorders, 43,* 208–219.

Rice, M. (1983). Comtemporary accounts of the cognition/language relationship: Implications for speech-language clinicians. *Journal of Speech and Hearing Disorders, 48,* 347–359.

Rice, M. (1986). Mismatched premises of the communicative competence model and language intervention. In R. Schiefelbusch (Ed.), *Language competence: Assessment and intervention* (pp. 261–280). Boston: College-Hill.

Roth, F. (1986). Oral narrative abilities of learning-disabled students. *Topics in Language Disorders, 7,* 21–30.

Roth, F., and Clark, D. (1987). Symbolic play and social participation abilities of language-impaired and normally developing children. *Journal of Speech and Hearing Disorders, 52,* 17–29.

Roth, F., and Spekman, N. (1984). Assessing the pragmatic abilities of children. Part 1. Organizational framework and assessment parameters. *Journal of Speech and Hearing Disorders, 49,* 2–11.

Roth F., and Spekman, N. (1986). Narrative discourse: Spontaneously generated stories of learning-disabled and normally achieving students. *Journal of Speech and Hearing Disorders, 51,* 8–23.

Rourke, B. (1983). Reading and spelling disabilities: A development and neuropsychological perspective. In U. Kirk (Ed.), *Neuropsychology of language, reading and spelling* (pp. 209–234). New York: Academic Press.

Rourke, B., Dietrich, D., and Young, G. (1973). Significance of WISC verbal-performance discrepancies for younger children with learning disabilities. *Perceptual and Motor Skills, 36,* 275–282.

Rourke, B., Young, G., and Flewelling, R. (1971). The relationships between WISC verbal-performance discrepancies and selected verbal, auditory-perceptual, visual-perceptual, and problem-solving abilities in children with learning disabilities. *Journal of Clinical Psychology, 27,* 475–479.

Rudel, R., Denckla, M., and Broman, M. (1981). The effect of varying stimulus context on word-finding ability. Dyslexia further differentiated from other learning disabilities. *Brain and Language, 13,* 130–144.

Schwartz, R., and Leonard, L. (1985). Lexical imitation and acquisition in language-impaired children. *Journal of Speech and Hearing Disorders, 50,* 141–149.

Slobin, D. (1973). Cognitive prerequisites for the development of grammar. In D. Slobin and C. Ferguson (Eds.), *Studies of child language development.* New York: Holt, Rinehart & Winston.

Snow, C. (1977). Mother's speech research: From input to interaction. In C. Snow and C. Ferguson (Eds.), *Talking to children: Language input and acquisition.* New York: Cambridge University Press.

Snow, C., Midkiff–Borunda, S., Small, A., and Proctor, A. (1984). Therapy as social interaction: Analyzing the contexts for language. *Topics in Language Disorders, 4,* 72–85.

Snyder, L. (1984). Developmental language disorders: Elementary school age. In A. Holland (Ed.), *Language disorders in children* (pp. 129–158). Boston: College-Hill.

Spekman, N. and Roth, F. (1982). An intervention framework for learning disabled students with communication disorders. *Learning Disability Quarterly, 5,* 429–437.

Stein, N., and Glenn, C. (1979). An analysis of story comprehension in elementary school children. In R. O. Freedle (Ed.), *New directions in discourse processing* (Vol. 1, pp. 53–120). Norward, NJ: Ablex Publishing.

Stockman, I. J., and Vaughn–Cooke, F. B. (1986). Implication of semantic category research for language assessment of nonstandard speakers. *Topics in Language Disorders, 6,* 15–26.

Strauss, A. A., and Lehtinen, L. E. (1947). *Psychopathology and education of the brain-injured child.* New York: Grune & Stratton.

Temple, C. (1988). Red is red but eye is blue: A case study of developmental dyslexia and follow-up report. *Brain and Language, 34,* 13–37.

Terrell, B., Schwartz, R., Prelock, P., and Messick, C. (1984). Symbolic play in normal and language-impaired children. *Journal of Speech and Hearing Disorders, 27,* 424–429.

Valletutti, P. (1987). Social and emotional problems of children with learning disabilities. In K. Kavale, S. Forness, and M. Bender (Eds.), *Handbook of learning disabilities.* Vol. I. (pp. 211–226). Boston: College-Hill.

Warren, S., and Kaiser, A (1986a). Generalization of treatment effects by young language-delayed children: A longitudinal analysis. *Journal of Speech and Hearing Disorders, 51,* 239–251.

Warren, S., and Kaiser, A. (1986b). Incidental language teaching: A critical review. *Journal of Speech and Hearing Disorders, 51,* 291–299.

Webster's seventh new collegiate dictionary. (1969). Springfield, MA: Merriam.

Wiig, E. (1986). Language disabilities in school-age children and youth. In G. Shames and E. Wiig (Eds.), *Human communication disorders: An introduction* (pp. 331–379). Columbus, OH: Merrill.

Wiig, E., and Semel, E. (1973). Comprehension of linguistic concepts requiring logical operations by learning disabled children. *Journal of Speech and Hearing Research, 16,* 627–636.

Wiig, E. H., and Semel, E. M. (1974). Logico-grammatical sentence comprehension by learning disabled adolescents. *Perceptual and Motor Skills, 38,* 1331–1334.

Wiig, E., and Semel, E. (1976). *Language disabilities in children and adolescents.* Columbus, OH: Merrill.

Wiig, E. H., Semel, E. M., and Nystrom, L. (1982). Comparison of rapid naming abilities in language-learning disabled and academically achieving eight-year-olds. *Language, Speech and Hearing Services in the Schools, 13,* 11–23.

Winitz, H. (1973). Problem solving and the delay of speech as strategies in the teaching of language. *Asha, 15,* 583–586.

Zimmerman, I., Steiner, V., and Evatt, R. (1969). *The Preschool Language Scale.* Columbus, OH: Merrill.

CHAPTER 11

The Special Education Teacher as Consultant

MARY McKNIGHT-TAYLOR

In response to federal and state legislation, and thus to a philosophy of mainstreaming and least restrictive environments, instructional programming and the role of teachers of children with handicaps have undergone massive changes. Meyers (1982) suggested that school consultation "involves a collaborative relationship between two professionals who view themselves as colleagues and work to solve the problem together." Two of the most important of these new roles are the special education professional as case manager and as educational consultant to regular classroom teachers in whose mainstreamed classes students with handicapping conditions have been placed. Although these roles have in some cases been separated into different positions, special education teachers must usually assume both functions, especially in small- and medium-sized school districts. Activities vital to the consultative role include those related to the administration and implementation of the total program planned for the care and education of children with special needs.

This chapter discusses characteristics and skills needed by the special education teacher for effective performance as a consultant/case manager. New demands for interaction with special education teachers have been created because of mainstreaming mandates and because local school districts are increasingly providing services for students formerly educated out of the district. Another factor in the expansion of the role of special educators is that the age for admission to public school has been lowered so that many systems provide all-day kindergarten, prekindergarten, and infant-stimulation programs. This chapter outlines various roles and services that may be part of the special educator's responsibilities above and beyond their direct service to children, and suggestions for meeting these demands with examples and resources are provided. Activities for the special education teacher in a consultative role to regular educators may be classified under five major categories. The special educator may alternately and simultaneously act as any or all of the following:

- case manager
- mentor
- advocate
- technical assistant
- resource person

THE SPECIAL EDUCATION TEACHER AS CASE MANAGER

The consultative role frequently requires case management and administrative skills. Not only are special education teachers responsible for children who remain in their rooms for the entire school day, they frequently must also monitor the educational and therapeutic programs of the children who are mainstreamed for part or all of the school day. In New York State, for example, the Special Education Committee (SEC), formerly the Committee on the Handicapped (COH), plays a major role in gathering data, setting goals, and establishing the Individualized Educational Program (IEP). In other states similar committees, bearing different names and alphabetical designations, perform the same functions. For example, in Maryland the committee is called the Admissions, Review and Dismissal (ARD) Committee. It is the special education teacher, however, who must usually monitor pupil progress, gather, record, and interpret data; document interventions and contacts; keep abreast of current issues in the field; and maintain complete records of special education and any other related services provided.

In the New York State Department of Mental Hygiene, these responsibilities are classified as those of a client coordinator. That person is responsible for reports that are personally generated, reports that are gathered from various disciplines and from contacts with the parents, other programs, and other facilities. In addition to these basic case-management responsibilities, regular reviews of student progress are conducted. In the absence of a case manager, the special education teacher coordinates all of these areas, as well as being responsible for classroom review, referrals, follow-up classroom management, and program evaluation.

Moreover, the case manager must acquaint parents with their rights under the law and must make certain that legal time lines are observed by the school system (these time lines are part of the legally established safeguards meant to protect children and their parents or surrogates). The case manager has the additional responsibility of making certain that due process procedures are observed whenever disputes or disagreements lead to administrative hearings and judicial appeals. Thus, the case-manager role is an emerging one for special educators who, unfortunately, are not typically prepared for this basically foreign function. Although case management is familiar to such professionals as social workers and rehabilitation counselors, it has not heretofore been part of the educator's professional mission.

Case manager responsibilities for the special education teacher as consultant include a great many of the responsibilities subsumed under the title of special needs coordinator in the Head Start System. The United States Department of Health and Human Services issued *A Guide to Model Head Start Position Descriptions* (1983). The guide lists fourteen responsibilities of the special needs coordinator, some of which are discussed here (parallels to the case manager role of the special education consultant are discussed where appropriate).

Although Head Start was designed primarily to serve children and families at or below the poverty level, its mission was expanded to include children with special needs. Ten percent of Head Start's enrollment must be set aside for children with special needs. In order to be in compliance with government regulations, all Head Start programs must demonstrate through staffing and recruitment patterns that they are, in fact, working toward meeting the service mandate for children with exceptional needs and their families.

To achieve this goal, specific assignments were made with clearly defined responsibilities. The Head Start special needs coordinator designs and implements the program for children with handicaps and is responsible for recruitment, enrollment, diagnosis, and provision of services to children with special needs. Although teachers as consultants do not recruit children, they do have a part in the decision-making process for admission to certain programs and for placement in both special education classrooms and mainstreamed settings (e.g., identifying which teachers might be better suited in temperament or teaching style to work with the child who has disabilities).

The second responsibility of the special needs coordinator is to develop the overall plan and budget of the program to ensure that it will meet the needs of children with handicapping conditions and their families in accordance with the performance standards set for the program. Special educators as consultants must develop ways of securing information about fiscal possibilities for the provision of services to children and their families, but they generally have no direct role in budget preparation.

The third responsibility of the special needs coordinator is, in some ways, part of the case-management responsibilities of the special education consultant, that is, obtaining a diagnostic report and confirmation of the handicapping condition by the appropriate professionals and service providers. Coordinators are also responsible for developing a follow-up plan for assistance. Both Head Start and special education personnel are responsible for developing an IEP through discussion of the diagnosis with an interdisciplinary team that includes teachers and parents. Both Head Start personnel and special education consultants are responsible for sensitizing their staff to the special needs of exceptional children, and both consult regularly with parents and staff on individualizing programs of the children. Additional responsibilities include the following:

- Assuming responsibility for arranging, coordinating, and monitoring films and publications for training and for circulation among staff members

- Conferring with and monitoring specialists employed to work with exceptional children

- Securing transportation or other needed services

- Determining what training or technical assistance is needed for children, parents, and others

THE SPECIAL EDUCATION TEACHER AS MENTOR

The concept of teachers as mentors has proved to be a successful method for training personnel in diverse fields. The concept is not a new one; it comes to us out of Greek legend, when Odysseus decided to entrust the development and education of his son to Mentor, a wise and learned man (Gray and Gray, 1985). The idea of training artisans and craftspersons under masters continues without significant change from medieval times when apprenticeships were a common practice.

The role of teacher as mentor to beginning teachers and to teachers returning to the profession after a significant lapse of time has received increasing attention in recent years largely because of the teacher shortage that has resulted from teachers taking higher paying or higher prestige jobs and from smaller numbers of college students selecting teaching as a career (The National Committee on Excellence in Education, 1983). Underlying the mentor-teacher concept is the premise that the mentor provides psychological and personal support as well as acquainting the new or returning teacher with the basic information of the trade. Psychological support is provided by the mentor in the role of coach (either for individuals or for a team), which may involve encouraging the teacher's efforts by tempering suggestions for improvement with praise (Neubert and Bratton, 1987).

The stress of a new job can cause anxiety for anyone; the stress of being a new special education teacher is enormous. Even when they are caring and reinforcing people, supervisors and principals can seldom provide the guidance and emotional support that can come from a fellow teacher. Beginning special education teachers need substantial help because of the nature of the students they teach, but they also need the assistance of a fellow special education teacher because most regular teachers are unfamiliar with the role and scope of the special education process and with the unique nature of the special class teacher. Even in these times, many regular educators fail to recognize that special education teachers require more training, greater knowledge, and more advanced skills that do regular teachers of nonhandicapped children.

The mentor-teacher concept has been implemented in many regular and special education settings, and it is one of the most personalized and cost-efficient options for training inexperienced or insecure teachers to work with children, particularly those with special needs. The role of mentor is complex Even though there are necessary supervisory and evaluative components inherent in the concept, the inevitable suggestions or critiques should be stated in the most positive and supportive terms possible. The major responsibility of the special education teacher as mentor is to provide an effective role model for new or returning teachers in terms of planning, instruction, and curriculum selection. According to Adkinson (1985), mentors must "have recent experience in classroom instruction . . . [and] have demonstrated exemplary teaching ability, including not only subject matter knowledge, but also communication skills and a thorough knowledge of instructional strategies necessary to meet the needs of pupils in different contexts" (p. 26). They must also establish an accepting, responsive atmosphere for the exchange of ideas, which can best be accomplished when the mentor "assumes that objective feedback given in a nonthreatening and supportive climate can improve teaching performance" (Garmston, 1987, p. 26).

Resource-room teachers and regular classroom teachers report three common problems in understanding the special education process. As reported by Kokaska (1985), these problems are the regular classroom teacher's inability to understand certain situations due to his/her lack of knowledge in special education, scheduling time in the resource room and the paperwork involved in teaching children with handicapping conditions. The mentor has an important role in helping solve these problems, in part, by providing sound philosophical and theoretical perspectives related to special education practices and by introducing coping skills that may help the novice special education teacher or the regular classroom teacher with mainstreamed students.

Lambert and Lambert (1985) described several roles for the mentor. One such role includes the mentor as one part of a comprehensive staff-development team: "The mentor teacher program has potential for becoming a vital part of comprehensive staff development programs, but not all schools and districts have such a coherent plan for promoting professional growth" (p. 30). The mentor teacher has the task of working on staff development projects such as identifying and defining the role of various members in the interdisciplinary team and providing guidance for persons facing new roles. In addition, mentors may guide new teachers in developing curriculum materials and help them evaluate the efficacy of using these materials with the child who has handicapping conditions. When they are called on to evaluate beginning or returning teachers, mentors must ensure by their comments and feedback that the teachers have a fair climate in which their developing skills can be evaluated. Thus the mentor-teacher protects the fledgling teacher from punitive or negative repercussions by explaining any weaknesses as well as identifying those steps to be taken to correct them. Further, the mentor preserves the confidential aspects of the process. In this way, confessed weaknesses, or those discovered by the mentor, can be addressed without fear of censure or dismissal. The selection of the mentor-teacher requires extensive evaluation of the role itself and of the personal and professional skills needed to fill it.

THE SPECIAL EDUCATION TEACHER AS TECHNICAL ASSISTANT

Special education services sometimes require the use of highly technical equipment and a familiarity with specialized medical and prosthetic devices. Children with handicapping conditions often need assistance in locking and unlocking braces or in using other prosthetic or assistive devices. Mainstream teachers may require technical assistance with regard to the positional requirements of children with paralysis, respiratory problems, or other conditions dictating a special position or frequent changes in position for comfort or for remediation of specific symptoms. Assistance may also be required in selecting inexpensive readily available equipment that will help the infant or young child learn from and interact with the environment. For example, Kasteri and Filler (1981) reported success in working with severely motorically involved infants and preschoolers, positioning them so that they could visibly locate, reach for, and play with toys in spite of severe muscular limitations due to lack of muscle tone, or hypotonia.

Increasing opportunities for children with poor postural and general muscle tone is important; the use of adaptive equipment helps facilitate learning and broaden the range of settings in which instruction can take place. The special education teacher as technical assistant helps the regular class teacher or other members of the interdisciplinary team choose and use appropriate assistive devices including equipment such as wedges, standing chairs, slant boards, and other equipment used for children with cerebral palsy.

However, the use of commercially produced equipment has several major drawbacks. Kasteri and Filler (1981) found that commercially produced equipment tends to be expensive, and although school budgets may permit their purchase, they are too expensive for home use. Adaptive equipment is often bulky and heavy, particularly the relaxation chair (or prone standers), and are therefore not easily moved from place to place. In many cases, adaptive equipment is designed for one individual and cannot be used to remediate problems in another child. Finally, the equipment may have limited use because the child may outgrow the unit with age or because the child's condition changes. Kasteri and Filler suggested using inflatable swim rings to provide an inexpensive, versatile, and portable alternative to some of the more expensive equipment that is available commercially. (See Chapter 9 for additional ideas about using inflatables for language-stimulation possibilities.) As technical assistants, special education teachers show parents and classroom staff the safe way to position children and how to place toys, books, or other stimulus material so that the child can compensate for physical limitations and is motivated to reach for, touch, or use the desired object.

Teachers may also supply parents or other caregivers with suggestions for materials and with some sources from which to secure them (Campbell, 1987). For example, some children may need transporters, crawlers, self-feeding equipment, head pointers, wheelchairs, tumbleforms, positioning aids, or scooters. Catalogs from J. A. Preston Corporation and other companies (see end of chapter for addresses) may be secured and made available to department heads, parents, administrators, and local charity groups who might wish to purchase (and donate) equipment to the school. A combination newsletter and catalog that provides additional technical help is put out by Handicapped Children's Technological Services (HCTS). They offer a basic system that has a timer, a tilt switch, and a control lead, allowing severely impaired persons, regardless of age, to control and operate cassette tape recorders or other battery-operated devices. The author/producer Edmond S. Zurmoski (1980) described how the equipment works. "The child grasps the Tilt Switch or it may be taped into his hand. Movement sensed by the Tilt Switch activates the 77-1A Timer which controls a tape recorder or a battery operated toy for eight seconds. The movement must be repeated to produce the sensory event again."

The role of technical assistant to the regular classroom teacher requires skill and a broad knowledge of methods and materials, with specific knowledge in the following areas:

- Technology (computerized instruction, mechanical teaching aids, assistive devices for hearing, alternative communication devices, and orthotic and prosthetic devices)

- Adapted assessment instruments for administration, scoring, and interpretation
- Classroom management strategies for grouping individuals
- Behavior modification strategies for the motivation and development of desired behavior and the extinction of undesired behavior
- Instructional and evaluation strategies
- Medical and emotional emergency intervention
- Audiovisual equipment
- Adapted art strategies
- Adapted physical education equipment and curriculum
- Self-help curriculum, particularly feeding, as it relates to strengthening and using the speech mechanism

In the role of technical assistant the special education teacher provides the following:

- Information about the specific nature of the child's language capabilities and help in establishing goals for instruction
- Goals based on assessments made by speech, language, and hearing specialists, as well as those based on recommendations made by psychologists, psychiatrists, and other relevant professionals
- Special management techniques for medical, behavioral, or psychological problems
- Motivational material and techniques that appeal to the child's interest and learning style
- Justification for needed specialized equipment and assistive devices
- Training in the use, care, and storage of specialized equipment and assistive devices
- Approaches for reporting to and interacting with parents of children with special needs
- Adapted evaluation procedures
- Methods for record-keeping strategies that save time and that provide documentation of the progress the child has made and of any problems that may not yet have surfaced
- Sample lessons for mainstreamed children with goals and materials outlined

- Sample schedules either for one lesson, for an entire morning, or for a week that show the time and structure needed to build language and communication concepts for a particular child

THE SPECIAL EDUCATION TEACHER AS ADVOCATE

In the role of advocate, the special educator seeks to protect special children from infringements on their rights as assured by the United States Constitution, and by state constitutions, and by federal and state legislation. The role of advocate also involves supporting the child through carefully planned and interpreted goals that may strain the boundaries of expected or already established limitations posed by that child's disability. Parents of exceptional children often need help accepting new and more challenging situations for their children, in some instances preferring to follow the safer, usual methods of care because they fear that their children will somehow be hurt or fail to hold the gains they have made. The literature on risk taking suggests the need for parent training or counseling if innovative program structures are to be used. In a mainstreaming effort, the special education teacher must structure the transition period so that parents, the special child, and the receiving teacher feel confident that continuing support will be provided.

There are materials and strategies that provide answers to questions asked by the child with special needs, by other children, and by regular classroom teachers about the child's special conditions. For example, Barbara Aiello's *The Kids on the Block* (1976) has puppets that represent different exceptionalities. Cerebral palsy, epilepsy, deafness, and blindness are among the conditions explained by the puppets in dialogue with each other and in response to questions from the audience. The puppets are presented by various theater groups and are shown in films as well.

In the role of advocate, the special education teacher helps parents and the regular classroom teacher establish goals for the child in other settings. This is an important service because the special educator helps frame the goals and provides the necessary resources for their achievement. These goals should be realistic and should be geared toward expanding the children's capabilities and toward giving them new opportunities for experiencing growth.

In the role of advocate the special education teacher provides the following:

- Ways to increase opportunities for children with handicapping conditions to interact with other students who are not handicapped

- Information and examples of student progress (for the student, other students, parents, administrators, and other teachers)

- Plans for normalizing experiences for as much time as possible and in as many activities as the child can manage, always considering any limitations resulting from physical problems

- New opportunities for students while monitoring safeguards for continued levels of service when students move to other teachers, programs, or situations.

- Needed information to parents as well as professional support in gaining guaranteed rights and services under PL 94-142 and other laws related to children with special needs

- Suggestions for home, school, and community members in an effort to foster cooperation on social and political issues that have some impact on the education and treatment of children with special needs

- Detailed records or research findings that document the success that has been met using strategies similar to those proposed

- Defense for schedules and settings of language instruction by documenting their proven effectiveness through the use of professional references and other published accounts by professionals in the field of speech and language development

- Examples of sessions that demonstrate effective behavior management strategies for working with various disability groups

- Evidence of gains that are made in language ability by their students (videotapes, audiotapes, newsletters, books, murals, and photograph displays)

- Opportunities for students to practice and demonstrate competence in language-related activities

THE SPECIAL EDUCATION TEACHER AS RESOURCE PERSON

Professional organizations concerned with various disabilities provide a rich source of material and resources for special teachers, for parents, and when shared properly, for regular educators as well. It is membership in umbrella groups such as the Council for Exceptional Children (CEC) and in more specialized groups such as the American Association on Mental Deficiency (AAMD), the Association for Children with Learning Disabilities (ACLD), and others that provides the special education teacher with knowledge and a sense of camaraderie.

Attending conferences provides contact with practitioners from various facilities having similar populations. Curricular strategies, which are often based on well-structured research, are available in the journals published by these organizations. Conference attendees are able to evaluate methods and materials that are appropriate for language stimulation; self-concept; and subject areas such as number concepts, reading readiness, and perceptual-motor instruction. When they are called on to provide support for other personnel, special educators are able to draw on the information gained from conferences with a sense of certainty about the effectiveness of specific approaches.

The special educator should pass along addresses of organizations, mailing lists, newsletters, and sources for free or inexpensive materials. References that supply medical, psychological, and special curricular information should be a part of the special teacher's resource files, and these files should be shared as situations require.

In addition to keeping files on local sources of financial, medical, or recreational support, the special education teacher should keep track of any eligibility requirements, exceptions that might be made, and so forth. Failure to screen information may lead to frustration on the part of the person seeking the special educator's help, and it may lead to a loss of faith in the special educator as a resource agent. Preface information with statements such as *This may be a source of help for you,* or *A family with similar problems was able to get help from* . . . Statements such as *This agency will need to have X, Y, and Z information in order to help you* allows the family to secure the necessary documents or to decide that they do not want to share that information. A resource file of diagnostic labels and resources should be made and updated constantly.

Special education classrooms are sometimes material rich. When the child is mainstreamed, it is helpful to send along with the child material that is familiar and with which successful learning has taken place. If enough of the same type of instructional material is available, send enough for a group. This makes the special child a contributor to the regular class and helps the host teacher integrate the child's goals into those of the class. Films and books that share the stories of children with handicapping conditions should be shared with other teachers so that storytimes incorporate adventures and problems of children who are like their peers except for one or more special areas. Books should be shared with teachers and regular classes so that these teachers and classmates will be sensitive to the needs of special children and appreciate the strength shown by special children in dealing with their disabilities and the demands of school and home. Instructional material adapted for a child's special visual or auditory needs should also be shared. Weiderholt, Hammill, and Brown (1983) suggested that follow-up on suggestions should be conducted on a regular basis: "Every time a resource teacher makes a specific recommendation that a teacher use a series of drills, a technique for managing an unwanted behavior, or a training strategy of any type, they should visit the classroom to see if the teacher is willing or able to implement the suggestions properly" (p. 43).

Educational prescriptions must be based on a solid understanding of a child's abilities, as well as on an understanding of those areas of weakness responsive to intervention. The consultant working with the regular teacher on facilitating language helps the regular educator gain a sharper picture of the child's communication ability, of workable approaches to teaching language, and of social settings that may facilitate learning. For example, a child who is beginning to respond to a stuffed animal might be ready not only to learn the animal's name but also to learn the sounds its real-life counterpart makes, the way it moves, and the words to describe its movement. Additional motivation for lessons centered on the stuffed animal might result if the sessions are fun and conducted like a game. Later, the toy could be used as a puppet, giving directions, asking questions, or generally reinforcing speech. The ability to organize and present information is basic to the development of other important consultative skills.

To the base of knowledge about children and their development should be added such factors as teacher attitudes, values, and a group of characteristics that may be labeled as a teacher's personal style. One of the most important skills for the consultant as case manager is the ability to communicate information about special children and about the goals for their care and education. Consultants must also be able to share these strategies and information for achieving established goals. Effective communication involves timing, format, content, documentation, and follow-up.

TIMING

Timing of contacts is especially important and should be done so that the consultant's role is as nonintrusive as possible. Requests for information from or for action by others should be made early enough to allow time for action and response. If requests are made of the special educator, responses must be early enough to be useful.

There is almost no "right" time to impart information that may be unpleasant or unsettling. Communication may involve additional demands on persons who are already overburdened or burned out. Even good news needs time in which to be digested and fully appreciated. Teachers are always desperate for time and often exchange information or requests as they pass in the halls, in the main office as they sign in or out, on lunch or playground duty, or in the teacher's lounge. In large schools, special classes may be located in wings or buildings separate from offices of personnel with whom contact must be made or from regular classes. Also, itinerant teachers, part-time personnel, and specialty teachers may only be reached on certain days for a limited time. In such cases, contact would be made primarily through notes left in their mailboxes.

Special education teachers have to make certain that there is adequate time for receipt of the communication, for action, and response. Overnight requests should be made only in an emergency. Hurried exchanges in the hallway or a quick call in the evening to numbers published in the school directory may set the stage for a more comprehensive meeting, may provide answers to questions already asked, or may pose new questions whose answers will be given at another time. When requests are made for information, for strategies to be used with a special child, or for material related to the special child in the mainstream, prompt and complete responses are required. Other educational personnel, parents, and professionals in related fields depend on the special education teacher for those pieces of information that complete the profile of the special child's functioning.

Timing refers to the following:

- Appropriateness of contact in terms of the schedule of activities and demands on teachers' time

- Not intruding by telephone outside of the school day (use home telephone numbers only with prior permission)

- Establishing contact for long-range requirements with periodic reminders (e.g., a calendar might be developed for the year with dates of special reports, testing, conferences, etc., and notes may be sent to remind the responsible person that the required action is due in two weeks, next Friday, etc.)

- Prompt responses to requests from others

FORMAT

A clear, concise format helps structure communication among members of the interdisciplinary team. Children with handicapping conditions may be involved with as many as six or seven disciplines at the same time. It is the special education teacher's responsibility as consultant to gather, unify, interpret, and disseminate information about the child's progress and needs. The format for referrals, requests for action, or requests for information will vary according to the purpose of the correspondence. All correspondence should contain certain basic identifying data about the child and the initiating person.

Short, form notes can be photocopied and then stapled to replies or used as the basis for replies. The following are examples:

- Here is the information you requested.

- I don't (know/have) the information you requested.

- I will (have/know) it by (date or time).

- I suggest that you contact (person's name) at (address or telephone).

- The best time to reach (person's name) is (date or time).

- I don't know what the best time might be to reach (person's name), but I have been successful by (calling X's office/calling X's home/dropping a note/leaving a message with a co-worker of X).

All correspondence should be dated, and the desired response date or time should be included.

Having a specific color for special education correspondence is helpful. Some systems routinely use color-coded correspondence for various personnel. This expedites correspondence, filing, and retrieval of information. In addition to color cues, the information should be organized so that there is a summary of the information upon which actions must be taken; then list the names of the persons who have a particular responsibility in the matter at hand. Those names, the actions to be taken, and the due dates may be further accented by italics, bold type, or magic marker highlights. Educators have large batches of mimeographed notices and flyers that must be sifted daily. A bold, eye-catching color or a uniquely shaped paper serves to identify special education correspondence, and if carefully chosen, it may give a lift to the reader. A sunny, yellow sheet of paper, a mock prescription pad, a music paper (with base or treble clef *and* notes), or an apple-red paper (even apple-shaped) might help make routine reading less so.

If a form is photocopied on plain white paper, a bright folder or mailing envelope can be used. The folder or mailing envelope option is a good one if mailing labels are included to redirect the completed material to the sender. A good format is one that saves time for everyone and gives as much help as possible in organizing responses so that they may be incorporated immediately into the total educational plan.

A four-part correspondence format is best. The original and carbon (or copy) go to the person being contacted: one copy goes to the child's folder; and one copy goes to a master folder for the class, being filed either under the area of concern (testing, placement, mainstreaming, home contact) or under the child's name.

Correspondence forms should be titled (see Figure 11-1). For example, assessment data might be titled:

- Test Results: Speech and Language Curriculum Implication

- Request for Testing

- Request for Test Results

- Test schedule for _____ (time period, days, etc.)

- Formal Tests (which will be administered by the Speech Pathologist)

- Informal Tests (to be administered at set intervals by classroom teacher after language instruction)

CONTENT

Confidentiality requirements must always be considered. Sensitive information about children and their families must be shared under very specific conditions. Requirements of PL 94-142 include such precautions as sealed envelopes, storage in locked files, and careful monitoring of access to records. These requirements are meant to safeguard the privacy of individuals and their families. Such requirements should pose no barriers to comprehensive communication when required.

Assessments made of students, opinions, and activities centered on the education and care of special children should be thoughtfully worded and expressed in professional terms. Public Law 94-142 also requires that the language in reports or communications to parents should be straightforward, not written in such technical language as to be untranslatable by parents and other lay persons. Comic characterizations, negative associations, or personal feelings should not be a part of communications. If the facts to be presented in the *Summary of Functioning* section are highly charged, a note may be made

Date: _____ Your name and title: _____

Child's name _____ Nickname _____

DOB _____ Current age (years and months) _____

AREA OF CONCERN

Schedule _____

Assessment _____

Medical _____

AREAS OF FUNCTIONING
(check those areas for which action is requested)

Speech and language ____

Perceptual/motor ____

Social/emotional ____

FUNCTIONAL LEVEL (category of disability)

M.R. ____   E.M.R. ____   TMR ____   Severe ____   Profound ____

L.D. ____   E.D. ____   P.H. ____   V.I. ____   H.I. ____

SUMMARY OF STATUS

1. Background information
2. Recent information
3. Crisis information

Information requested   _____

Action requested _____

Reason for request _____

Person requesting action or information (may be parent, another discipline,
   COH, SEC*, or other) _____

Desired response date: _____

Desired response mode: _____

Please respond by
   Telephone (H) _____ (O) _____
   or
   1. On the form provided ____
   2. Tear-off ____
   3. In space provided ____
   4. On the back of this form ____

* Committee on Handicapped, Special Education Committee

Figure 11-1. Sample Correspondence Format

there saying, "See me for further information," or "Consult confidential folder for Social Work notes, Psychologist report, or Medical history form."

The following should be included in the communication:

- A summary of pertinent facts (past and recent) that pertain to the communication

- A statement of actions you expect to be taken

- A statement of actions you have taken or will be taking

- The due date for response, if one is required

- The most convenient way to contact you

Be certain that the information you give is current and accurate. Keep abreast of legislative activity on the local, state, and federal level. Make certain that the person with whom you are communicating is the person responsible for the actions or information you seek.

DOCUMENTATION

Accountability requires not only that teachers perform assigned duties conscientiously but that teacher's efforts be documented either by changes in the students for which the teacher is responsible or by proof of the activities in which the teacher is engaged. Lesson plans (annotated with successes, failures, changes, and special conditions such as fire drill, child's illness or absence, etc.) are one way to monitor teacher activity. Another way is to keep a log of activities for each child — a record of consultative activities and the dates when they were initiated or the dates when responses occurred or are expected.

FOLLOW-UP

Careful documentation helps make follow-up less difficult. A master calendar that can be posted and coded helps teachers remain focused and meet deadlines. Each member of the interdisciplinary team has a heavy set of responsibilities, many contacts, schedules to make, and deadlines to meet. To help those members respond to the special educator's requests, follow-ups must be pursued. Reminders of what is due and when should be sent out in a timely fashion. Reminders may include a second mailing of the material, which may have been misplaced or left at home. Deadlines must be met by the special educator with respect to materials or actions required by others.

Caution — beware of overload. Have plans for action, back-up plans, and alternatives to both. Create a file of materials, references, and resources on which to draw. Give persons needing help direction to those resources (with that person assuming responsibility for carry-through). To questions about available strategies or resources, give responses such as: "I believe that the local library has a reference book entitled _____. It would help you find _____. The library is open from _____ to _____. The telephone number is _____." The same information might be typed and photocopied for quick help to those needing it. Keep listings of specialized agencies as a part of your resource file. Valuable time is saved when resources are cross-indexed according to subject, disability group served, and any other special feature such as whether it is a private or public facility and the scope of services provided.

THE SPECIAL EDUCATION TEACHER AS CONSULTANT TO SPECIAL OR REGULAR CLASSROOM PERSONNEL

The personnel included are teacher aides, interns, volunteers, tutors and student teachers. Administration and supervision are key responsibilities for the special education teacher, and include both a directive and a nondirective role. Directive roles include assignments to certain duties, general information about the class and the children, and specific information such as class rules, methods of instruction, and expected behaviors for other personnel. The flow of communication here either contributes to or inhibits the success of the teaching/management efforts. Nondirective behavior involves careful observation and good listening skills.

Good listening skills include the ability to extract hidden meanings from casual and sometimes emotion-laden comments. Personnel dissatisfaction, excuses, resistance, and failure to carry out directions, may be the result of unstated personal problems, professional jealousy, and a lack of understanding about special children and their needs or about the methods employed by the special teacher.

Critical responses to an assignment, such as *I'm not supposed to do that!* or *You always give me the worst children,* may really be a function of, *My son/daughter didn't come home last night; I'm afraid he/she is on drugs* or *I'm waiting for results from a medical screen for me/for my son/for my loved one* or *I don't know how to do that.*

Sensing an unwarranted air of resistance, a skillful teacher will (1) set aside time to review goals and procedures, (2) check assignments of responsibility to see whether the charges have merit, or (3) modify or substitute assignments. Teachers may (1) change the group with which the person usually works to one that presents fewer problems or is generally less demanding; (2) compliment the person by expressing awareness of and gratitude for responsible actions and skill in past classroom work; (3) recognize that adults need time out too by giving the person an extra off-task period; or (4) reinforce the team concept and the value of each member, for example, by telling the person(s) *We couldn't get nearly as much done as we do in here if you didn't faithfully check and record assignments,* or *if you didn't keep the children in your group involved.* Competence in the supervisory role involves the following:

- Setting up areas of responsibility for all persons involved and making certain the responsibilities are known
- Modeling expected instructional and management strategies
- Providing a broad range of materials and strategies for developing language
- Scheduling language-rich activities as part of each day's program
- Establishing a warm, interesting, fun-filled environment for language learning
- Maintaining a balance between spontaneous instruction (taking advantage of unscheduled but teachable moments) and structured, routinized skill-building sessions
- Maintaining a supportive and reinforcing relationship with support personnel and personnel-in-training

Listening stations that shut out extraneous sounds might be shared with regular educators whether or not they currently have a special child in their classrooms. When they are approached to accept a special youngster, they might be more willing to try to work with the youngster if they feel secure in initiating the methods and procedures that have already been shared with them. Computer programs for drill and practice may be shared to show how timed visual information can be used to increase attention and to diversify the drill and practice for both the teacher and the student.

BARRIERS TO THE SUCCESS OF THE SPECIAL EDUCATION TEACHER AS CONSULTANT

Special education teachers must walk the proverbial tightrope when working with others. They must maintain their role as specialist, but they must not appear to be know-it-alls. They may have to face hostility from regular teachers who have 26 students compared to the special education teacher's six or eight.

PROFESSIONAL COMMITMENTS

Involvement in organizations dealing with various aspects of exceptional conditions, searching for new teaching strategies, upgrading personal skills, and trying to stay abreast of technological advances may leave the special education teacher stretched too thin to be effective as a consultant. Gaining access to resources may pose additional problems. Money for transportation or special events may be limited, or there may be a lack of available resources.

RECORD KEEPING

A related skill for effective communication is the ability to establish, maintain, and use records of the history, assessment results, and general functioning of the special child. Competence in this area depends on the teacher's ability not only to maintain but also to interpret records; appropriate intervention is the likely result. The credibility of teachers is linked to their ability to support with hard data the judgments, suggestions, reports, referrals, and other decisions made about children. Beginning with diagnostic information, teachers must establish well-ordered, clearly labeled files that present a detailed profile of a student's functioning in at least three major categories: physical, cognitive, and social-emotional. Medical reports should be included with major points highlighted, especially those relating to physical stamina, neurological measures, and intactness of body systems, particularly lips, tongue, teeth, gums, and respiratory functioning. Vision and hearing evaluations should be included with an interpretation of what the test scores mean in terms of instructional procedure and adaptation of the curriculum or the teaching environment.

CONCLUSION

The role of consultant requires that special educators be skillful teachers and caregivers for exceptional children. In addition, they must demonstrate competence in their classrooms, be able to use their competencies as a basis for communicating the goals of special education, and assist others in achieving them.

The roles of resource persons contribute to the quality of care, ensuring that the delivery of service will be coordinated, consistent, and appropriate. The following sources may prove helpful:

- Achievement Products for Children, P.O. Box 547, Mineola, NY 11501 (Transporters, crawlers, self-feeding equipment, head pointers, and so forth)

- J. A. Preston Corporation, 60 Page Road, Clifton, NJ 07012 (Wheelchairs, tumbleforms, positioning aids, scooters, and so forth)

- Handicapped Children's Technological Services (HCTS), RFD 2, Box 60B, Foster, RI 02825 (Newsletter/catalog providing additional technological assistance)

REFERENCES

Adkinson, R. (1985). Selecting the best teacher mentor candidates: A process that worked. *Thrust, 14,* 26–27.

Administration for children, youth, and families, Head Start Bureau. (1983). *A guide to model Head Start position descriptions.* Washington, DC: U.S. Department of Health and Human Services.

Aiello, B. (1976). *Making it work: Practical ideas for integrating exceptional children into regular classes.* Reston, VA: The Council for Exceptional Children.

Campbell, P. H. (1987). Physical management and handling procedures with students with movement dysfunction. In M. E. Snell (Ed.), *Systematic instruction of persons with severe handicaps* (pp. 178–187). Columbus, OH: Merrill.

Garmston, R. J. (1987). How administrators support peer coaching. *Educational Leadership, 44*(5), 18–26.

Gray, W. A., and Gray, M. M. (1985). Synthesis of research on mentoring beginning teachers. *Educational Leadership, 43,* 37–43.

Kasteri, C., and Filler, J., Jr. (1981, September). Using inflatables with severely motorically involved infants and preschoolers. *Teaching Exceptional Children,* pp. 22–26

Kokaska, C. J. (1985). Resource teachers have problems too! *Academic Therapy, 21,* 189–192.

Lambert, D., and Lambert, L. Mentor teachers as change facilitators. *Thrust, 14,* 28–32.

Meyers, J. (1982). *Consultation skills: How teachers can maximize help from specialists in schools.* Washington, DC: Association of Colleges for Teacher Education.

The National Committee on Excellence in Education. (1983). *A nation at risk: The imperative for educational reform* (pp. 1–65). Washington, DC: U.S. Department of Education.

Neubert, G. A., and Bratton, C. (1987). Team coaching: Staff development side by side. *Education Leadership, 44*(5), 29–33.

Wiederholt, J. L., Hammill, D. D., and Brown, V. L. (1983). Basic teacher competencies for resource teachers. In J. L. Wiederholt, D. D. Hammill, and V. L. Brown (Eds.), *The resource teacher: A guide to effective practices* (pp. 31–43). Boston: Allyn & Bacon.

Zuromski, E. S. (1980). *Active stimulation program system 77-1A times, 77-2 tilt switch, control lead.* Foster, RI: Handicapped Children's Technological Services.

Index

Page numbers followed by "(t)" and "(f)" refer to tables and figures, respectively.